ARCHAEOLOGY IN
BRITISH TOWNS

ARCHAEOLOGY IN BRITISH TOWNS

From the Emperor Claudius to
the Black Death

Patrick Ottaway

London and New York

First published 1992
by Routledge
11 New Fetter Lane, London EC4P 4EE

Simultaneously published in the USA and Canada
by Routledge
a division of Routledge, Chapman and Hall, Inc.
29 West 35th Street, New York, NY 10001

© 1992 Patrick Ottaway

Filmset in Monophoto 10/12pt Palatino by
Selwood Systems, Midsomer Norton
Printed in Great Britain by Butler & Tanner Ltd,
Frome and London

British Library Cataloguing in Publication Data

A catalogue record for this book is
available from the British Library.

Library of Congress Cataloging in Publication Data

Ottaway, Patrick.
Archaeology in British towns: from the Emperor Claudius to the
Black Death/by Patrick Ottaway.
p.   cm.
Includes bibliographical references and index.
1. Excavations (Archaeology)—Great Britain.   2. Cities and towns—
Great Britain—History.   3. Urban archaeology—Great Britain.
4. Great Britain—Antiquities.   I. Title.
DA90.O86   1992
936.1—dc20   91–41071

ISBN 0–415–00068–8

To my mother, Mary and Nick with love

CONTENTS

ILLUSTRATIONS

Figures

Plates

PREFACE

Everyone relishes a secret, some little piece of knowledge which is reserved for a chosen few. It is no surprise, therefore, that archaeology, which offers us the chance of discovering the long-forgotten secrets of the past, has a perennial attraction. In an urban context we can acquire the three-dimensional vision to travel below the familiar townscape of today to a mysterious underworld of decayed buildings, lost streets, ancient refuse tips and ghostly burial grounds. On emerging from these nether regions the archaeologist brings back tales, a thousand years old and more, of the men and women who made the modern city. They are tales which are eagerly told, for while there is pleasure in having a secret it can never compare with the pleasure of sharing it.

The idea for this book grew out of a series of evening classes I ran a few years ago for the University of Hull, which were rather grandly entitled 'British Towns: The Archaeological Story'. The course attempted, first, to introduce students to some of the principal discoveries made in urban archaeology between the late 1960s and the late 1980s and, second, to outline some of the principles and problems of excavation in towns. As a period of economic downturn in Britain has brought with it something of a lull in archaeological activity, the spring of 1991 seemed a good time to review the ideas I explored during the course and commit some of them to print.

This is a somewhat unusual book about archaeology because it attempts to cross the great intellectual divide which yawns so dauntingly between the study of the Roman and post-Roman periods. My explanation for daring to leap from one side to the other, however, lies in the peculiar environment in which urban archaeologists work. Although most of my colleagues, guided by either choice or circumstance, specialise in the study of a particular period of the past, becoming Romanists, Anglo-Saxonists and so forth, the archaeologist in the fortunate position of working in an historic town must be prepared to have a competence in all the periods in which that site was occupied, from the mid-first century, or earlier in some cases, to the present day. While unravelling the superimposed layers and structures of the past, however, the urban archaeologist becomes a specialist of a rather different kind, one who studies the development of a complex and distinctive institution over many centuries. In the following chapters I have, therefore, tried not only to describe archaeological discoveries on a period-by-period basis, but also to identify features which make the settlements we call towns stand out from those around them, irrespective of historical circumstances.

While beginning at the beginning with the first Roman towns, I have chosen to bring the story to a close in about 1350. I am aware that many important archaeological discoveries in towns have been concerned with later periods, but the mid-fourteenth century marks something of a watershed, with the effects of the Black Death bringing to an end the great surge to urbanism which characterised most parts of medieval Britain. By this time, moreover, the number of written sources has become so large that archaeology can no longer claim to be the principal source for urban history.

In a book of this size, which covers a long period of history, one must obviously be selective in terms of both themes and places, or risk presenting an account which is doomed to be excessively generalised. According to a recent report by English Heritage, as many as 150 towns in England have been subject to some form of archaeological excavation in the last ten years with over fifty enjoying a continuous programme of work.[1] The Scottish and Welsh figures would doubtless increase the totals significantly. In the face of such a mass of archaeological activity, I hope I need make no apology for having chosen to concentrate, for the most part, on a dozen or so towns, where what I consider to be the more important themes in early urban history and topography are currently under investigation. In doing this I have inevitably ignored the work of many colleagues, but hope that the very fact of having to make a choice is seen as a comment on the success of the urban archaeological enterprise in this country.

This success has, of course, not been achieved without a struggle, and I have tried to tell a little of the story behind the emergence of permanent archaeological organisations in this country, both in my first chapter and at intervals in subsequent chapters. At a time when access to sites and funding for excavation are usually taken for granted, it is hard to realise that the context in which urban archaeology takes place has changed immeasurably even during the relatively short career of this particular member of the digging profession.

York, 5 June (Derby Day) 1991

ACKNOWLEDGEMENTS

In writing this book I have been assisted by numerous friends and col-
leagues around the country who have kindly spared the time to discuss
their work with me. I therefore wish to express my warmest thanks to
Brian Ayers, Philip Barker, Paul Bennett, David Bentley, Martin Biddle,
Peter Carrington, Philip Crummy, Brian Durham, Richard Hall, Chris
Henderson, Philip Holdsworth, Bob Jones, Mick Jones, Richard Kemp,
Harry Kenward, Ailsa Mainman, Gustav Milne, Alan Morton, Charles
Murray, Michael Ponsford, Ken Qualmann, John Schofield, Judith Stones
and Gill Stroud.

I am particularly grateful to Philip Crummy and Ailsa Mainman who
read through the draft text and made many useful comments. Any errors
of fact and judgement are, of course, my sole responsibility.

The plans, other than those acknowledged below, were prepared by
Glenys Boyles, whose efficiency, skill and kindness are greatly appreciated.
Generous assistance with photography was provided by Mary Ottaway.

I would also like to take this opportunity to acknowledge with the
deepest gratitude the assistance and encouragement I have had from Peter
Addyman, Martin Biddle, Philip and Nina Crummy, and Ken Qualmann
in pursuing my career in urban archaeology.

Finally I owe special thanks to all those people who have attended my
evening classes and lectures over the years; it is their enthusiasm and
forbearance which has encouraged me to see this project through to its
conclusion.

Illustrations

I am indebted to the following for permission to reproduce copyright
material:

Department of Urban Archaeology, Museum of London: Figures 1.2, 3.6, 6.10; Plates 1.1, 3.3, 3.4, 3.5, 5.5, 6.6, 6.11.

Martin Carver and Worcestershire Archaeological Society: Figure 2.3.

York Archaeological Trust: Figures 2.4, 2.5, 5.10, 6.12; Plates 2.2, 2.4, 2.5, 2.6, 4.1, 4.2, 4.3, 4.4, 4.8, 5.3, 5.6, 5.7, 5.8, 5.9, 6.7, 6.13.

Winchester Museum Service Archaeology Section: Figures 2.1, 3.9; Plates 2.1, 3.6, 3.7.

City of Aberdeen Art Gallery and Museum Collections: Figures 2.2, 6.5.

East Riding Archaeological Society: Figures 2.6, 6.8.

Colchester Archaeological Trust: Figures 3.2, 3.3, 4.4.

Canterbury Archaeological Trust: Figures 3.7, 3.8, 4.5; Plates 4.7, 6.12.

City of Lincoln Archaeological Unit: Figure 4.3; Plates 2.3, 4.5, 4.6.

Exeter Museums Archaeological Field Unit: Figure 4.2; Plate 3.1.

Southampton City Museums, Archaeology and Heritage Management Section: Figures 5.1, 5.2; Plate 5.1.

Winchester Research Unit: Figures 5.3, 5.4, 6.1; Plate 6.5.

Oxford Archaeological Unit: Figures 5.5, 5.6, 6.7, 6.13.

Norfolk Archaeological Unit: Figures 5.11, 5.12, 6.2; Plates 6.1, 6.4.

Kingston-upon-Hull Museum: Figure 6.3.

Scottish Urban Archaeological Trust: Figures 6.4, 6.6; Plate 6.3.

City of Bristol Museum and Art Gallery: Figure 6.11; Plates 6.8, 6.9.

City of Chester: Figures 5.7, 6.9.

Ashmolean Museum, Oxford: Plate 5.2.

Courtauld Institute: Plate 5.4.

Humberside Archaeological Unit: Plate 6.2.

Southampton City Museums: Plate 6.10

ABBREVIATIONS AND DATES

Abbreviations

AAI	Area of Archaeological Importance
CBA	Council for British Archaeology
DOE	Department of the Environment
DUA	Department of Urban Archaeology at the Museum of London
RCHM	Royal Commission on Historical Monuments
YAT	York Archaeological Trust

Dates

Where possible I have referred to actual dates or to centuries. In other cases I have adopted the following terminology which corresponds with most, if by no means all, current practice.

AD

43–c. 410	Roman
43–c. 200	Early Roman
c. 200–c. 410	Late Roman
c. 410–1066	Anglo-Saxon
c. 410–c. 650	Early Anglo-Saxon
c. 650–c. 850	Middle Anglo-Saxon or Anglian (for York and Lincoln)
c. 850–1066	Late Anglo-Saxon or Anglo-Scandinavian (for York and Lincoln)
1066–1485	Medieval

Figure 1.1 Map of Britain showing the location of towns referred to in this book.
Towns marked with open circles are for information only
(drawn by Glenys Boyles)

xvi

1

ARCHAEOLOGY IN TOWNS

Once upon a time the word archaeology would have conjured up images of baggy shorts, solar topis, Lawrence of Arabia, Ur of the Chaldees or Tutankhamun; in other words glamorous exploration by the privileged few in hot countries around the Mediterranean or in the Near East. One could argue that when Britain ruled a quarter of the world archaeology became a cog in the wheels of empire, as the British sought to associate themselves with the great imperial civilisations of the past by digging them up. On the disappearance of this country's role as a great power, however, and as the redevelopment of Britain's cities and countryside proceeded apace after the Second World War, her archaeologists began to turn their attention more and more to their own land.

As a result of the 'rescue archaeology' boom which began in the late 1960s, there can be few fields of academic inquiry, at least in the humanities, which have grown so rapidly as British urban archaeology, both in terms of data gathered and numbers of people involved. As an illustration of the contrast between then and now, we might note that for most of the 1960s there was but a single field officer employed by the Guildhall Museum in London to cover the archaeology of sites threatened with redevelopment in the City.[1] At the beginning of the 1990s the Museum of London had a Department of Urban Archaeology which might, at any given time, have over 200 staff engaged in excavation or related research. Outside London, most of the other historic towns of Britain have acquired a permanent archaeological team based either in the local museum or in an independent unit.

The importance of archaeology for the study of towns in Britain is that it is virtually the only source of detailed information on the first thousand years or so of their history and, in most cases, the principal source for, perhaps, the following three to four hundred years. We must recognise, moreover, that such written sources as there are for the Roman, Anglo-Saxon and medieval periods are very selective in what they tell us and tend to reflect the preoccupations and biases of the upper echelons of society. Archaeology's value is that it can put us in touch with the vast

1

majority of people in the past who would otherwise be invisible and unheard.

The principal purpose of this book is to give some impression of what the great explosion of archaeological activity in Britain's towns in the last 25–30 years has taught us about their early development. We might first of all reflect, however, that, although most of us now live in places we would call a town or city, urban living in this country has a relatively short history when seen in global terms. If we take the Roman colony at Colchester, founded in c. AD 54, as our first town (see pp. 49–50), it has a history of less than 2,000 years, whereas in other parts of the world towns have existed for two or three times as long. Until relatively recently, moreover, the spread of urbanism in Britain has been a slow process and an intermittent one; no place founded as a town in the first century and a half of Roman rule has remained continuously urban since that time, and the town as a home for more than 10 per cent of the population can only be dated back to, perhaps, the seventeenth century. Moreover, until the growth of Tudor London to a population of about half a million, all Britain's towns were very small. At the time of the Domesday Book in 1086, for example, even London is unlikely to have had as many as 10,000 inhabitants, and by the fourteenth century barely more than 40,000.[2] It remains the case, however, that from the early Roman period onwards towns as centres of economic and social activity had an importance which far outweighed mere numbers of inhabitants. An underlying theme of urban history is a recognition of this fact by emperors, kings, princes and the like, who have, by turns, coveted and feared the power and wealth of townspeople.

At this point we must try to make clear what we mean when we call a settlement a town and thereby set it in a class apart from all other settlements. Although size and density of population, and the presence of important public buildings, such as cathedrals, town halls, or sports stadia, may come immediately to mind as distinguishing features, when we look in any detail at the question it becomes more complex. We may know what a town looks like when we see it, but it is much more difficult to define.

One school of historical inquiry has defined towns primarily on the basis of legal and administrative concepts drawn from contemporary written sources. In the Roman period a framework of analysis has been provided by the three grades of settlement: *colonia* (colony), *municipium* and *civitas* (or, to be more precise, *civitas* capital). These terms occur in literature and inscriptions and appear to have described settlements of urban character, albeit of differing status based on the rights of their inhabitants.[3] In the study of the medieval period, settlements have had to meet requirements such as those employed by Beresford, who accepts as a town:

any place that passes *one* of the following tests: had it a borough charter? did it have burgages, was it called *burgus* in the Assize Rolls, or was it separately taxed as a borough? did it send members to any medieval Parliament?[4]

In the intervening Anglo-Saxon period the problems of defining the nature of settlements referred to in written sources by terms such as *wic* (see p. 120) and *burh* (see p. 139), or Latin terms such as *civitas* and *urbs*, have rendered an approach based on legal status much less easy to follow. It is only with the emergence, in the last 20–30 years, of extensive archaeological data, therefore, that the Anglo-Saxon town has become an organised field of research.

Legal definitions are important for urban history because the way that contemporaries regarded the status of a place might have considerable bearing on its social and economic role, and on many aspects of its appearance. We must also be aware, however, that the role a settlement actually played in relation to those around it may have had little relation to legal status. It is, for example, doubtful whether places founded by the Romans as *coloniae* and so forth in the first and second centuries were fully urban in the 10–20 years or so before Roman rule ended in the early fifth century. In medieval times there were plenty of places which passed the Beresford test, but might best be described as 'rotten boroughs' rather than towns in any meaningful sense. If we think of the status of settlements as a product of the relations between them, which are in turn based on the day-to-day attitudes and behaviour of men and women, we are well served by Fernand Braudel's conclusion that:

> the town stood, above all, for domination and what matters most when we try to define or rank it, is the capacity to command and the area it commanded.[5]

For an archaeologist the study of economic and social relations underlying the ability to command presents rather different problems from those faced by a historian like Braudel, who worked with statistics on trade or immigration to show the influence of a settlement on its region. The archaeologist must deal primarily with physical remains whose meaning is often open to many interpretations. I suggest, however, that archaeologists and historians alike may consider labelling a settlement as a town if, when compared to others in its region, it had, first, a relatively large and dense population, and, second, a distinctive and diverse range of economic functions, which might include, but were not dominated by, agriculture. In addition, we should expect evidence, including the appropriate amenities, for a distinctive role in administration, politics and religion (see Figure 1.2).[6]

Figure 1.2 Towns as centres of government and administration: an artist's impression of the forum and basilica in second-century London (based on a study by Peter Marsden). Recent research by Trevor Brigham and Gustav Milne has shown the need for revision in a number of details, but Ronald Embleton's painting gives an excellent impression of both the scale of the building and the aspirations of second-century Londoners.

From an archaeological point of view these are features which can be readily recognised in both quantitative and qualitative senses. In the first place we may excavate buildings whose number, organisation, form and internal arrangements will betray information about both the size and density of a settlement's population, and the range of activities in which it was engaged. In the latter respect particular significance attaches to evidence for specialists, whether in administrative, commercial or other activities, who could only be supported by a settlement of some wealth and status. Among the specialists in a town we would expect, above all perhaps, to find a merchant class engaging primarily or exclusively in trade. Facilities for trade and the exploitation of communications, such as bridges, markets and quays, must therefore be counted as characteristic urban features (see Plate 1.1). Merchants, and other specialists such as government officials and religious leaders, also form an important component of the relatively complex social hierarchy to be found in towns. One manifestation of this is likely to be a diversity of dwellings, including examples of unusual size and quality.

The greater the number of actual or intended buildings, and the greater the diversity of their functions, the more likely it is that a settlement's inhabitants will exhibit concern for internal spatial organisation. Some form of regular street system, usually on a grid plan which allows for the easy measurement and sub-division of space, is a common feature of towns through the ages. At the same time settlement growth may be accompanied by a dispersal of functions into zones for dwellings, industry, religion and so forth. Settlements of some size and prosperity might also seek to erect defences both to protect themselves against their neighbours and to assert their distinct status by a display of architectural splendour. Walls and ramparts are, therefore, another archaeologically identifiable indicator, although not a universal one, of the existence of a town.

Complementing buildings and streets in our search for archaeological indicators of urban status are the artefacts recovered from within and around them. They will also indicate the range of activities performed in a settlement, particularly in the spheres of crafts and trade. The diversity and quantity of goods manufactured, and the extent of the trading network over which they were dispatched, are crucial factors for determining the capacity of a settlement to dominate its immediate region and have an impact beyond it. The excavated evidence for goods which could have been exported from a settlement will probably consist largely of items, such as iron tools or pottery vessels, manufactured for day-to-day use, while the bulk of imports purchased in return will be locally produced building materials and subsistence foods. At the same time, however, we may find, if only in small quantities, luxury consumer goods, such as silk textiles or exotic foodstuffs, which are evidence for those unusually

Plate 1.1 Towns as centres of trade: the late-first-century Roman quay under Cannon Street railway station in London (scale 0.50m/c. 1 ft 6 ins) (Photograph: Museum of London)

wealthy families, at the head of the typical urban social hierarchy, who had exceptional tastes and purchasing power.

It will be clear that the definition of how a town may be recognised which I have attempted here is essentially multi-dimensional. It allows for no exact measurement of, for example, size, and does not require the unfailing presence or absence of any particular feature, such as a circuit of walls or a grid of streets. While such an approach is intended to be appropriate to the diverse nature of the evidence, it inevitably throws open to debate the status of many settlements which lie on the margins of urbanism. It is as a result of the problems of definition that scholars in archaeology and other disciplines are continuing to put their minds to more elaborate classifications of settlement role and status, in recognition, of the fact that a place may have some distinctively urban functions, but cannot be classified as a town in other respects.[7]

One of the most important and distinctive aspects of the archaeology of places with a long history as towns is the potential they offer for the detailed study of social and economic change, which may have a significance far beyond towns themselves. The reason for this lies in the depth and complexity of the superimposed layers of buried material, or strata, which are testimony to the intensive and varied nature of occupation in towns over past centuries. At least two metres of strata are quite common in the centre of historic towns, but up to eight or even ten metres (26–33 ft) may be found in York and London.

This great build-up derives primarily from two sources. The first is the disposal of rubbish, the undigested remains of the voracious urban appetite for building stone, timber, farm animals and any number of other commodities. In the days before municipal collections which take refuse out of town, much of the debris from domestic and craft activities was simply dumped in backyards, either in surface middens or in deliberately dug pits (see Plate 2.2). In the cramped conditions of many early town centres, streets and other open spaces, as well as the rivers, would also be used. To quote just one example, it is reckoned that, thanks to refuse dumping, the level of the backyards of the Anglo-Scandinavian buildings at 16–22 Coppergate, York (see p. 149) rose about two metres (6 ft) in the tenth century.[8]

The second major source of buried urban strata is superimposed buildings. Today construction usually involves thorough clearance of the site, but, until relatively recently, a town building which was no longer required was in many cases just levelled, the remains were then spread about and the next building was put on top, with little or no deep excavation for footings. This is, in turn, of course, one reason why Roman and medieval buildings, especially in materials other than stone, often had short lives. The process of building and rebuilding in early towns could soon give rise to a considerable accumulation of structural remains. Other causes of rising ground level in towns include deliberate dumps, often with a high refuse and building-rubble component, to combat floods or to create terraces for building. Natural processes such as flood deposition and the gradual accumulation of soil from decaying organic matter may also make a contribution, especially during episodes of desertion in urban areas.

We have so far been thinking of archaeological remains as buried, but an ancient building which still stands above ground is as much an archaeological site as its buried counterpart. Although few buildings, other than medieval churches and castles, survive in Britain from before, perhaps, the fourteenth century, those which do, and many from later periods, will repay careful study along archaeological lines to uncover what may be a very complex and unrecorded sequence of construction and alteration. Hiding behind modern façades there are still many fragments of as yet unknown ancient buildings, and their discovery and detailed study during renovation or demolition are an important part of the urban archaeologist's work.

The nature of urban archaeological sites, both above and below ground, should become more apparent in the following chapters, but I also hope to show how discoveries relating to topography, buildings and daily life can be used to examine wider themes, leading to a greater understanding of human behaviour in the past. These themes include the way man interacts with his natural environment, whether in the siting of towns, the exploitation of natural resources or the combating of natural hazards, such as a rise in river levels. At the same time we may look at how successive generations have interacted with the man-made environment of their forebears and, whether their town grew or contracted, how it was adapted to suit changing circumstances.

The direction of these interactive processes has, for the most part, been in the hands of society's leaders. Just as towns dominated their regions, so certain social groups dominated the towns and created the physical surroundings to express this through the form and arrangement of buildings, monuments, and even cemeteries. Nothing, for example, is more evocative of the conquest of Britain by the Romans than the form of the Roman town dictated by imperial officials, with its rectilinear streets and monumental buildings at its core embodying all forms of power, secular and spiritual. Similarly, the transformation of Anglo-Saxon towns by the construction of castles and cathedrals in Norman French style by William the Conqueror's lords and bishops effectively symbolised his new regime. We need not, however, always think of society's leaders as emperors, kings and the like; in medieval towns, for example, the creation of zones inhabited primarily by the practitioners of particular crafts may be seen as one aspect of attempts by their leaders to acquire or defend a monopolistic position in the market by the physical exclusion of interlopers.

Finally, archaeology allows us to capture something of the powerful attraction town life has exercised over the minds of people of all social stations through the centuries. In medieval times towns were known as 'consumers of men' because of the frequency and intensity of epidemics of fatal diseases, largely caused by poor sanitation in overcrowded dwellings. It is only recently that urban populations have become able to sustain themselves without regular influxes of immigrants. While there have certainly been episodes, from time to time, of immigration forced on people by harvest failure or eviction, most immigrants have probably taken on the risks of urban living willingly. In part, of course, this has been because towns have offered the opportunity of financial gain. In part also they have offered the chance of personal freedom away from the rigid social hierarchy or oppressive feudal duties of rural settlements – 'Stadt Luft macht frei', as the German proverb has it. Finally, let us not forget the increased opportunity for entertainment and social intercourse. From attending the theatre or enjoying the pageantry of religious ceremonies to drinking with friends or choosing a husband or wife, town life was attractive because it was fun.

Urban history from archaeology – genesis and growth

The systematic study of urban history through archaeology is perhaps only 25–30 years old. Prior to the late 1960s, data from excavations were sparse, especially for post-Roman periods. This is, of course, not to say that the early history of towns had been completely neglected. Historians and historical geographers in this country have a long tradition of using written sources, architectural evidence and the discoveries of local antiquarians to reconstruct the topography, economy and society of the urban past. Without the careful study of both structural sequences and of artefacts in relation to their buried context, however, such reconstructions can only be partial.

The earliest examples of what we might recognise as the archaeological investigation of towns can probably be dated to the second half of the nineteenth century, when work took place on the deserted town sites of Roman Britain. At Wroxeter Thomas Wright excavated the baths from 1859 to 1862,[9] and at Silchester, between 1855 and 1878, the Reverend J.G. Joyce, one of a long line of great nineteenth-century clerical antiquaries, undertook an extensive programme of excavation which was continued by the Society of Antiquaries between 1890 and 1909.[10] Although it was poor by our standards, the nineteenth-century work at Silchester was on such a large scale that the plan which emerged from the excavations is still the most complete there is of a Romano-British town in its heyday when the majority of the buildings had stone foundations. Post-Roman towns were of less interest to Victorian excavators, although the first investigation of a medieval town site may be that which took place in 1877 before the construction of the Examination Schools in Oxford High Street. A number of refuse pits were examined and interpreted, erroneously, as the remains of a 'British village'.[11]

The next great period of archaeological work in towns, again the focus being on the Roman period, was the 1920s and 1930s, when some of the best-known excavations were undertaken by R.E.M. (later Sir Mortimer) Wheeler at Colchester[12] and Verulamium (Roman St Alban's).[13] Whereas previously the Roman town had been considered as an entity unchanged in form and function over the 350 years or so of Britain's inclusion in the empire, Wheeler began to present evidence for change through time. He was able to do this because of his great innovations in archaeological method which allowed the understanding of complex sequences of buried strata. Wheeler was also a great communicator of his results to both an academic and non-specialist audience, even if he was sometimes guilty of over-rapid interpretation – 'celeritas wheeleriana' as Sheppard Frere has called it.[14]

Before the Second World War the concept of 'rescue archaeology', the excavation of sites threatened with redevelopment, was more or less unknown, although the work in 1930 by Christopher Hawkes at Sheepen, Colchester (see pp. 47–9) in advance of the Colchester by-pass, should probably be considered the first urban-rescue dig.[15] Since the war, rescue has gradually become the main context in which urban archaeology has taken place, initially, in the late 1940s and early 1950s, on sites cleared by enemy bombing. In London, for example, Professor Grimes made such important discoveries as the Cripplegate Roman fort and the Temple of Mithras.[16] In Canterbury Sheppard Frere's work provided a framework for the study of the Roman and medieval town, and also found vital and hitherto unsuspected evidence for Anglo-Saxon occupation.[17] In Southampton the first steps were made towards understanding the middle-Anglo-Saxon site of Hamwic.[18]

Excavations continued sporadically in a number of towns in the 1950s and early 1960s, with Roman sites, notably Verulamium, excavated by Frere, again receiving greatest attention.[19] The archaeology of Anglo-Saxon and medieval towns remained largely unexplored, although at Thetford in the late 1940s Group Captain Knocker's extensive excavations provided the only large body of archaeological information on a late Anglo-Saxon town for nearly twenty years.[20] In the mid-1950s Oxford was the scene of an important step forward in medieval urban archaeology when, in advance of redevelopment of the Clarendon Hotel site in Cornmarket, work on both below-ground archaeology and standing buildings provided a model for the city's growth from the Anglo-Saxon period to the later middle ages.[21] Meanwhile at Southampton work continued uninterrupted, and in 1953 attention moved from Hamwic to the medieval walled town,

thereby laying the foundations for one of the most extensive urban archaeological programmes in Britain.[22]

In spite of the developments I have briefly outlined, it is fair to say that
as late as the mid- or late 1960s urban archaeology had a low profile.
Resources and trained personnel were few and public enthusiasm apparently limited. If, however, we are to identify the beginning of a new era
in terms of academic approach, strategic ambition and, ultimately, public
awareness, we can do no better than quote Martin Biddle in the second
interim report on excavations at Winchester published in 1964. Describing
the aims of the newly-formed Winchester Excavations Committee. Biddle
wrote:

> the committee was formed to undertake excavations, both in advance
> of building projects, and on sites not so threatened, aimed at studying
> the development of Winchester as a town from its earliest origins to
> the establishment of the modern city. The centre of interest is the city
> itself, not any one period of its past, nor any one part of its remains.[23]

From this time onwards Biddle was, in many ways, to take on the
mantle of Wheeler as Britain's leading field archaeologist; indeed one of
his earliest experiences of excavation had been under Wheeler at the great
Iron Age enclosure site at Stanwick in North Yorkshire.[24] After National
Service in Palestine, during which he was assigned to one of Dame
Kathleen Kenyon's digs at Jericho, Biddle had started work in Winchester
while a Cambridge undergraduate, directing an excavation on the site of
the Anglo-Saxon New Minster. This brought home to him:

> the untapped wealth of the city's archaeology and the extent to
> which it was threatened with elimination through the demands of
> modern development.[25]

Some impression of this wealth will follow in subsequent chapters, but in
the organisational structure of the Winchester Excavations Committee,
and subsequently the Winchester Research Unit, and in the standards set
by the great field campaigns at Cathedral Green, Lower Brook Street, the
Castle and elsewhere, a model was created for other historic towns to
follow. Before this occurred, however, there were some disastrous episodes
when lack of funds and refusal of access led to the destruction of archaeological sites in towns with little record, most notoriously, perhaps, in
1973 on a site in London dating back to the Anglo-Saxon period in New
Palace Yard, on the doorstep of Parliament itself.[26]

In 1971 leading archaeologists came together to form 'Rescue', a pressure
group whose aim was to bring to the attention of public and politicians
alike the scale of the threat to archaeological sites, particularly in towns.[27]
The problem was outlined in the Council for British Archaeology (CBA)

publication entitled *The Erosion of History*,[28] which produced such alarming, and, it must be said, somewhat exaggerated, conclusions as:

> Of the historic English County Borough towns half have already been archaeologically destroyed; of the remaining 29, 24 are seriously threatened, and 5 less severely. Of the 55 towns in this category, only 10 are being adequately investigated archaeologically.

This was followed shortly after by Rescue's publication of *The Future of London's Past*,[29] focusing on the particular problems of the capital. As a result of the campaign by Rescue and of pressure from within the Department of the Environment Ancient Monuments Inspectorate, a substantial increase in central government funding became available to support the fledgling urban units in places such as Oxford (set up in 1967), York (1972) and the City of London (1973). My own involvement in urban archaeology began in the early 1970s and there is no doubt that it was an exciting time to be digging, since it appeared, however briefly, that it rested on a single generation to salvage what was left of the buried remains of our historic towns.

In the event, although destruction of archaeological sites in towns has proceeded at a rapid rate over the last twenty years, most of them were excavated in a controlled manner before development and a great deal of archaeology still survives. In the same period the context in which urban archaeology takes place has changed radically. The days of desperate attempts to investigate sites with inadequate resources while faced with unhelpful and suspicious site owners, and indifferent public authorities, are largely over. Access to sites for archaeological work before development is now accepted as a matter of course, and funding, while never secure and rarely entirely adequate, is available at unprecedented levels. In the 1970s and much of the 1980s the principal source of funds was the public purse, either from local authorities or from central government, which works through an Ancient Monuments Inspectorate with responsibility for rescue archaeology, now no longer based in the Department of the Environment, but in three quasi-independent agencies: English Heritage (also known as the Historic Buildings and Monuments Commission), Cadw (Welsh Historic Monuments) and, the most recently created, Historic Scotland. In the late 1980s and early 1990s it has become routine for the grants from central government to be supplemented, or completely replaced, by funding from site developers themselves, often to the tune of several hundred thousand pounds on deeply stratified urban sites.

The changing climate has, above all, been a result of the success of archaeologists, on the one hand, and local and national government, on the other, in integrating archaeology into the town- and country-planning process (see Plate 1.2). This should be seen in the context of a general movement towards a greater concern for environmental and 'heritage' matters in planning in recent years. Following the barbarism of the immediate post-war period there has been a search for approaches to the management of urban change which are sensitive to townscapes which

Plate 1.2 Archaeology as a local government function: corporate image at Southampton

may have taken one thousand years or more to develop. At the same time, it is more widely appreciated that these townscapes are part of a community's consciousness of its past, which is vital to stimulate a healthy understanding of where it is today and a sense of purpose about where it is going tomorrow. Archaeology as a discipline which describes and interprets the development of the urban fabric is, therefore, in a unique position to assist planning authorities to adapt rather than disrupt the character of historic towns. Archaeology has, in other words, joined the mainstream of urban conservation which can have such a positive economic and social benefit.

The most important aspect of the local government involvement in archaeology is that for some years now it has been standard practice in most authorities for archaeologists to see all planning applications at an early stage. This allows any archaeological implications of a new development to be given due consideration. In addition, an awareness of archaeology has been a feature of many county and local structure plans. Declarations of intent are often made operational through a Section 106 (formerly Section 52) Agreement under the terms of the 1971 and 1990 Town and Country Planning Acts, whereby an element in the granting of planning permission is an arrangement between the developer and local archaeological body for site access on the basis of a reasonable timetable of work and some financial contribution. There is no question, however, of making either access or funding mandatory by law. While most planning authorities now expect a developer to fund an archaeological site assessment before submitting a planning application, Department of the Environment Planning Policy Guidelines issued in 1991 specifically state: 'Planning authorities should not include in their development plans policies requiring developers to finance archaeological works in return for the grant of planning permission.'[30]

At the same time, archaeologists and developers have sought to head off potential conflict through a voluntary code of practice agreed in 1986 by the Standing Conference of Archaeological Unit Managers (SCAUM), and the British Property Developers Federation which represents most major operators. The code's objective is to put archaeologists on the same professional footing as other bodies with whom developers deal, and to integrate archaeology into construction programmes, while, at the same time, committing archaeologists to plan their work to take account of commercial requirements. The goodwill which has resulted has, in many cases, led to a greater degree of cost-effective working on both sides.[31] This co-operative approach clearly has much to recommend it when government policy is, on the one hand, to place greater reliance on self-regulation than legislation, but, on the other, favours the idea that, in environmental matters, the 'polluter' should pay.

The only significant change in legislation relating to urban archaeology in recent years has been Part 2 of the 1979 Ancient Monuments and Archaeological Areas Act which provides for the designation of Areas of Archaeological Importance (AAI) in which access to sites was guaranteed statutorily – for four-and-a-half months – for the first time. In the event, however, only five towns were designated – Canterbury, Chester, Exeter, Hereford and York – and no further designations appear likely. Prevailing opinion in central government is that local planning arrangements are sufficient to safeguard the interests of archaeology. Nevertheless, in the five towns the legislation has, on the whole, succeeded in focusing the minds of developers and planners, and has led to a more positive approach to ensuring proper site access.

In spite of improvements in access and funding, long-term preservation of important archaeological deposits in towns remains some way off. The Scheduled Monument legislation, reviewed most recently in the 1979 Act, is still primarily concerned with the preservation of countryside field monuments such as barrows and hillforts. Some urban monuments, such as defences, are scheduled, but it remains the case that much of the urban archaeological resource is still, in a sense, threatened with destruction, if only in the long term. Furthermore, as we shall see at sites in London (see pp. 68–71) and York (see pp. 91–3), serious conflicts of interest can still arise when archaeological excavations result in major discoveries, arguably worthy of *in situ* preservation.

While urban archaeology still confronts many problems, there is, none the less, good reason for us to be positive and, as we look back over the last twenty-five years or so, we should celebrate the fact in this time excavations have revolutionised our knowledge of almost every aspect of the early history of towns. To appreciate how this has been done, however, we must endeavour first of all to understand some of the increasingly subtle and sophisticated techniques of modern field archaeology.

2

URBAN ARCHAEOLOGISTS AT WORK

Site evaluation – why dig here?

One of the commonest questions an excavation director is asked by members of the public is 'how do you know where to dig?' In most urban situations this can be answered briefly by saying that an excavation almost anywhere inside or immediately outside the town centre is bound to produce archaeological discoveries, since the place has probably been intensively occupied for 1,000 years or more. It must be added, however, that, while there are bound to be some areas which are more interesting than others, archaeologists cannot dig anywhere that takes their fancy. Most urban archaeology today takes place on sites threatened with redevelopment, where the buried remains face destruction by new buildings, roadworks and so forth. In other words sites are, up to a point, chosen for archaeologists by factors beyond their control. It should be noted, in addition, that threatened sites are usually the only ones for which funds, from government or the developers themselves, are available. In recent years there have been very few sites in towns dug purely for research reasons, where there has been no time constraint and no immediate danger of destruction. While this can be frustrating from an academic point of view, it is likely that for the foreseeable future archaeologists will have enough to do to cope with threatened sites. It is arguable, moreover, that unthreatened sites should, if possible, be preserved for future generations who will probably have greater resources and better techniques than we do.

Within the 'rescue' framework, archaeologists still face a whole range of decisions about where and what to dig before a shovel is put into the ground. It is simply not possible to excavate every last piece of threatened archaeology and sometimes sites or parts of sites have to be written off altogether. Archaeologists must continually aim to use what are often very restricted resources to address the academic problems a site presents by examining a sample of its buried remains. Defining the optimum sample requires application of a battery of techniques of site evaluation. In the early years of the urban units the archaeology of most towns was largely

16

unknown and virtually any site within the historic core was likely to reveal new and important information. Gradually, however, as the outlines of the early development of most larger towns, at least, have become clearer, more detailed statements of objectives and the means of achieving them have become possible. This has allowed the allocation of resources between and within sites to be planned more effectively. The success of an excavation project, however, still depends on the archaeologist's ability to predict, if only in general terms, what will be found before time and money are committed to it.

A relatively simple tool of evaluation is the distribution plan, showing the location of building remains or artefact finds in an urban area, which will give an idea of the location and intensity of settlement in different time periods. A relatively detailed example showing Roman discoveries in Colchester appears on page 51 (see Figure 3.2), but only recently a distribution plan of no more than a handful of finds revealed the location of middle-Anglo-Saxon London in a hitherto unsuspected area outside the Roman walls (see pp. 127–8).[1] The information for distribution plans may be derived from a variety of sources including both commercial and archaeological excavations. The latter are, of course, the most useful, but the former can also be of great importance. In Canterbury, for instance, the work of the City Engineer, James Pilbrow, in the 1860s revealed a great deal about the Roman town during the laying of the first main sewers.[2]

Although they can only be summarised here, important aids to planning archaeological work are the documentary sources of which there is a vast, if disparate, range for the study of early urban history and topography.[3] For the Roman period there are a few official sources which refer to towns, including the *Antonine Itinerary*, a road book giving routes and distances between places in the empire, and the *Notitia Dignitatum*, a list of the dispositions of military and official personnel in the late fourth century.[4] In addition, there are occasional references in such historical works as *The Agricola*, *The Histories* and *The Annals of Imperial Rome*, written in the first century by Tacitus. For the post-Roman period there are again historical accounts, such as Bede's *History of the English Church and People* and the *Anglo-Saxon Chronicle*. Early state archives include the tenth-century Burghal Hidage, giving provision for the defence of towns and other sites in Wessex.[5]

The medieval period produced the first extended descriptions of towns. Most remarkable, perhaps, is the account of London in the twelfth century by William Fitzstephen in his life of Thomas à Becket.[6] State archives also become more detailed after the Norman Conquest. The Domesday Book permits some estimates of eleventh-century urban populations to be made, and illustrates the impact of the Norman Conquest by, for example, references to houses destroyed to build the new castles. The main purpose of the Domesday Book, however, was to assess the country for taxation, and many of the crown's records from the twelfth to thirteenth century onwards also give information on urban fortunes and layout through tax data. The topography of medieval Hull, for instance, can be understood in some detail because it was largely royal land after 1293, when Wyke, as it was then known, was acquired by Edward I (hence Kingston-upon-Hull). The crown kept control of its investment through a remarkable series of fee-farm rentals which cover almost every property in the town.[7] In crown records there are also murage grants, which allowed towns to levy taxes to fund construction of defences, and they can be used today to determine the chronology of the work.

In many towns the church was the principal landowner and its records of ownership and rents are often very informative. Much of the twelfth-century geography of Canterbury, for example, has been reconstructed from the rentals of the cathedral priory.[8] Municipal archives, which survive in many cases from the thirteenth century, include enrolled deeds, which are records of property transactions by the town itself, its large land-owners, and even individual citizens. The Norwich Survey, for example, used the city's fine collection of enrolled deeds to make a detailed study not only of the geography of property ownership between 1284 and 1346, but also the occupation of the owners and the nature of their buildings.[9] This has been set alongside the archaeology to develop an unusually detailed picture of a great medieval town. A similar project has been

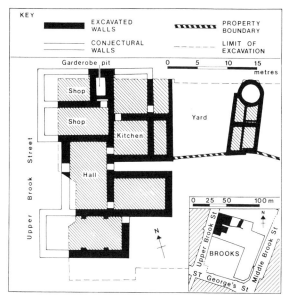

Figure 2.1 Interpretative plan of John de Tytyng's House, Winchester (see Plate 2.1) (Winchester Museum Service Archaeology Section)

undertaken in Winchester,[10] and in 1987, at the Brooks site, it was possible to identify a property occupied by one of the city's leading late-thirteenth-century merchants, John de Tytyng. Complete excavation of the house, yards, and outbuildings, including the privy, complete with wooden toilet seat, has produced an unusually vivid picture of the man's life and times (see Figure 2.1 and Plate 2.1).[11]

Although there are no Roman or medieval examples, early town plans are of particular interest to archaeologists. The first to contain any useful topographical information is probably that of Bristol dated c. 1480, although there is little else before the great series of plans made by John Speed in the early 1600s to accompany his maps of English counties. From Speed's time onwards, however, town plans gradually become more common and until early this century often reveal a townscape which is little changed from medieval times (see Figure 2.2). Similarly artists' views (see Figure 6.3) and even early photographs of towns can convey a wealth of information relevant to the archaeologist's search for vanished buildings and streets.

Armed with the knowledge of previous finds and the evidence of documentary sources, the archaeologist can make a start on compiling a framework of priorities in which to set individual projects. This will also be informed by the knowledge, first, that some sites may be more representative of a town's history than others, and, second, that survival of buried deposits and structures may vary considerably, and unpredictably, from one part of an urban area to another.

Even in towns such as Winchester and Southampton, which have been relatively well explored archaeologically, no more than c. 3 per cent of the historic core has been excavated. If we are, therefore, to be confident about using archaeology to generalise about even the broad outlines of a town's early history, excavation sites should, if possible, be well distributed geographically so as to give an impression of the nature and history of occupation over the whole of the urban area. Second, sites should allow the investigation of a range of functions: residential, industrial, religious and so forth. Among the more crucial sites, perhaps, are those of public buildings, such as Roman fora or medieval churches, whose form and development will be a good indicator of a town's economic fortunes and of its status as a settlement distinct from others in its region. Equally important are the defences, which may not only reveal episodes of exterior threat, but also give some impression of the extent of settlement at particular times, and indicate occasions when new civic status was achieved. Finally, streets may represent the history of an urban site in microcosm, indicating, for example, the extent of town planning and, in their standard of upkeep, the degree of communal discipline and civic wealth.

Our ability to predict the location of particular types of site will vary according to the amount of previous work and extent of documentary

Plate 2.1 Late-thirteenth-century town house belonging to the merchant John de Tytyng as excavated at the Brooks site, Winchester,

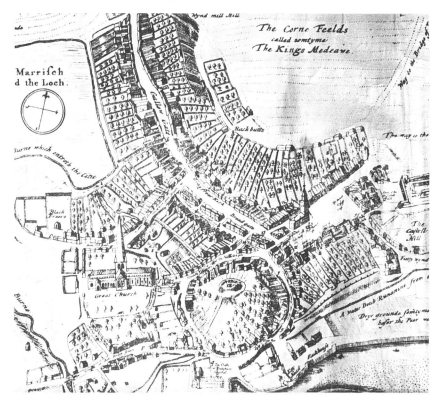

Figure 2.2 Part of Parson James Gordon's map of Aberdeen dated 1661, but showing an essentially medieval layout with long narrow tenements end-on to the streets. St Nicholas's church is on the left and the castle site on the right. Castle Street is the wide street to the right of centre; Broad Street and Gallowgate run to the north (City of Aberdeen Art Gallery and Museum Service)

information, but even if the location of the desired type of site can be found, it is equally important to know if anything actually survives in the ground. In towns where occupation has been more or less continuous for a thousand years or more the problems of survival are very complex. There is usually little indication on the modern surface of the overall depth of strata or shape of the landscape at any particular period in the past, since human activity over the years may have radically altered the natural contours. One force for change is deposition, and so at York, for example, much of which sits on two filled-in river valleys, there are up to 10m (33 ft) or more of archaeology in places. Removal of strata may also have taken place on a grand scale, and in Norwich, for example, post-medieval landscaping of the castle area meant that while in some parts of the recently excavated Castle Mall site the archaeology was very deep, in others it was unexpectedly shallow.[12] A problem everywhere is that Victorian and modern buildings with deep cellars and basements, often not recorded in any detail, may have removed virtually all the archaeology in areas which might otherwise be considered of archaeological interest. Even if a considerable depth of archaeological deposits does exist, there is no guarantee that there is equally good survival from each of the periods in which the town as a whole was occupied. It is not uncommon, for instance, to find that medieval rubbish pits have substantially destroyed Anglo-Saxon or Roman deposits, or for ancient stone buildings to have been extensively demolished once they became redundant, leaving little but footings for the archaeologists.

The survival of archaeological deposits is also affected by the underlying geology and groundwater regime. On well-drained subsoils, such as sandstone and gravel, the organic component of deposits will not only decay due to bacterial action, but will also be washed away or leached out; as a result, the buried strata may be relatively shallow. On more impervious subsoils, such as clay, this leaching process may be more restricted and depth correspondingly greater. If, moreover, the water table is above subsoil level, normal decay processes may be very substantially impeded and the preservation of organic matter, including structural timbers, may contribute to an unusual depth of deposit such as those to be found in the centre of York or on the banks of the Thames in London.

A survey of previous excavations is again a necessary starting point for assessing the survival of deposits in a town and the archaeological potential of particular sites. Ideally an ongoing process in every historic town should be the development of three-dimensional plans showing, first, the depth of archaeological deposits overall and in the major historical periods, and, second, the location of major disturbances. A good example is the maps of London in *The Future of London's Past*,[13] which gave a stark indication of the extent of destruction of the city's buried past, yet also revealed the archaeological potential of such areas as the Thames waterfront. More recently, work by Professor Martin Carver in Worcester[14] and other West Midlands towns has shown the value of deposit-survival maps for pinpointing areas where specific aspects of the urban past such as structures, organic-rich deposits and cemeteries may be best investigated, and at the same time for developing strategies for the preservation of archaeological strata as a resource comparable to ancient buildings standing above ground (see Figure 2.3).

In most towns the accumulation of information on ancient topography, survival of deposits and location of settlement through time is possible because archaeologists are able, by working in close co-operation with local planning authorities and public utilities, to monitor every significant disturbance of the ground and record any archaeology revealed. Small-scale observations, or 'watching briefs', are often unglamorous, but they

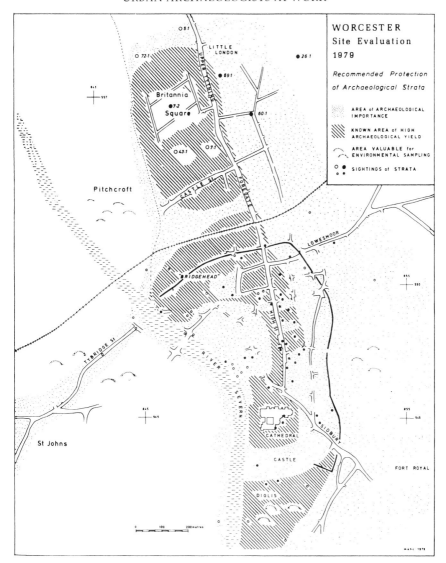

Figure 2.3 Evaluation as a basis for preservation: plan of Worcester showing areas of well-preserved archaeological deposits (Worcestershire Archaeological Society)

are an absolutely vital component of an urban unit's work. It is surprising how much basic topographical and historical information can be recovered from examining areas of ancient building fabric revealed in small-scale renovation, or from looking down the trenches for building footings, sewers and the like. A watching brief may, in fact, be the only way of looking below ground at some parts of the modern town, such as, for example, the main streets.

In Gloucester, Patrick Garrod, Field Officer with the museum's excavation unit, has spent over twenty years in watching-brief work, the value of which was summed up in the volume appropriately bearing his name – *Garrod's Gloucester* – as follows:

> Since 1973 the greater part of his time has been dedicated to the observation and recording of all ground disturbances, whether during building construction or the laying of service trenches.
>
> Long familiarity with excavations, prior to and throughout the city redevelopment, has enabled Garrod to relate even the smallest stratigraphic section to the known archaeological sequence. The process of archaeological retrieval under these circumstances has been highly cost-effective.[15]

Once all archaeological and historical sources have been assessed, it is usual practice, as the final stage in the evaluation for any major project, to undertake some limited trial excavation on the site itself. Both archaeologists and site developers now realise that at the earliest possible stage test trenches should be dug to assess potential in detail and indicate appropriate level of funding. While there are methods of remote sensing, which can detect buried features by measuring either changes in the ground's resistance to electronic impulses or in its magnetic field (using a proton magnetometer), they are rarely of value on urban sites because of the difficulty of coping with the great depth of superimposed strata, and are better suited to rural sites which are relatively shallow.

Strategy and method

Urban archaeological sites come in all shapes and sizes depending on academic objectives, available resources, practical constraints or, most commonly, some combination of the three. The scale and scope of work will inevitably, however, have an important bearing on the value of the results. Until the early 1960s the vast majority of excavations on deeply-stratified urban sites were small, narrow trenches, useful primarily for determining sequences of occupation rather than for revealing the development of the urban landscape. Archaeologists today will, of course, still employ narrow trenches for evaluation, but much more useful for studying the interrelationship of buildings, streets, yards and so forth, is what has come to be known as 'area excavation'. This may involve the examination of several hundred square metres at a time, with results that are, as we have already seen at John de Tytyng's house, extremely rewarding. In spite of the cost of such projects one can be forgiven for concluding that, on the whole, 'big is beautiful' in urban archaeology.

Systematic area excavation had its genesis in this country with Wheeler at Verulamium and elsewhere in the 1920s and 1930s. Within his areas, however excavation took place in a series of regular box trenches usually c. 3m (10 ft) square divided by unexcavated baulks, c. 1m (3 ft) wide.[16] This strategy had a certain practical and organisational value, especially when, as on Wheeler's sites in India, large numbers of relatively inexperienced workers were involved; but, unless the baulks were meticulously removed, matching the sequences of the strata between boxes was a problem, and the excavator was never able to get an uninterrupted view of, for example, a building's plan. After the Second World War excavation by 'open area' was developed, with few or no baulks, one of the pioneering sites again being Verulamium during Sheppard Frere's excavations in the 1950s.[17] The open area approach is now standard on large sites and can be seen in operation in many of the photographs in this book.

While the great value of urban archaeological sites lies in their super-imposed layers of structural material, refuse, etc., unravelling them in excavation is a complex and time-consuming business. Much of the actual digging is, of course, done by the famous 'archaeologist's trowel' (to be exact, the 'W.H.S. mason's 4-inch pointing trowel'), but also by pick and shovel, tools of surprising subtlety in the right hands. During excavation an archaeological site, with its uneven ground surface punctuated by holes and trenches of varying sizes and depths, often resembles a lunar landscape or a gruyère cheese. Faced with this incomprehensible scene, the casual visitor may turn to the archaeologist and ask questions along the lines of 'why did you dig deeper over here than over there?' It should be possible to reply that nothing on the site (except the baulks) is an original creation of the excavators, but is a result of revealing what was created by people occupying the site in the past. The ever-present pits, for example, were probably dug by householders for refuse or cess and the archaeologist has merely emptied them out (see Plate 2.2).

The basic principle of stratigraphic excavation in archaeology is to remove the structures or deposits, either on the surface or in cut 'features', such as ditches or pits, in the reverse order of their creation or deposition until undisturbed subsoil or 'natural' is reached. In this way we get a picture of the site as it developed over time, by a process rather like running a film slowly backwards. During excavation each layer, cut feature or structure, or, as they are generically known today, 'context', is given a unique number and its details are recorded. Artefacts found in each context are kept separate and recorded under their context number.

The establishment of these simple principles owes a great deal to Wheeler.[18] Prior to his work most excavations proceeded by digging off spits of arbitrary thickness, which might comprise a mixture of many different contexts. The primary objective in excavations, such as those in the nineteenth century at Silchester, was to reveal stone walls and other

Plate 2.2 The rubbish or cess pit – this is a tenth-century de luxe wicker-lined model from 16–22 Coppergate, York (scale 2m / 6 ft 6 ins) (Photograph: York Archaeological Trust)

solid structural remains, and to recover artefacts. The depth and position of discoveries were recorded up to a point, but with little attempt to relate them to a sequence of stratification, which in turn made it difficult to relate them to an exact historic and cultural context.

Stratigraphic excavation is, of course, more difficult to organise than spit excavation. There is, first of all, the logistical problem of ensuring work proceeds across the site on layers which are roughly contemporary, while keeping the team fully occupied. As Wheeler noted: 'idleness is both costly and infectious.'[19] Secondly, there is the problem of defining the individual layers and features. This often baffles inexperienced, and occasionally experienced, excavators as they struggle to determine where one context ends and another begins. In some instances contexts are well defined; stone walls, for example, are usually easy to identify, even by the inexperienced, but in many other instances edges are difficult to spot as they may depend on slight differences of deposit colour or texture. While the problem of context definition is one important reason why archaeology is so time-consuming, it should be stressed that even the most marginal differences may be of enormous importance in revealing the occurrence of major events. For example, the remains of what were substantial timber buildings in Anglo-Saxon Southampton can only be found by very careful trowelling of the natural brickearth to reveal the stains which give away the location of rotted posts or ground beams (see Plate 5.1). At Wroxeter, where earlier excavators dismissed the possibility of learning anything of the fourth-century town,[20] the recent discovery of late and post-Roman timber buildings on the baths basilica site has only been possible by meticulous cleaning and recording, stone by stone, of spreads of finely broken-up rubble.

Recording – the unrepeatable experiment

Since it is self-evident that archaeological excavation is also destruction, a crucial aspect of the job is recording.[21] The theory and practice of archaeological recording may seem an esoteric subject to the lay person, but the way recording is carried out may profoundly affect what can be learnt about the past from excavation. Because of this it has raised and continues to raise strong passions in the archaeological community. One of the principal issues is the extent to which it is possible to make an objective record free from the subjective bias of the excavator. A related issue is the extent to which recording can be delegated by the site director or supervisor to the more junior members of the field team. Setting these issues in a wider context, the first can be seen against a background of the growing links of archaeology with the natural and physical sciences, which would liken excavation to a form of experiment. The second can be seen in the context of the democratisation of society in the twentieth century, with weakening of class distinctions between the rulers and ruled.

Recording takes two basic forms: one is the written word and the other is illustration by means of drawings and photographs. Since both require the excavator to make decisions of some sort about what is included in the record, and because, once excavated, it is not possible to put the site back and start again, there is inevitably scope for endless argument about what constitutes correct practice.

The basic written record is a description of each context with some indication of its location, dimensions and, in the case of deposits and structures, its composition. Equally important is a record of the context's relationship with others found immediately above and below it or dug into it. Each context, from the smallest spread of mortar to the largest wall, is given equal value at this stage and may be seen as a building block which will be used to reconstruct the site and its history after the excavation is over. For this reason an element of consistency is required in the way contexts are dealt with and it is common practice today for the written record to be on a pro forma sheet which prompts the excavator by a series of questions about the layer or feature in hand (see Figure 2.4). In an attempt to preserve objectivity, the excavator's thoughts on interpretation are kept separate from the description of what he or she observes.

One component of the drawn record is the cross-section, a scale drawing of superimposed deposits as revealed in the baulks or sides of trenches (see Figure 2.5). In addition there is the plan, a record in the horizontal plane related to a fixed site grid. Until, perhaps, the mid-1960s plans were usually only made of major structural or cut features. The systematic planning of the surfaces between them was largely ignored, indeed there was no option when the job of recording was reserved for a few trained staff. As a result the subtle patterning of soil colouring or the disposition of stones which might, for example, give away the presence of major timber buildings, was often missed. As far as urban archaeology is concerned, the detailed recording of surfaces was another of the great innovations of Biddle's Winchester excavations[22] and was soon universally copied. Current practice is to make a detailed scale drawing of every individual context, again regardless of its presumed importance during excavation (see Figure 2.4).

A systematic approach to recording is vital to ensure a good and consistent standard on large urban sites where responsibility for recording cannot be undertaken solely by a few supervisors, but has to be delegated to many members of staff. A high degree of comprehensiveness and objectivity is important because archaeologists today are increasingly ambitious about what they can learn from excavations and because the growing number of research specialisms means that the significance of many aspects of a site may not become apparent until after the event. It is no longer possible for excavation recording to be executed, as it was until quite recently on some sites, by a single all-seeing director and a few trusted assistants who, with a combination of experience and inspiration, would integrate description and interpretation in their recording in a way which can be hard to disentangle by others wishing to check the results. It may be fair to say, however, that the organisational implications of current methods have robbed archaeology of its romantic heroes who literally made history as they went along, and replaced them with teams of highly-skilled technicians with a more matter-of-fact approach.

While there is no doubt that excavation records are more comprehensive than they have ever been, the human element ensures that they are by no means without subjective bias, since it is simply impossible in practical terms to describe and quantify every aspect of an archaeological site. It follows, therefore, that although delegation of recording tasks is an organisational necessity and fulfils a vital training function, there is no

YORK ARCHAEOLOGICAL TRUST	Site Code 01 1988·24	Area or grid 02 VII	CONTEXT NO 03 7599

Length 04 11·54 m	or dims. N-S	Width 05 8·90 m	or dims. W-E	Highest OD 06 7·54	Lowest OD 07 6·99	Pottery date 08 C10th–11th

Context Type

CUT type 09

STRUCTURE type 10

DEPOSIT type 11 Demolition rubble   Deposit Munsell 12

Description 13 Friable light-brown/yellow mortar

Inclusions 14 Frequent limestone fragments and larger blocks (up to 50cms long) – some faced. Occasional cobbles.

Relationships

Physically 15 Below 7418, 7458, 7609, 7702, 7571   Physically 16 Cut by 7529 7556

Physically 17 Above 7614, 7618, 7657, 7663, 7626   Physically 18 Cuts

Strat. 19 Below 7529, 7556, 7609, 7702   Butts/Butted by 20

Strat. 21 Above 7614, 7618, 7657   Bonded to 22

Contains 23   Fill of/ 24 Part of   Same as 25

Interpretation 26 It is possible that this layer derives from the demolition of the adjacent Roman wall 72528, but none of the limestone pieces is burnt as in the wall itself. It is also suggested that 7599 was deliberately laid down as a surface for a medieval timber building (cont. over)

Excavation method (tick) 27 Trowel ✓ Spade ☐ Machine ☐   Plan nos. 28 7599   Plan Zone(s) 29 B, C, E, F, H, I

Section nos. 30 37, 43   Sample nos. 31 2021–4, 2032–3   Finds 32 △19853–5 Ae coins △19856–7 Pb objects △19858 bone comb.

Photo ref. nos. 33 M 887500–9 C 889113–889120   Site book ref. 34   Date excavated 20·10·88

Compiled by P.J.O.

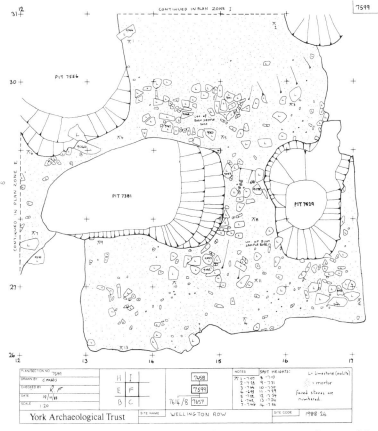

Figure 2.4 Recording the urban past: 1. Pro forma context recording card (top) and field plan of archaeological deposit (bottom) (eleventh-century rubble and mortar spread-cut by later medieval pits, Wellington Row site, York)

ROUGIER STREET 1981

Figure 2.5 Recording the urban past: 2. The section; north-west face of a trench at 5 Rougier Street, York, showing c. 6m (20 ft) of deposits with the Roman layers highlighted; note also the medieval pits cut down into the top of Roman layers (drawn by T. Finnemore, York Archaeological Trust)

sense in which current systems allow an excavation to function as a community of equals in which one person's opinion is as valid as another's. Experience soon tells us that some people are, by any standards, more perceptive than others and more accurate in recording what they perceive. Ultimately responsibility for the conduct of the excavation lies with the director, romantic or otherwise, who must not only ensure the making of a full and consistent record, appropriate to clear research objectives, but also evaluate and interpret that record to the best of his or her ability.

Chronology and dating

If archaeologists are to use their carefully recorded sequences of deposits and structures to make a significant contribution to the writing of history, then it is clearly crucial that they develop techniques for accurate dating. In practical terms, the generation of a sequence of events from the records of what may, on a complex urban site, be many hundreds or thousands of contexts, begins by retaining the concept of each one as a building block of equal value. Using the records of relationships between contexts established on site, the most convenient way of illustrating the sequence is in a diagram showing the contexts linked together, the earliest at one end and the latest at the other.[23] The preparation of these diagrams, or 'Harris matrices' as they are often known after their eponymous inventor, is the first task to occupy an excavator after completing work on site. In due course contexts can be grouped together into episodes of construction, pit digging, etc.

Once the sequence has been resolved, however, we still only have the contexts as they relate to each other as earlier or later; the next task is to give them 'real' dates and make up groups under period headings such as Roman, Anglo-Saxon, etc. In urban archaeology man-made artefacts remain the principal tools for dating, as opposed to scientific techniques. Coins are of particular importance because, although they did not bear dates in this country until the sixteenth century, numismatics is so well-developed a field of study that the minting date of most coins, whether Roman or later, can usually be pinned down to a few years if not a single year. In addition to coins there are other objects whose dates have been established by association in archaeological contexts either with coins or with the remains of known datable historical events, such as the burning of Colchester by Boudicca in AD 60 or the erection of Norman castles in the late eleventh century.

The problem with relying on coins for dating is that they are not usually found as frequently as one would like. It is only coins of the later third and fourth centuries, when inflation was rampant in the Roman empire, that are at all common as site finds. The most important artefact for dating

31

urban archaeological contexts is therefore pottery. Because pottery was usually cheap to produce in the past and because a pot is fragile and frequently broken, while the material itself is virtually indestructible, pot sherds are plentiful on most urban excavations. At the same time, pottery exhibits considerable diversity of form, fabric, decoration and finish, so that it lends itself to the development of detailed time-related sequences or 'typologies'. It is for this reason that a vital member of every archaeological unit is the pottery specialist, who may appear to have an unglamorous life spending year upon year ploughing through bag after bag of dusty old sherds, but in the end is the member of the team on whom all the others rely.

Until recently the study of Roman pottery has been rather more advanced than that of the post-Roman periods, reflecting again the initial pre-eminence of Roman studies in British urban archaeology. Dating Roman pottery is also easier, in a sense, because of the relatively large numbers of coins found in Roman contexts and the existence of samian ware. This is the shiny red tableware made in Gaul in the first to third centuries, whose distinctive forms, decorations and potters' stamps have been so extensively studied that the manufacturing date of most pieces can be given to within twenty to thirty years. It is not usually possible to date the less immediately inspiring 'coarseware' so accurately, but this material is now the principal subject of analysis. The dating of post-Roman pottery, especially of the later Anglo-Saxon period is, by contrast, very much a product of the last twenty to thirty years. Indeed it would be fair to say that one of the great unsung achievements of the urban archaeology units has been to use their long stratigraphic sequences to develop a post-Roman pottery typology for most regions of the country (see Plate 2.3).

At this point we must note that one of the principal characteristics of urban archaeological deposits is their mixed origins. It is in the nature of the human occupation of towns that there are continual disturbances of the ground with the digging of pits, foundations and so forth. As a result, artefacts may be redeposited on many occasions after initial loss or discard before finding their final resting place. A typical urban deposit may therefore contain objects made in many different time periods. To date the deposit itself it is necessary to identify the latest objects, the others then assume rather less importance and are described as 'residual'. Because of the problem of redeposition, dating with pottery is something of a numbers game in the sense, first, that a high percentage of sherds in a deposit are likely to be residual, so that it is necessary to have a relatively large group before one can be really confident of having at least a few which are more or less contemporary with the deposit itself. Second, the various attributes of pottery, especially locally-made earthenwares, may only change slowly and irregularly, so that dating relies on a consideration

Plate 2.3 A group of late Anglo-Saxon (early-eleventh-century) pottery from Lincoln. Rear: bowls and pitcher; front: crucible, lamp and bowl (Photograph: City of Lincoln Archaeological Unit)

of statistical trends in form, decoration and so on, rather than on spotting particular features.

In theory scientific dating techniques which do not rely on the judgement of a pottery specialist appear attractive, but their use has been limited in urban archaeology because they rarely give sufficiently precise results. On a prehistoric site where there are few datable finds and where accuracy to within fifty to a hundred years or so either way is acceptable, radiocarbon dating, for example, comes into its own, but in the Roman and post-Roman periods where one is usually aiming to work within much shorter time frames, it is not so useful. There is one scientific technique, however, which is proving of enormous value for urban archaeology: dendrochronology or tree-ring dating.[24]

The cross-section of a tree trunk reveals a sequence of concentric rings, each representing a year's growth; a ring's thickness depends on climatic factors, especially rainfall, which vary annually so that each year has a more or less unique ring 'signature'. Dendrochronology is based on measurement of the rings on ancient timbers and comparison of the size pattern with patterns or 'curves' dated in absolute terms by radiocarbon and other means. The development of the technique is now so well advanced as to allow the felling date of oak to be determined to within a few years for much of the last 2,000 years, in at least some parts of the country. For an ancient timber to be dated accurately, however, it should have at least 50–80 growth rings to enable exact matching with the master 'curve' and the rings should include the last to form (i.e. the outermost) on the original tree, although this so-called sapwood, being relatively soft, is usually removed from timbers used for structural purposes.

The application of dendrochronology depends, of course, on the survival of timber in the ground, which in turn depends largely on waterlogging. This occurs on a relatively small number of sites, but these do include London's Roman and medieval waterfronts (see pp. 64–7 and 189–94) which have produced the raw material for one of the most extensive dendrochronology projects in Britain. The results are particularly valuable not only for accurately dating the structures themselves, but also for dating the large number of artefacts directly associated with the landfill behind them.

Finds – 'anything interesting?'

The most common question an archaeologist has to field from members of the public is 'have you found anything interesting?' By this the questioner does not usually mean Roman walls or medieval streets or any of the other structural features which absorb the excavator, but small objects, preferably made of silver or gold, although a human skeleton will also give satisfaction. It is an unfortunate, if understandable, consequence of the way archaeology was conducted in foreign fields or foreign deserts in the past that the subject is still very much associated in the public mind with treasure or 'loot'. Our materialist western society relentlessly fetishises ancient and antique objects on the basis of their monetary value while ignoring what they can tell us about the lives of the human beings who made and used them.

Most archaeologists are, of course, thrilled by digging up beautiful and precious objects. Such finds are, however, unusual and it is worth outlining what the finds from urban archaeological deposits are likely to consist of and why. The vast bulk of finds include: first, building materials, such as stone, bricks, tiles, mortar and plaster; second, potsherds; third, animal bones, deriving primarily from food consumption; and fourth, industrial waste, usually metalworking slag, which is perhaps the most unloved item in the excavator's finds tray. Iron objects can occur in quite large numbers, although a substantial proportion will be nails, but, otherwise, man-made artefacts in metal, bone, glass or more exotic materials, such as amber or jet, are rare. The reason for this is simply that what we are usually digging up in and around the buildings and streets of our ancient towns is refuse: material which was thrown out as being of no further use.

Until relatively recently, of course, the vast majority of people had very few material possessions. What they had was carefully looked after and if it was possible the material was recycled when the object itself was no longer usable. This pattern of rigorous 'curation' remains common today in many Third World countries. Objects will, of course, be dropped in even the poorest communities, and, if they are small and the floors of buildings and yards are muddy, they will be hard to recover even if their loss is noticed. Most 'small finds' from archaeological sites are, therefore, exactly that, small, and also of low value, then and now. On occasions in the past, however, objects were deliberately buried as grave offerings, for religious purposes or as hoards for safekeeping during times of danger. As a result of such practices archaeologists can have the good luck to find objects of great artistic merit and monetary value. It should be stressed, however, that this is very exceptional and such finds are primarily of value for what they tell us about the past and not for what they can fetch at auction.

We have looked briefly at the study of artefacts for dating purposes, but as any specialist will tell you, this is only the beginning of a process which can lead to an understanding of the technology, economy and social organisation of the community producing them. As an example we may consider the use of pottery for studying trade, a crucial aspect of the urban economy. Most trade in which early towns were involved would have been in perishable goods, such as food and textiles which rarely survive in the ground, but some indication of trading networks can be indicated by pottery, providing its source can be determined. The easiest wares to source are usually those imported from foreign countries which stand out in terms of form, decoration and so forth from the local types. The best way to source the latter is to discover the kilns where they were produced. Failing this, distribution maps can indicate market centres which were probably close to the kiln sites themselves. We can also use scientific techniques such as thin-sectioning. This involves treating ceramic like a geological specimen and studying the quantity and types of mineral in the clay, which can then be related to clay beds in the ground.

A vital role in artefact research is played by the conservator (see Plate 2.4) who is another of the growing number of archaeological specialists with a scientific background.[25] Although one part of the conservator's job is to ensure that objects do not decay or disintegrate after excavation, there is much more to it, since in the process of preserving an object it is necessary to investigate the nature of its material and the way it has been manufactured. As an example of the role of conservation in artefact research, we may look at the treatment of iron objects. They are relatively common finds on urban sites because the metal was used by townsmen for a wide variety of purposes; there were tools for trades and crafts, fittings for doors, chests and other furniture, and horse trappings and weapons.

Before the industrial revolution made the blast furnace universal, iron was made by the 'direct method'.[26] This involved heating, or smelting, the iron ore with charcoal and a flux, usually limestone, to absorb the impurities. In this process the iron was never molten as simple furnaces

Plate 2.4 Archaeological conservation in action: Erica Paterson, conservator at York Archaeological Trust, with heavily corroded medieval iron coffin fittings and X-ray plates (Photograph: York Archaeological Trust)

could not develop sufficient heat, although many of the impurities flowed away before congealing into amorphous lumps of slag. The bloom, or iron lump, produced by smelting in this way was inevitably somewhat heterogeneous both in terms of the composition of the metal itself and because of the remaining slag it contained. All objects made from iron smelted by the direct method, as opposed to cast iron, have a slightly fibrous appearance created by thin strings of slag.

Since the technology did not exist to get iron hot enough to cast in moulds, every object had to be forged individually by hand. One of the smith's particular skills, however, was to make the iron, which in pure form is a relatively soft if ductile metal, into harder more rigid steel suitable for bladed tools (see Plate 2.5). This involved the introduction of small quantities of carbon, usually by heating the iron in charcoal from which carbon diffused into the metal. Although a slow process, it had to be judged to perfection since overdoing it would create a metal which was too brittle. Cooling the hot metal required skill also and usually involved rapid quenching in water since allowing slow cooling would mean loss of carbon. In short, like all the processes of smithing, making steel relied on the skill of the smith's eye and hand, informed by experience and based on knowledge handed down from father to son. This tradition has now been largely destroyed by the mass production of steel, so that archaeologists studying the working of iron made by the direct method are studying a technology, and a sophisticated one at that, which has largely disappeared.

Plate 2.5 The art of the tenth-century smith and the twentieth-century conservator: knives (handles missing) from 16–22 Coppergate, York (the longest is 135mm/c. 5 ins) (Photograph: York Archaeological Trust)

One of the problems of rediscovering the traditional smith's art is that when iron objects come out of the ground they are usually heavily corroded, often appearing as unexciting, reddish-brown amorphous lumps. To determine the identity of an iron object it is first X-rayed. Just as a medical X-radiograph will show bones under the skin, so an archaeological X-radiograph will show the form of an iron object under the corrosion, along with any non-ferrous plating and such technological features as weld lines. The X-radiograph can then guide the conservator in the careful removal of the corrosion layer. This is a highly skilled job requiring great patience and the ability to recognise features which may not be apparent on an X-radiograph, such as the remains of textile or leather which has corroded on to the metal. Finally the object will be stored in environmentally stable conditions with moisture and temperature strictly controlled to prevent further corrosion and preserve it in good condition for further research.

Organic finds – from beetles to bodies

In our discussion of finds we have so far concentrated on man-made objects, but another important development in archaeological research in recent years is the analysis of organic material, which includes not only the bones of humans and other animals, but also plant remains, insects and even micro-organisms such as parasite eggs. The science of what is usually called environmental archaeology has opened up immense new vistas on the past, bringing us into contact with its natural environment, but more especially with the way in which humanity exploited that environment and its resources.[27]

The extent to which organic matter survives varies considerably and is dependent on the burial environment. On most urban sites bones survive quite well, although they can be largely destroyed by acid soil. Other material will be much more poorly preserved unless the processes of decay caused by bacterial action have been hampered and this requires a burial environment in which oxygen is excluded. Wells and pits sealed immediately after use can provide localised pockets of good organic preservation on any type of site, but the best environment for preservation on a large scale arises where refuse disposal practices have created compacted layers of organic debris which have then become waterlogged. This combination can be found on one of Britain's richest sites for the study of the early urban environment, the Anglo-Scandinavian town at York (see pp. 146–55), where deposits excavated at sites such as Lloyds Bank (6–8 Pavement)[28] and 16–22 Coppergate consisted entirely of organic matter, including wood, all manner of plant remains and dung from various sources. As anyone who has worked on these deposits will know, they are quite unlike anything else in archaeology, if only because of the smell which will be guaranteed to get you a seat to yourself on the bus home!

Even on predominantly 'dry' sites the form of organic matter may be preserved by its replacement in the ground by non-organic minerals. Faeces, for example, provide suitable micro-environments for the chemical processes involved, and ancient stools, or coprolites as they are known, which appear as light, greyish pellets are quite common, although usually canine rather than human (see Plate 5.9). The corrosion of metal objects will also mineralise and preserve the form of organic items, including plant remains and textiles, buried in contact with them. Finally charring has a preservative effect, and charred grain, for example, which may result either from accidents or deliberate destruction of infested stores, is another common find.

The recovery of organic matter requires special techniques. Bones, for example, can be hand-collected during excavation, but this will not provide a very representative assemblage since those of smaller mammals, birds and fish will be largely missed. To ensure full recovery of bones and other categories of finds, deposits have to be carefully sieved. This can be done on site, but the recovery of smaller more delicate organic material such as insects (see Plate 2.6) or pollen grains will require the transfer of soil samples from the rigours of the excavation to the laboratory for careful disaggregation.

Plate 2.6 The wonderful world of environmental archaeology: tenth-century fly puparia from the Lloyds Bank site, York (average length 8mm/c. $\frac{1}{3}$ in.) (Photograph: York Archaeological Trust)

Environmental archaeology can, on occasions, tell us about natural phenomena. Changes in river regime, for example, can be determined by the occurrence of micro-organisms preferring greater or lesser salinity. We can also learn about the faunal and floral surroundings of a town: the plants that grew by the river banks and on patches of waste ground, the trees in the local woods and the birds that flew about in them. We must be aware, however, that, by and large, these surroundings were not entirely natural, but man-made or at least man-affected. Environmental archaeology in an urban context, therefore, tells us primarily about the way man exploited nature with cultivated crops and domesticated animals, and about the effect of man's activities on the local fauna and flora. As we shall see in both Roman York (see pp. 89–91) and medieval Oxford (see p. 179), the process of urbanisation is matched by marked changes in the ecosystem, with, for example, increased occurrence of the insects, fleas and lice which enjoy life on human beings themselves and on their decomposing refuse.

A substantial proportion of organic finds derives, in one way or another, from food, and few aspects of archaeology have more general appeal than the study of what our ancestors ate. We will touch on this subject again in the following chapters, but in general terms our knowledge of meat-eating is quite comprehensive because of the good survival of bones.[29] The frequent occurrence of bran and grain also shows that a high-fibre diet was standard for early townspeople. The preservation of fruit and vegetables is less good, but a wide variety is known, with a range of pulses and legumes; some of the latter, like the splendidly named Fat Hen and Good King Henry, are usually considered as weeds, but would have provided a highly nutritious addition to the diet of the urban poor.

Food remains are good indicators of how standards of living varied over time and can indicate social distinctions between different parts of towns. In medieval Southampton, for example, the thirteenth century saw a marked change in diet,[30] at least for the rich merchants living near the quayside. Compared to their forebears in the twelfth century they had a much greater variety of meat including veal and sucking pig. The bone material showed, moreover, that the meat was no longer cut off the carcass on the premises, but arrived as small joints prepared on a commercial basis by a specialist butcher. Other dietary novelties included a range of game birds and imported figs and grapes.

Deserving a place in our attention equal to that of food is the subject of cleanliness and sanitation. Insect remains are of particular value in this respect because, while animals and plants may move or be moved from their natural habitat, insects usually die where they lived. This subject has been studied extensively in York and the insect assemblages appear to show that, while the Roman town was usually, but not always, kept fairly tidy, the Anglo-Scandinavian and medieval town – until perhaps the fourteenth century – was full of decomposing organic matter, deriving from a variety of sources including the disposal of food, defecation, and plant material used as floor covering.

The evidence of diet and living conditions can give us some impression of the health and well-being of ancient townspeople, but of particular interest, of course, are their own mortal remains. The systematic study of human skeletons is, like that of other organic materials, one of the more recent developments in archaeology. Until recently burials were only of interest to antiquaries and archaeologists if they were interred in an elaborate coffin or accompanied by artefacts. Unfurnished burials, usually surviving simply as a skeleton in a bath-shaped pit, which were common in Roman times and the norm from the middle Anglo-Saxon period onwards, received scant attention. The situation in the early 1960s was summed up by the authors of the report on the church of St Mary-le-Port, Bristol as follows :[31]

> The general impression, including the 'official' view of central government and local museum sponsorship, was that we knew all we needed to know about Christian burial, that in any case they had no finds, and that there was an element of impropriety in disturbing or even looking scientifically at interments of a community whose religious beliefs and mortuary practice were at least nominally those of our own day.

Matters were not helped by various unfortunate episodes in the city:

> There had in the 1950s been some scandal in Bristol about the destruction of cemeteries (notably one in the Horsefair), when the skeletons were taken away unceremoniously in lorries. This was stopped only when some fell off a lorry, were picked up by children and taken to show their schoolteachers.

In spite of such setbacks, however, archaeologists and palaeo-anthropologists have gradually developed methods for excavating and analysing human remains and have thereby created a respectable scientific discipline.[32] At the same time propriety has been ensured by the Burial Grounds Amendment Act of 1981 which requires developers proposing to disturb burials to have them removed from site in a seemly fashion at their expense.

The study of a skeleton, providing it is reasonably complete, will reveal, first of all its sex and approximate age at death. Secondly, although the fleshy parts are missing we can get some idea of the physical appearance of our forebears from their bones, and one easily measurable dimension is height. Contrary to popular belief there is no evidence for any substantial change in the stature of townspeople over the centuries until after the Second World War, since when, thanks to better diet, we have become on average slightly taller. Examination of bones can also reveal responses to various forms of stress.[33] This may be manifested as a chronic response, such as osteoarthritis which is very common on the skeletons of early townspeople and is probably a product of the general wear and tear of

41

life rather than any particular occupational or environmental conditions. Acute responses to stress may be manifested as wounds or fractures. The cause of a person's death is only rarely detectable from the skeleton, although presumed fatal blows to the skull have been detected. Some evidence may appear for growth abnormalities such as rickets, and one of the earliest known cases was recently found in an Anglo-Saxon skeleton at Norwich.[34] Infectious diseases only affect the skeleton occasionally, but one of the most gruesome sights for an archaeologist is a tubercular spine where the vertebrae have become distorted and fused together.

The study of the bodies themselves is, of course, only half the story as far as cemeteries are concerned since they are also cultural artefacts which in many ways reflect the structure of living society. We know from our own time that the way a person is buried, from cremation in the municipal cemetery to burial in Westminster Abbey, says a great deal about a person's status and rank in life. Similarly, from the study of where ancient people were buried and with what degree of ceremony, we may get an impression of how society treated such social divisions as those between men and women, young and old, or rich and poor. Some understanding of this point can be gained in almost any church and churchyard today, where the burials in the building are usually of the rich and landed while lesser mortals are interred outside.

Reconstructing the urban past

It often comes as a surprise to the general public that archaeologists do not spend all their time digging, and that much more time – and money – is spent in the office or laboratory writing up the results of fieldwork. As research methods and analytical techniques have improved and archaeologists have become more ambitious about what can be discovered, the 'post-excavation' process has become more and more expensive and time-consuming, and the comprehensiveness expected of archaeological reports is now much greater than it has ever been. This is not to say that reports produced in the early years of field archaeology were necessarily poor, rather that they often suffered from a lack of resources of both a financial and technical nature.

However much one might, on occasions, agree with its sentiments, it would, none the less, be difficult for an archaeologist today to offer as an excuse for a report's shortcomings that once used by Wheeler:

> The mechanical, predictable, quality of Roman craftsmanship, the advertised humanitas of Roman civilisation, which lay always so near to brutality and corruption, fatigued and disgusted me so that my Verulamium report fell short in some parts of its record.[35]

In Wheeler's defence, of course, one could say that few archaeologists today are able to write with the gusto, style and imagination of the great man. Indeed, anyone expecting a good read out of the modern archaeological site report will probably be disappointed. The reason is that, very properly, reports have as their primary function the presentation of information on strata, finds and so forth which is often of a very detailed and specialist nature. The production of such a report with its accumulation of facts is, however, not the end of the archaeologist's work. The final step is to interpret these facts, to infuse them with some meaning so that we may gain a new understanding of the past.

A fundamental aspect of the process of interpretation is the reconstruction of the physical environment in the past, either in the form of an individual structure (see Figure 2.6) or the entire townscape (see Figure 5.2). There are a number of illustrations in this book which show how effective the reconstruction of buildings is as a means of interpretation, but the exercise is not without problems, since it is rare for a buried urban structure to survive in such good condition as the twelfth-century merchant's house recently excavated at St Martin-at-Palace-Plain in Norwich (see p. 181).[36] More often than not structural remains are extremely vestigial, existing, perhaps, as walls which are largely demolished, patchy floor surfaces and a few post holes. Occasionally there are below-ground features, such as cellars or garderobe pits, and even more occasionally such superstructural elements as collapsed walls and roofs. It is often impossible, therefore, to come to valid conclusions about a building's original plan, let alone its overall appearance and function. Should sufficient survive, however, archaeologists may employ not only the excavated evidence itself as a basis for reconstruction, but also analogues in the form of surviving buildings of the period which appear to share common features with the buried example. The existence of useful analogues, of course, varies considerably. At one end of the scale there are, for instance, quite a number of major Roman public buildings still standing in the former empire, so that it is possible to reconstruct the theatre at Canterbury (see Figure 3.8) or forum at London (see Figure 1.2) with some degree of confidence. Similarly, later medieval timber-framed and stone-built houses, albeit principally of the upper classes, survive in some numbers, allowing valid reconstructions of excavated examples (see Figure 2.6). At the other end of the scale, however, are the dwellings of the mass of population of all the periods covered in this book, which are the most commonly excavated, but of which few if any examples survive. Interpreting their remains inevitably brings the archaeological imagination more strongly into play, but, whether there are analogues to help or not, the archaeologist who would attempt the reconstruction of buildings must also become something of an architect and civil engineer, and acquire some understanding of the load-bearing capacities of timbers of particular sizes, methods of supporting roofs and so on.

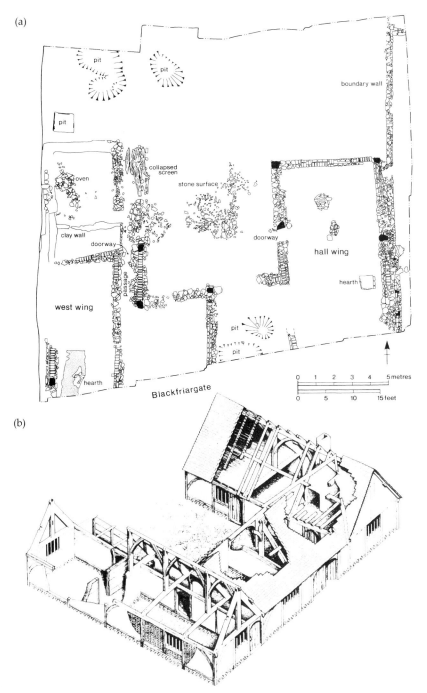

(a)

pit

pit

pit

boundary wall

oven

collapsed
screen

stone surface

clay wall

doorway

doorway

hall wing

passage

hearth

west wing

hearth

pit

pit

Blackfriargate

| 0 | 1 | 2 | 3 | 4 | 5 metres |

| 0 | 5 | 10 | 15 feet |

(b)

Figure 2.6 Reconstructing the urban past: (a) excavated plan of the Wytelard property, Monkgate, Hull in the early to mid-fourteenth century (after Armstrong and Ayers 1987, Figure 31); (b) the archaeologist's reconstruction of the building based on the plan and on standing buildings of the period (East Riding Archaeological Society)

When we move from reconstruction of overall structure and external appearance of buildings to that of their internal appearance, similar approaches apply. Archaeological evidence relates, of course, primarily to features at ground level, and one of the most common discoveries is the hearth, which may simply be an area of burnt clay or a more solid brick or stone-built structure. The detailed examination of internal surfaces by modern archaeological techniques can, however, allow the plotting of both formal divisions of space by walls and other partitions, and less formal divisions revealed by the distribution of distinctive artefacts and wear patterns on the floors.

Archaeological remains of furniture and fittings are more elusive than walls and floors. Not only were they made of perishable material, primarily wood or textile, but they were usually removed before buildings were abandoned or demolished. We must hope, therefore, for the remains of disasters, fires or sudden collapse, which took the inhabitants by surprise such that they left their possessions behind, as in the case of a bed burnt in Boudicca's attack on Colchester.[37] The use of analogy with standing buildings to reconstruct interiors in the past is difficult since the latter are more sensitive to changing social needs. The use of rooms and fashions in decor may change frequently while the basic structure remains the same.

While reconstructing the physical appearance of early towns – their buildings, streets, defences and so forth – absorbs much of the urban archaeologist's time, we must also remember that, in the well-known words of Mortimer Wheeler, 'the archaeological excavator is not digging up things, he is digging up people'.[38] From the remains of buildings, their surroundings and associated artefacts and organic finds, urban archaeologists try to create as vivid a picture as possible of townsmen and townswomen in the past as they went about their daily lives sheltering and feeding themselves, caring for their children, making a living and, of course, dumping their refuse. We may also glimpse leisure hours spent carving bone, playing musical instruments, gambling on board games and enjoying the company of pets. Finally we can gain some insight into religious beliefs, from-day-to-day superstition, which might involve the burial of a pot under the floor of a Roman building, to sophisticated theology manifested in the organisation of an Anglo-Saxon cathedral.

Although the scope of archaeology to reveal the past is great and increasing, this chapter should not be concluded without reminding the reader that the nature of the evidence constrains archaeology to be primarily concerned with men and women as communal and social beings. It is rare that it can tell us about a particular named historical personality in any detail. Of course it is exciting when an inscription or artefact allows this, but by and large archaeology is about the people who do not figure in the history books, in short it is about the lives of people like you (probably) and me.

3

EARLY ROMAN TOWNS

The colony at Colchester – 'the citadel of their servitude'

On approaching the Essex market town of Colchester by road, you will be greeted at the town boundary by a sign which bears the words 'Welcome to Colchester – Britain's Oldest Recorded Town'. The visitor may, however, be forgiven for asking what this town consisted of. To the classical scholar the '-chester' element in the modern name, derived from the latin *castra*, a camp, suggests a Roman origin, but virtually all that is recognisably 'historic' in Colchester is a few stretches of town wall and the Norman castle. The disappearance of the tangible remains of Colchester's past is, of course, largely due to the growth and accompanying rebuilding of the town in the twentieth century, which has culminated in some major redevelopment projects in the 1970s and 1980s. It was in advance of these redevelopments, however, that a remarkable series of excavations made discoveries vital not only for understanding Colchester's Roman past, but also the origins of urbanism in Britain.

In essence Roman civilisation was an urban civilisation based on a network of city states which acted as centres for all the economic, political, social and religious life of their region. As we have already noted, these cities were graded according to legal status and this in turn determined the inhabitant's status, including tax liability and level of punishment in the event of wrongdoing. Every town in the empire was, up to a point, organised along the lines of Rome itself, with a town council, or *ordo*, nominally made up of one hundred *decuriones* who qualified to serve on the basis of a property qualification. They elected four magistrates annually, two to act as justices and two to carry out public works.[1] Although Rome itself did not have much of a clear and ordered plan, provincial towns usually bore some resemblance to a Roman ideal. The principal streets were laid out on a rectilinear grid pattern which divided the urban area into what were known as *insulae* (islands). The central *insulae* were occupied by the public buildings which included the forum, essentially a large courtyard, often used as a market, which was enclosed on three sides by shops or offices behind a colonnaded portico and on the fourth by the basilica, a hall in which administrative and judicial business was conducted. In adjacent *insulae* there would usually be a public bath house, temple to the Roman gods and, on occasions, a theatre.

In Britain the Romans encountered a country without towns, a country where the vast majority of the population lived in small villages or isolated farmsteads. In order to conquer, govern and tax the Britons, therefore, the Roman administration had to create towns. This involved stimulating a taste for urban living, and a willingness on the part of the leaders of native British society to adopt the Roman custom of paying for public works as a way of expressing their social status. A reference to the problem of changing the life-style of the native Britons is specifically made by Tacitus in a well-known passage in his biography of Agricola, Governor of Britain from AD 78 to 84:

> Agricola had to deal with people living in isolation and ignorance, and therefore prone to fight; and his object was to accustom them to a life of peace and quiet by the provision of amenities. He therefore gave private encouragement and official assistance to the building of temples, public squares, and good houses.[2]

In the light of this passage it is, perhaps, no accident that one of the earliest mosaics in the palace at Fishbourne, near Chichester, probably built to ensure the loyalty of a native British king, is a simplified representation of a Roman town with walls, gates and a street grid.[3] It is, to a great extent, by the success of urbanisation that we may measure the success of the Roman conquest of Britain.

Armed with this yardstick, we may now ask why the Romans chose to start at Colchester. The answer is that one of the principal centres of British resistance to the Roman invasion in AD 43 was a site at Gosbecks, now on the south-western outskirts of the modern town (see Figure 3.1).[4] This was the headquarters of the Trinovantes, one of the dominant peoples of south-eastern England in the early first century AD. They were ruled in 43 by the sons of King Cunobelin who had been leader of the Catuvellauni, another important tribe with a base at Verulamium. All that survives above ground today of the native capital at Colchester is a series of prominent linear earthworks, or dykes, and a burial mound known as the Lexden tumulus. These sites have been the subject of considerable speculation since at least the eighteenth century, and in 1759 they were drawn and mapped by the famous antiquary William Stukeley, inventor of druidic mythology, who also suggested that The Mount, a surviving Roman burial mound, was Cunobelin's grave.[5]

Systematic examination of the dykes and the areas within them has its origins in the 1920s and 1930s, and major excavations by Christopher Hawkes and Rex Hull, curator of the Castle Museum, took place at Sheepen, five miles north of Gosbecks on the banks of the river Colne.[6] In

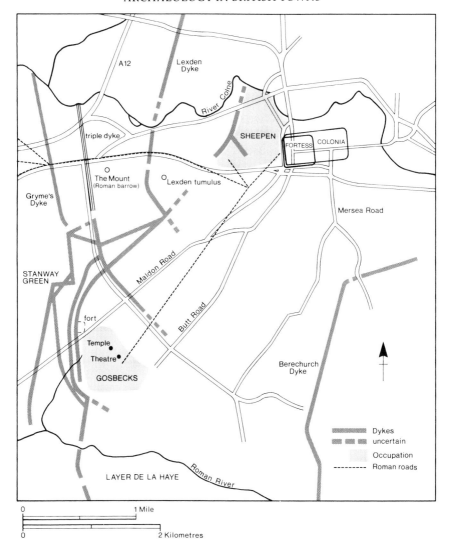

Figure 3.1 Plan of the principal sites of the late Iron Age and Roman periods in the Colchester area (drawn by Glenys Boyles; Colchester Museum)

addition to native huts, pottery kilns and numerous coins of Cunobelin were found, indicating a manufacturing and trading centre. Of particular importance was the discovery of moulds for making coin flans, which indicated that this was the site of a mint, presumably under royal control.

Two Roman temples were also found at Sheepen which were of 'Celtic' type, square in plan, with a small central shrine surrounded by an ambulatory.[7] The principal native cult site may, however, have been at Gosbecks,

48

where a farmstead within a large ditched enclosure has been identified as a royal residence. Close by was another temple of Celtic type set in a colonnaded precinct near which a fine statue of Mercury was found. A Roman theatre in the area may also have been used for religious ceremonies as well as secular entertainments. The temples were probably successors to native versions, of which no trace has been found, and may have been allowed and even encouraged by the Romans, with the aim of reassuring the Britons by retaining an element of continuity in a rapidly changing world.

The Gosbecks/Sheepen complex can probably be characterised as one of a small group of Iron Age sites in southern Britain known as *oppida*, which were not strictly urban, but had a number of distinctive economic, political and ceremonial functions dependent on a native royal establishment. The exact nature of the relationship between the *oppidum* at Colchester and the walled Roman town on higher ground to its northeast was, however, obscure until relatively recently.

The recording of Roman discoveries in and around the centre of Colchester has a long history.[8] The earliest systematic account of the Roman town was written by the Reverend Philip Morant in 1748.[9] He was an acquaintance of Stukeley and wrote at a time when there was fierce controversy as to the location of the Roman site referred to by Tacitus as *Camoludunum*.[10] As a Colchester man, it is, perhaps, not surprising that Morant gave way to hyperbole when he supported the town's claim by concluding:

> There are more Roman remains in and about this town than in any other part of southern Britain; nay I may justly affirm, than in any other part of Europe out of the Italian dominions, where stood Rome, the centre of glory, and the metropolis of that great empire.[11]

Morant was, of course, ultimately proved correct and *Camulodunum* did indeed refer to the British *oppidum* at Colchester, adjacent to which the 20th legion established a base which was subsequently replaced by the *Colonia Claudia Victricensis*. The title *colonia* (colony) indicates a Roman town of the highest rank whose essential component was a substantial body of Roman citizens. In the four British *coloniae* (Colchester, Gloucester, Lincoln and York) most of these people were legionary veterans and their families who would have been given land in the surrounding region in return for which they were expected to promote the interests of the Roman state. Sponsored, appropriately, by the Morant Club, it was on the north side of the Castle Park that the first large archaeological excavation in Colchester took place in 1920, with the express intention of giving some topographic framework to the large collection of artefacts from the town.[12] The director was the young Mortimer Wheeler. Amongst the earliest remains of houses and streets, Wheeler found burnt debris which he associated with the revolt, described by Tacitus, of Queen Boudicca (then known as Boadicea) of the native Iceni people in AD 60.[13] Wheeler and Dr Laver, an active local antiquary, also identified the walls of the 'vaults' under the castle as foundations for the podium of the great Roman temple where the colonists made their last blood-stained stand against Boudicca.[14]

The pace of new building in Colchester quickened after the second World War and in 1963 the Colchester Excavation Committee was revived to record threatened sites. Of particular interest was work in 1965 on North Hill where, in addition to the discovery of houses with fine mosaics, early Roman buildings were found of a type to suggest the presence of a military base associated with the 20th legion.[15] The breakthrough in making the crucial link between the Gosbecks/Sheepen native settlement and the Roman town itself, however, came during excavations directed by Philip Crummy, director of the Colchester Archaeological Trust, at Lion Walk in 1972.[16] The earliest remains on the site included two ditches, – one running east–west, the other north–south – of classic Roman military type with a V-shaped cross-section. Enclosed by them were the remains of elongated, rectangular buildings which could only be barracks; the fortress of the 20th had finally emerged.

The Lion Walk site showed that the fortress had had a short life. The ditches were deliberately backfilled and a street, clearly part of the *colonia* plan, was found running across the north–south line. Further large-scale excavations on the Culver Street site showed that some fortress buildings had been demolished to make way for another *colonia* street, but others remained standing. Crucial at both Lion Walk and Culver Street was the recognition once again of extensive burnt debris datable to Boudicca's attack; not only did this material overlie the fortress ditches, but also the streets and remains of buildings. The overall sequence was now clear: in AD 43 a fortress had been built on high ground to the north-east of the native site. Some six years later the legion moved on and, after perhaps another five years, its defences were levelled and the Roman *colonia* was laid out. The western half was on the same site as the fortress whose street plan was largely retained; the eastern half had streets on a slightly different alignment (see Figure 3.2). In the former fortress some of the barracks were re-used as dwellings for the veteran settlers before being burnt by Boudicca.

At the same time as these discoveries were made at Colchester, a similar picture of the re-use of a fortress site for a *colonia*, although later in the first century, emerged from excavations at Gloucester.[17] There is no clear evidence at Gloucester for the re-use of buildings and streets, but it is worth quoting a comment made by Sheppard Frere in 1975:

the discovery at Colchester and Gloucester that far from being settled in a pleasant new urban development, these old soldiers were

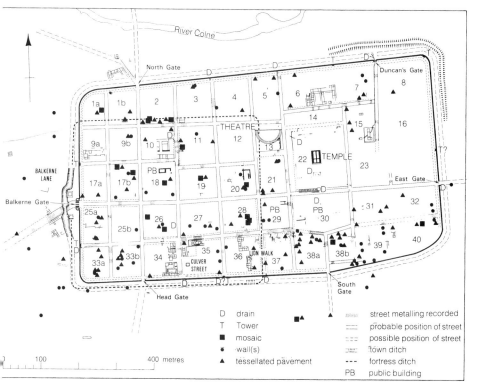

Figure 3.2 Plan of the Roman *colonia* at Colchester showing the line of the Roman fortress defences and location of principal buildings and other finds (Colchester Archaeological Trust)

crammed into re-used barracks left over from the days of military occupation comes as something of a shock: no site elsewhere in Europe or the other provinces of the Roman Empire had prepared us for this situation.[18]

After these words were written, Exeter also produced evidence for the re-use of a fortress for civilian purposes. In c. AD 75 the men of the 2nd legion moved to Caerleon in south Wales and some ten years later their base was converted into *Isca Dumnoniorum*, capital of the *civitas*, or territory, of the *Dumnonii* people.[19] The legionary baths were replaced by the town forum and basilica (see Plate 3.1) and well-preserved remains of both buildings were found in excavations west of the cathedral in the late 1970s. Indeed they still survive and it is to be hoped that they may one day be re-excavated for public inspection.

At Lincoln (see Figure 4.3), where by c. 96 a *colonia* had succeeded the fortress, there is, as yet, no indication of the fate of the barracks, but

Plate 3.1 Exeter: from fortress to town. The *pilae* (floor supports) of the *caldarium* (hot room) of the fortress baths and (right) the steps up from the forum courtyard to the basilica built over the remains of the earlier building (scale 2m/c. 6 ft 6 ins) (Photograph: Exeter Museums Archaeological Field Unit)

excavations on the St Paul-in-the-Bail site have shown how the site of the fortress headquarters, or *principia*, was reoccupied in the early second century by the forum and basilica.[20] Where the *principia* had faced east, however, the forum was shown to have faced south. It then became clear, first, that a line of Roman columns, discovered in the late nineteenth century and known as the Bailgate colonnade, supported a portico on the east side of the forum. Secondly, one of Britain's most important, but least known and least-visited, Roman monuments, the splendid Mint Wall, still standing over 8m (13 ft) high above the footings, was shown to have formed the rear wall of the basilica on the north side of the forum court-yard.

Constructed in the eastern part of the new colony at Colchester were the public buildings, intended as a model for the Britons to admire and emulate. Chief amongst them was the temple for the worship of the spirit, or *numen*, of the Emperor Claudius on which work probably started immediately after his death in AD 54. The idea, cynical though it may seem, behind the Roman state's deification of its emperors was to provide an emotional and spiritual focus for the increasingly disparate peoples of the empire which would also serve the underlying political purpose of securing loyalty to the ruling house. Although nothing survives above the foundations, the temple of Claudius was clearly one of the few built in classical style in Britain, resembling, perhaps, the famous Maison Carrée in Nîmes, with a raised podium and colonnaded façade. The Colchester temple is also known from excavations to have been surrounded by a large open area enclosed by a precinct wall with a monumental arcade on the south side.[21] Another public building erected at much the same time was the theatre, some footings of which were recently discovered in Maidenburgh Street where they can still be seen.[22]

In the new colonies at Colchester, Gloucester and Lincoln we begin to see how Roman imperial power was exerted through the careful selection of new urban sites. The extensive native settlement at Gosbecks/Sheepen, with its royal enclosure, protected by dykes, had clearly been a focus of both political and religious authority, and a centre for trade and manu-facturing. To emphasise the change of regime the Romans took a new, but adjacent site and transferred to it the functions of the old site, organised in a new way and populated by a hard core of people who had an interest in promoting the new order.

The appearance of the colony, with the first monumental stone buildings ever seen in England, must have been astonishing to the Britons, but it was also a potential source of resentment as traditional economic and social relations were disrupted – 'the citadel of their servitude' as Tacitus called it.[23] It is no surprise, therefore, that when Boudicca rebelled she made straight for the colony and burnt it down. Excavations have con-firmed Tacitus' reference to a lack of defences[24] which had clearly made the queen's task easier. For archaeologists, however, the fire has provided a distinct charred layer which, as we have seen, has made discovery of the town's early history possible. In this deposit, moreover, material is preserved which would otherwise decay to nothing, so that, for example, sections of building-wall survived at Lion Walk, where the timber had disappeared but the clay coating had baked hard leaving the voids of uprights and clear impressions of wattles. More remarkable discoveries were the textile covering and stuffing of a bed and the charred remains of dates, imported as luxuries, but never enjoyed by the customer.

After Boudicca's revolt had been crushed, the colony was gradually rebuilt, this time with defences, a classic case of shutting the stable door after the horse has bolted. Here our attention must move to the west side of the Roman town, to the site at Balkerne Lane, now developed for the inner ring road. It lies in a cutting parallel to the town walls, but goes across the line of what was originally the main Roman road to London which left the town from what is known today as the Balkerne Gate (see Plate 3.2). Boudiccan fire deposits were again recognised in excavation, overlying the backfilled fortress ditch, but cut by a new ditch to defend the colony.

While working on this site Philip Crummy turned his attention to the Balkerne Gate itself. This had originally been examined by Mortimer

Plate 3.2 Part of the upstanding remains of the Balkerne Gate at Colchester showing the opening into the southern guard chamber (see Figure 3.3)

Wheeler as a young army captain in 1917, when he was asked to complete some previous investigations. As Wheeler put it:

> My modus operandi was to detail, evening by evening, three or four volunteers from my battery and, with their aid, to make what sense I could of the untidy furrows. The nucleus of my gang was my groom ... and one of my gunners.[25]

Part of the gate lies underneath a pub named 'The Hole in the Wall' hence Wheeler goes on:

> To these a variety of bodies were added, attracted less by archae-ological research than by the homely noises of – and subsequent participation in – the revelry of the tap-room overhead.

Philip Crummy was able to reinterpret Wheeler's work and show that what he had regarded as a secondary rebuilding of the gate was in fact the remains of a free-standing monumental arch, which had been incorporated in the gate when the town wall was built (see Figure 3.3). Until recently the wall was thought to be early third-century and to have been erected as part of the widespread movement to defend Roman towns at this time (see pp. 95–7), but it is now clear that the wall and rampart are not contemporary. The wall was built free-standing no later than AD 65–80 and was presumably a response to the Boudiccan revolt.[26] While one possible context for the erection of the arch is the defeat of Boudicca, since it was typical Roman practice to erect commemorative monuments in such circumstances, it is more likely, in view of the date of the town walls, that construction took place c. 50. The Colchester arch may, there-fore, be seen as marking the foundation of the *colonia* or even the conquest of Britain itself.

The walls are made of septaria, a form of clay which is vulnerable to erosion and frost, and this explains the extensive rebuilding in medieval times, but well-preserved stretches of Roman wall can still be seen in a number of places standing up to 4m (13 ft) high. It is sad to record, however, that in 1987 a huge service basement under the Culver Street shopping centre required the removal of a fine 10m (33 ft) stretch of Roman work. Although it has been reconstructed nearby, it is now at a 90 degree angle to the true line.[27] It is hard to believe that the shopping centre will last for more than a small fraction of the nearly 2,000 years of Britain's first town wall.

Early Roman London – 'a centre for businessmen and merchandise'

While the *coloniae* at Colchester, Gloucester and Lincoln were deliberately founded by the Romans to bring 'civilised' values to Britain, the cir-cumstances surrounding the origins and early growth of London, where

Figure 3.3 An imaginative reconstruction of the Balkerne Gate, Colchester (c. AD 275) showing the triumphal arch expanded to form the town gate. Note also the temples and extensive suburb alongside the London road (drawn by Peter Froste)

urban development began at much the same time as Colchester, may have been rather different.

The pace of modern construction in and around the City of London, whose boundaries are virtually the same as those of Roman *Londinium*, has been more rapid in recent years than almost anywhere in Europe, but this has brought enormous opportunities for archaeological research.[28] (See Figure 3.4 for the location of archaeological sites in London.) It is now thought that, although there may have been some military involvement in the choice of the site itself, London's early development was largely undertaken by civilians. Most of them were presumably immigrants, either from other parts of Britain, seeking to escape hard, dull lives in native villages, or from Gaul and other Roman provinces, seeking new commercial opportunities. Many of these people clearly became prosperous as a result of trade, in some cases sea-borne long-distance trade

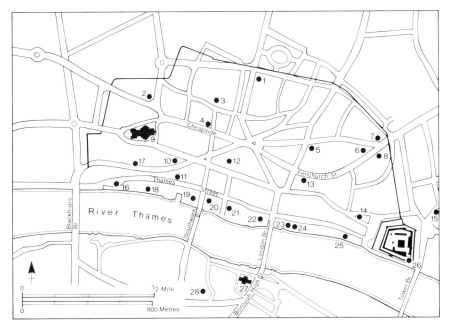

Figure 3.4 Principal excavation sites in London referred to in this book (drawn
by Glenys Boyles)
Key: 1 15/35 Copthall Avenue/43–4 London Wall; 2 GPO Newgate; 3 Guildhall Yard;
4 36–7 King Street; 5 Leadenhall Court; 6 94–7 Fenchurch Street; 7 9 Northumberland
Alley; 8 Aldgate 1972/Holy Trinity Priory; 9 St Paul's Cathedral; 10 Watling Court;
11 Huggin Hill; 12 Temple of Mithras; 13 5–12 Fenchurch Street; 14 Church of All Hallows
by the Tower; 15 East Smithfield; 16 Baynard's Castle; 17 223–5 St Peter's Hill; 18 Trig
Lane; 19 Vintry House; 20 Thames Exchange; 21 Cannon Street Station; 22 Seal
House/Swan Lane; 23 St Magnus House (New Fresh Wharf); 24 Pudding
Lane/Billingsgate Lorry Park; 25 Old Custom House; 26 Tower of London; 27 Southwark
Cathedral; 28 Courage Brewery

with the rest of the empire. This is apparently confirmed by Tacitus
who records that London was 'an important centre for business-men
(*negotiatores*) and merchandise'.[29] A successful economic role was closely
followed by the assumption of a political role, as London replaced Colchester, perhaps following the Boudiccan revolt, as the provincial capital
of *Britannia*.

The City of London as the Romans found it was a site occupied by two
low hills on the north bank of the Thames, separated by a small river now
known as the Walbrook which still runs in a culvert below the street of
that name. On the river bank was a shelving foreshore, ideal for the
drawing up of small boats.[30] Human activity over the centuries has, of
course, radically altered the natural contours and riverside, but the hills
would have been more prominent to Roman eyes than might be supposed

today, since the Thames is now at an appreciably higher level than it was in the first century.

London ousted Colchester as capital because it was a better communications centre. The Thames was a natural highway to the coast and continent, and London is the lowest point where the river can be easily crossed, before it reaches the sea, on the road from the ports at Richborough and Dover to the interior of the province. While it is not clear if the Romans appreciated this at the time of the invasion, and one theory is that a crossing was made upstream at Westminster, they soon found that by using a natural causeway over the low sandy islands on the otherwise marshy south bank of the Thames, a more satisfactory river crossing could be made close to where present-day London Bridge now stands. Excavations in Southwark have shown that the main road from the south lay immediately to the west of Borough High Street and was probably in existence by AD 50.[31] Of particular interest in these excavations has been the discovery of numerous irregular coins of the Emperor Claudius, which were minted in Colchester for purposes of army pay when official coins were in short supply. Their presence in Southwark not only gives a date for the early roads, but suggests the involvement of the army in construction.

Although the nature of the site and its communications has long been apparent, at least in general terms, it is fair to say that a detailed understanding of the history and layout of Roman London is very much a product of the last twenty years or so of excavation. We should not, however, ignore a long tradition of scholarly inquiry into the Roman city.[32] Sir Christopher Wren, for example, noted Roman remains at St Paul's Cathedral and elsewhere during the rebuilding of London after the Great Fire of 1666, and William Stukeley made the first attempt at a plan of Roman London in 1722.[33] It was during the nineteenth century, however, as the Victorian building boom took hold, that a great increase in Roman discoveries occurred. Among the antiquaries of the period, Charles Roach Smith, a chemist by trade, is the best known, and from 1834 to 1855 he observed building sites and sewer trenches in a number of areas,[34] often in the teeth of opposition from the City Corporation anxious to press on with development. Among his more important discoveries was masonry in Upper Thames Street which he took to be a Roman riverside wall. This idea was subsequently dismissed by archaeologists only to be proved correct in 1974 (see p. 101). Roach Smith also urged the creation of a museum for the City, and the forerunner of the present Museum of London was opened by the Corporation in 1868. Subsequently its collection of antiquities grew rapidly and from time to time structures were recorded, but as Mortimer Wheeler put it in 1930:

The mere salvage of Roman relics in London is no longer of more than secondary importance. The pressing need is now for the scientific observation and record of these relics in situ, in relation to the various structures and strata on the history of which they are capable, if seen in position by a trained eye, of throwing a new light and interest.[35]

The first systematic excavation programme had, however, to wait until after the Second World War, when Professor William Grimes, under the aegis of the Roman and Medieval London Excavation Committee, but with very modest resources, worked on sites cleared after bombing, especially around St Paul's.[36] He undertook important investigations of the Roman and medieval defences and in the process he found the early-second-century Cripplegate fort which had probably accommodated the provincial Governor's personal bodyguard. In 1954 Grimes made the famous discovery of the Temple of Mithras, with its unique collection of cult sculptures, on the banks of the Walbrook. This attracted enormous public attention – 'The New Craze: our glorious past' shouted the *News Chronicle*[37] – but sadly produced few extra funds for excavation.

In 1962 the Excavation Committee was wound up and responsibility for field work passed to the Guildhall Museum. For much of the next ten years a single field officer attempted to respond to threats created by London's building sites. Access was frequently refused and funding remained inadequate. At crucial times, however, there was, in the best British tradition, a large number of enthusiastic volunteers who made many major discoveries, including the Governor's Palace and large parts of the forum. In 1972 matters came to a head over the destruction of important medieval waterfront deposits at the Baynard's Castle site. The public outcry and the campaign headed by the Guildhall Museum led, in due course, to the establishment of a full-time rescue unit in 1973, known as the Museum's Department of Urban Archaeology (DUA), funded initially by the City Corporation and Department of the Environment. One reason for the DUA's great success, however, has been the policy developed by the first Chief Archaeologist, Brian Hobley, and his successor John Schofield, of asking every developer for a financial contribution to excavation. This began to bear fruit in 1979 and has secured grants for over 200 sites. In 1988–9 77 per cent of the DUA's income came from developers.[38] In 1983 the Museum acquired a second archaeological unit, the Department of Greater London Archaeology, run on much the same lines, to excavate in 23 of the 32 outer London boroughs.

In 1973 the scale of the destruction already done to London's archaeology and the imminent threat to it were brought into focus, with the publication of *The Future of London's Past*, which concluded that:

Over about one quarter of the City the archaeological deposits have already been totally destroyed; over a further three-fifths they have been at least partially damaged, usually with the loss of the later deposits.[39]

As far as Roman London was concerned, it was clear that, although it was better researched than the Anglo-Saxon and medieval cities, many problems remained, most crucially, perhaps, those of its origins, its early occupation and the process by which the original nucleus became the later town.

Paradoxically, an advantage of the extent and pace of recent development in and around the City is that they have provided opportunities to excavate in virtually every part of the Roman town. This has allowed archaeologists to understand its layout and the variable nature and intensity of occupation in a manner rarely possible in other historic towns where statutory conservation of buildings and monuments prevents access to many areas. Furthermore, the remains of Roman London are usually better preserved than those of later periods which have often been substantially disturbed by modern basements. It is ironic, therefore, that although the DUA deliberately set out to redress the imbalance of previous work towards Roman studies, their Roman discoveries have, in many ways, been the most spectacular.

The nature of the Roman presence in London between the conquest in 43 and 50 remains uncertain, but the only suggestion of a fort comes from the Fenchurch Street–Aldgate area, where three sites have produced two sides of an enclosure with a ditch of military character.[40] No contemporary buildings are known, but the handle of a soldier's sword was found in the ditch fill.

Between 50 and 60 it appears that settlement was located primarily on the hill to the east of the Walbrook around two streets running east–west, the northernmost being linked to the main roads, east to Colchester and west to Verulamium (see Figure 3.5a). These streets were linked by another at right angles to them leading to the riverfront and crossing. Excavations in the central area around the principal streets are now beginning to tell a consistent story of dense occupation, largely surviving as the remains of buildings with timber frames and walls of wattle and daub.[41] Their plans show that they were amongst the earliest examples of the typical Roman town building known to archaeologists as the 'strip building' (see Figure 3.6). This may be defined as an elongated rectangular structure up to 30m (100 ft) long, whose longer axis was at 90 degrees to the street; the front of the building served as a shop and/or workshop, while domestic quarters lay in the rear. The idea behind this arrangement was to maximise the number of units which could be fitted on to a street frontage – an important consideration from a commercial point of view. Since the rooms often appear to be of standard sizes it is likely that the timber frames were prefabricated, reducing costs and allowing rapid erection.

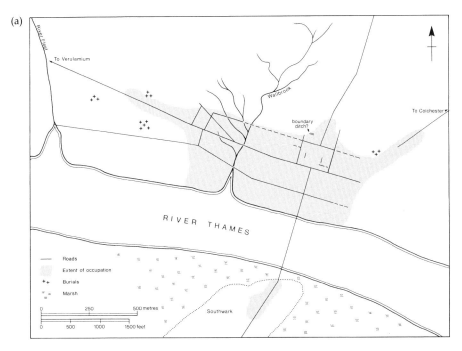

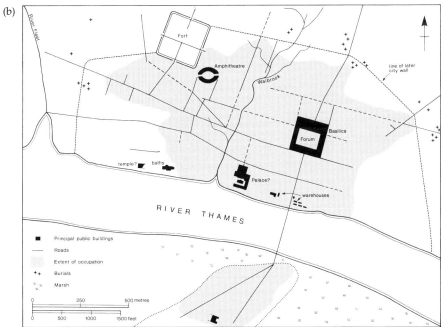

Figure 3.5 Growth of a Roman provincial capital: (a) London c. AD 60; (b) London c. AD 150 (drawn by Glenys Boyles; Museum of London)

61

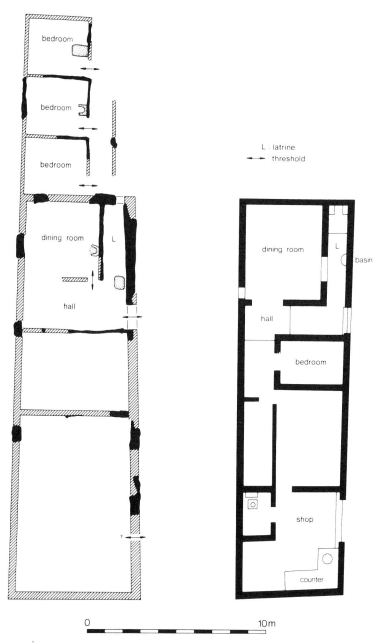

Figure 3.6 The influence of Rome: the urban strip building – comparative plans from GPO Newgate, London and Herculaneum with suggested functions for some of the rooms (Museum of London)

As at Colchester, the extent of early Roman settlement in London can be traced by the presence of burnt deposits associated with the revolt of Boudicca who, after destroying the colony, brought her chariots down the Roman version of the A12. Burning at London appears concentrated in a strip between the two east–west streets, with outlying patches on sites to the west of the Walbrook. While a great deal of blood may have been shed in the fledgling community, one of the more gruesome pieces of London's archaeology traditionally associated with the queen's exploits can no longer be seen as her work. This is the collection of human skulls, some fifty surviving, which have been found on a number of occasions in first-century deposits filling the upper Walbrook. In the late nineteenth century General Pitt-Rivers, one of the founding fathers of British archaeology, but not a physical anthropologist, asserted that the skulls had been forcibly severed from their bodies; Mortimer Wheeler suggested that this was the work of Boudicca. Recent analysis by human-bone specialists has shown, however, that the skulls are unlikely to be from beheaded massacre victims, but come from bodies which had been carefully defleshed and dismembered.[42] The skulls' presence in the Walbrook is probably the result of native religious practices which often focused on the worship of human heads and water spirits.

Although archaeology suggests that recovery from the Boudiccan revolt was slow at first, the Flavian period (i.e. from the accession of the Emperor Vespasian in 69 to the death of Domitian in 96) was one of rapid growth, as it was in many of the other Roman towns of southern England. As far as London is concerned, the population may have been increased by people evicted from their villages and conscripted for forced labour as the Romans took reprisals for the revolt.[43]

The emerging plan of Roman London appears to be a little different from that of many other towns in not being a unitary grid covering the whole settled area. Expansion seems to have taken place in a series of discrete planned stages designed to fit the local topography. At the Leadenhall Court site, for example, a formally laid-out block of strip buildings was found, dated to c. 80, on a site previously unoccupied, north of the original settlement.[44] It is on the western hill, however, that growth seems particularly strong at this time. At 36–7 King Street another planned development was found, based on streets radiating out from a crossing over the Walbrook. Reclamation of a previously marshy area further north (at 15–35 Copthall Avenue and 43–4 London Wall) allowed the construction of strip buildings associated with industrial activities.[45] Further strip buildings were found on the Watling Court and GPO Newgate sites which, unusually, had rooms with mosaic floors and walls with painted plaster. This not only indicates a certain prosperity, but also, perhaps, the tastes of inhabitants who came from more sophisticated parts of the empire.[46]

The scale of development in late-first-century London must indicate official funding and organisation rather than purely private enterprise, and nowhere has this become more apparent than on the waterfront, with its unified system of quays, terraces, streets, buildings and drains. Virtually nothing was known of this, however, until 1973 when the first waterfront excavation took place at the Old Custom House site.[47] Since then, one of the DUA's most spectacular achievements has been to plot the development of the north bank of the Thames over some 2,000 years.[48] Before looking at some of the details of the discoveries, we should note that there are two particularly striking features of all the sites excavated. The first is that they show how the river bank has advanced southwards over the centuries by deliberate reclamation – up to c. 50m (160 ft) in the Roman period, and c. 50m (160 ft) more since then. The Romans' principal objective was probably to win new land for settlement, which would be level and therefore preferable to the steep slopes of the hills behind. During reclamation in the first and second centuries the ground was also built up to combat a rising river level, and this, in part, accounts for the great depth of archaeology. Although the river level probably fell after c. 200, it has been rising again since late Anglo-Saxon times, so that the second feature of riverfront sites is that the timberwork of quays and other structures is very well preserved in waterlogged ground.

Excavations on sites around the north end of London Bridge have shown that to the west of it in c. 70 the line of the waterfront was advanced by up to 15m (50 ft) with an artificial terrace retained at the front by great timber baulks. Immediately east of the bridge a substantial rectangular timber structure has been interpreted as a pier of the original Roman bridge. By c. 90 it stood at the end of a quay, similar to that to the west of the bridge, behind which two small open-fronted warehouses, *horrea*, were constructed (see Plate 3.3). Another contemporary quay has recently been recorded near and actually under Cannon Street station (see Plate 1.1), suggesting that London's principal harbour at this time was between the bridge and the Walbrook. The discovery in excavations on the Courage Brewery site in north Southwark, of the plank floor and parts of the walls of a timber warehouse, has shown, however, that there were also waterfront facilities serving the community on the south bank.[49]

Our knowledge of the early quayside is now so good that if you stand at the top of Fish Street Hill or Pudding Lane near London Bridge, it is easy to imagine yourself back in the last decade of the first century AD, watching the Thames (or *Tamesis* to the Romans) flowing by, while out in the channel, newly arrived from Boulogne, perhaps, is a single-masted ship, about 20m (65 ft) long (similar to one whose remains were excavated at County Hall in 1910),[50] waiting for the small ships drawn up on the foreshore to go out and fetch its cargo of Gallic wine. Stretching across the river to your right, supported on its great timber piers, is the bridge

Plate 3.3 Late-first-century timber quay at the Pudding Lane site, London, with the remains of warehouses in the background (vertical scale 1m / c. 3 ft 3 ins) (Photograph: Museum of London)

Plate 3.4 Roman wooden scoop handle
with negroid head from the Thames
Exchange site in London (overall length
of object 269mm/c. 10 ins) (Photograph:
Museum of London)

carrying men and oxcarts slowly moving back and forth with innumerable
burdens. It might not be as grand as the stone bridge at Trier, but Londoners no doubt believed they would match the Germans soon enough!
All around you is a busy, noisy throng of people from many nations.
Under the keen eye of the Roman harbourmaster, and aided by his clerks,
there are native Britons working as seamen and porters, merchants from
Gaul and the Rhineland, probably in the wine trade, and here and there
are dark-skinned men from the east selling spices and discussing the latest
religious ideas from as far as Antioch or Ephesus. Then there are the
imported goods themselves brought to satisfy the tastes of the upper

classes of the new self-confident city. We have cases of shiny red samian pottery from southern Gaul, now all the rage on local dinner tables. In the warehouse are stacked great amphorae from Spain containing olive oil or *garum*, an exotic fish sauce, and alongside are jars of the local imitation made from herrings and sprats.[51] The sacks piled up probably contain grain from the great British harvest so vital for feeding the Roman army, and making a commotion in the next room are a pack of fierce hunting dogs so widely prized all over the empire. As this little scene fades into a darkening sky and the rain begins, the harbourmaster and his assistants run for cover, no doubt wishing they were back in Ostia or Narbonne, but they know that the empire has foreseen even the hazards of the local climate as the timber-lined drains, which will be so lovingly excavated 1,900 years later, are filling up and doing their job.

In the early second century, after a serious fire which affected both the waterfront and many other areas of Roman London, the riverfront advanced a further 15m (50 ft) to a new line now under Thames Street. Excavations at the Seal House and Swan Lane sites west of the bridge suggest that shortly afterwards the central stretch of the waterfront advanced a further 20m (66 ft), again with quays fronted by massive timbers. In the later second century evidence for advancement east of London Bridge was found at the Old Custom House site, where the most sophisticated quay construction techniques yet known were employed. They involved a system of prefabricated timber boxes made of great oak baulks cut to a standard size with neat dovetail joints. The structure was much more economical in the use of materials than earlier quays, but at the same time was strong enough to survive the insistent changes in the course and level of the river.

At the same time as these major developments on the riverfront were taking place, London's political and administrative role was being given physical expression in a number of other structures (see Figure 3.5b). Provision of a civic centre for London[52] began with a forum and basilica, built c. 80, occupying only c. 0.6ha (1.5 acres), which was relatively modest when compared to roughly contemporary fora elsewhere. The life of this building was, however, brief and in c. 100 work began on a successor over five times larger and worthy at last of the ambitions of Londoners, who must have believed they were building one of the empire's great cities (see Figure 1.2). It is not known if this was primarily a public enterprise or if, in the preferred Roman manner, private finance was used. In any event it may have been difficult to keep the momentum of construction going, as the excavations in 1984–6 at the Leadenhall Court site[53] suggest that some 20–30 years may have been required to complete what became the largest Roman building north of the Alps.

Another collection of disparate Roman discoveries, this time between Cannon Street and Upper Thames Street, a little downstream from the

Walbrook, has been interpreted as the palace of the Governor of the British province, erected between 80 and 100.[54] Its superstructure and architectural appointments must be largely conjectural, but it certainly commanded splendid views of the river and would have included reception halls, residential chambers and an ornamental garden with pools. The palace's residents and visitors would no doubt have enjoyed spending their leisure hours watching traditional Roman games and sports, which often assumed a fairly robust character as they included bear baiting, mock hunts and gladiatorial combats. The principal venue would have been the amphitheatre, but until as recently as July 1987 no trace of such a building had been found in London. The search ended, however, at the Guildhall Yard site in the north-western part of the town, close to where Professor Grimes had located the Cripplegate fort.[55]

At a depth of 6m (19 ft 6 ins) below modern ground level, a shallow curving wall footing was found. After the discovery of further walls it became clear that what had been found were the remains of one of the ceremonial entrances, with perhaps accompanying shrines, for an amphitheatre of typical elliptical plan. The earliest building had been of timber, but it was subsequently reconstructed in stone. Careful analysis of the walls and others found nearby, but not previously understood, showed that London had the largest of the dozen or so amphitheatres known from Roman Britain. It measured 130m (426 ft) by 110m (360 ft) and originally the walls probably stood as much as 20m (66 ft) high, with tiers of seats inside leading down to the arena, as can be seen most vividly in Britain today in the amphitheatre outside the fortress at Caerleon.

Another requirement of what the Romans regarded as civilised life was the bath house. This was not just a place for getting clean but functioned as what might be described in modern municipal jargon as a 'leisure centre', where sports, games and social events took place. The largest of several bath complexes in Roman London lay on artificial terraces in the Huggin Hill area. This is west of the Walbrook and close to a natural spring line from which fresh water could be taken, and close to the river into which spent water could be discharged. The site lies near the western limit of the contemporary city, apparently a little apart from centres of population, but perhaps in an area dedicated to places of public assembly, religious observance and entertainment.

The importance of the Huggin Hill site to Roman London has recently been demonstrated in the glare of publicity showing that the balance between the requirements of development and archaeology is a delicate one which can easily be upset when unusual discoveries, arguably worthy of preservation and display, are made.[56] The first sighting of major Roman buildings on the Huggin Hill site was made by Roach Smith in 1845, but the first excavations took place in 1964 and 1969 when, in advance of redevelopment, the remains of a major bath complex erected in the late first century were revealed.[57] It had been extensively rebuilt with a large new steam room or *caldarium* in the early second century, perhaps at a time when Hadrian, alarmed at the use of Rome's baths for prostitution, forbade mixed bathing. As a result of the excavation, the baths complex was made a Scheduled Monument, in theory securing its long-term preservation.

In 1986 a planning application was submitted for the development of Dominant House – the 1964 site – and permission was granted subject to Scheduled Monument Consent. Trial work by the DUA showed that Dominant House had done remarkably little damage to the archaeology, but the Secretary of State, on the advice of English Heritage, gave Scheduled Monument Consent, allowing destruction after a delay of six months for excavation. This was generously funded by the site owners to the tune of £500,000.

The principal discovery of the excavation was a previously unknown, large heated room of cruciform shape with walls up to 3m (10 ft) high and over 100 of the *pilae*, or pillars, which held up the floor allowing hot air to circulate beneath (see Plate 3.5). Alterations in the second century included the construction of a massive stone structure standing 5.5m (18 ft) high and over 3m (10 ft) thick, forming, perhaps, the base of a tower or monumental arch.

When it became clear that the remains were well preserved, a press view led to an outcry over impending destruction, prompting Labour MP Tony Banks, for example, to declare in the Commons:

> 'I don't see why a bunch of property speculators behaving like up-market Arthur Daleys should be allowed to put their wretched profits before our history.'[58]

Unfortunately, however, there seemed to be no way of preserving the remains through scheduling without bankrupting English Heritage with a compensation claim. As David Keys wrote in *The Independent* on 15 April 1989:

> The most impressive and best preserved Roman remains found in London this century are to be destroyed within the next two months, because of shortcomings in the law and the lack of a preservation strategy for the capital's archaeological heritage.[59]

Although the developers did alter their foundation plans to minimise damage to the *caldarium*, which has been buried under sand, there was no question of displaying the remains. The tower or arch base was almost totally destroyed and dumped as rubble. The comments of Peter Rowsome and Kevin Wooldridge of the DUA in *Rescue News* may serve as a conclusion to the sorry affair:

> As for the preservation of remains it seems that only the 'oxygen of

Plate 3.5 Huggin Hill baths in London showing the *caldarium* with the *pilae* around which hot air circulated. The great arch or tower base is at the rear on the left-hand side (Photograph: Museum of London)

70

publicity' and public outcry can gain even the minimum of success. London as the Roman provincial capital will continue to lack any substantial visible building to represent it.[60]

It is rare for a town at any time in its history to experience continuous growth at the pace experienced by early Roman London. It is no surprise, therefore, that by the middle of the second century *Londinium*'s years of expansion, fuelled both by new commercial opportunities in the region and the great public building programmes, were over. The building and occupation sequences come to an end on sites in many areas of Roman London in the mid- to late second century.

Overlying the latest building remains, deposits of what are usually known as 'dark earth' are found. This material has recently been described in more detail as 'a dark grey, rather silty loam with various inclusions, especially building material'.[61] Similar deposits have been found in other Roman towns, but the origin of the dark earth remains a matter for debate. It would seem, however, that in many cases it was created from decaying vegetation and strata of other kinds which had been mixed up by agricultural activities in the later or post-Roman period. It is possible that this mixing has destroyed the remains of late Roman timber and clay buildings, but at present the evidence of large areas of dark earth is usually interpreted as indicating a sharply reduced population in third- and fourth-century London. As such this has been one of the most surprising discoveries of the city's archaeology in the last twenty years, prompting a major rethink on its role in the later Roman period.

Provincial capitals – 'the amenities of a classical city'

Although the three first-century *coloniae* and London are vital to our understanding of the origins of Roman urbanism in Britain, it should be stressed that, because of their unusual role and status, they are not necessarily typical of the towns of Roman Britain and we must now look at the *civitas* or regional capitals.

As Britain was absorbed by the Roman empire, it was divided up into self-governing regions, or *civitates*, based on pre-Roman tribal divisions. At the centre of each *civitas* was a deliberately created town or *civitas* capital whose inhabitants were not Roman citizens, but of lower status and known as *peregrini* (aliens).[62] In many cases the location of these towns was determined by previous use of the site by the military, either as forts or, in the case of Exeter and Wroxeter, legionary fortresses. Most capitals were also, like the *colonia* at Colchester, close to important native centres where urban functions were already beginning to develop. The earliest capitals, including Canterbury and Verulamium, were founded in about AD 50. More were created in the Flavian period, including Chichester, Cirencester, Exeter, Silchester, Winchester and Wroxeter. Finally, in the early second century towns such as Caerwent and Aldborough were created in areas more distant from the original sphere of Roman colonisation.

Returning to the earliest foundations, evidence dating from the mid-first century for a characteristic Roman urban layout was found at Verulamium by both Wheeler and Frere.[63] By AD 60 the town had the status of a *municipium*, meaning its people had special rights and privileges, although not full Roman citizenship.

In Frere's excavations immediately south-east of the theatre, he found a row of timber-framed strip buildings of classic form. A colonnade ran along the Watling Street frontage and Frere commented: 'It is evident that an attempt was being made to provide the town with the amenities of a classical city, if only in timber.'[64] After destruction by Boudicca, Verulamium acquired further amenities in timber, then in stone. Rather than reviewing these developments in detail, however, we may look instead at the important work, much of it recent, which has taken place in rescue excavations at Canterbury (*Durovernum Cantiacorum*).[65]

As in London, opportunities for archaeology in Canterbury arose after the Second World War as a result of extensive bombing. The enemy target was the cathedral which was fortunately missed, but a large area immediately to the south, around St George's Street, was devastated. In 1944 a series of short summer digging campaigns began, largely staffed by unpaid volunteer helpers, which continued until 1957 under the direction of Sheppard Frere.[66]

Although work was based on small trenches rather than area excavation, a reliable outline picture of the development of the city from pre-Roman times was produced. It was shown, for example, that before the Roman town there had been late Iron Age occupation which probably focused on a ford across the River Stour. Although Frere found no evidence for a fort at Canterbury, and none has been found since, he pointed out that the three Roman roads which converge on the town change direction here, suggesting that it was an early focus of Roman settlement, again relating to control of the river crossing. Frere also found traces of streets, houses and public buildings including the baths in St Margaret Street, but one of his greatest achievements was to put together a plan of the great stone-built theatre,[67] one of only four known in Roman Britain. This is a rare piece of evidence in the province for a taste for the drama and music of classical culture, and an indication that Roman Canterbury bore a closer resemblance to the more sophisticated towns of Gaul than many others in Britain which were more remote from continental influence.

The discoveries made by Frere have been substantially added to by the work of the Canterbury Archaeological Trust which came into being in April 1976. As a result of being rather later on the scene than the other major urban units, the Trust suffered from acute financial difficulties in the late 1970s and early 1980s when the principal source of funds for urban archaeology was central government.[68] Thanks to the efforts of its first director, Tim Tatton-Brown, and his successor, Paul Bennett, in securing funds from site developers, however, the Trust has not only survived, but has undertaken a wide range of successful field projects covering all aspects of the past of the city and its region. Within the walls, sites have been particularly concentrated in areas where the public buildings of the Roman town were located (see Figure 3.7).

Further evidence has been found for intense occupation in the immediate pre-Roman period, which indicates the presence of a native royal site, similar to Gosbecks at Colchester, and numerous coin finds suggest a trading centre and mint. Soon after the Roman conquest, however, it appears that a start was made on demolishing the native settlement and laying out the town, although this was to be quite a lengthy process, perhaps demonstrating the initial reluctance of the Britons to contribute to civic projects. The earliest gravelled streets, which are probably mid-first-century, include the two principal north–west/south–east routes, running, in modern terms, from Burgate to Westgate (this is Watling Street or the London–Richborough road) and from Riding Gate to London Gate. Connecting these two streets was one or more running north–east/south–west. Other elements in the plan appear to be late-first- or early-second-century. The public buildings do not appear to have been completed until the Hadrianic period. Nevertheless, when this was done they must have been a truly impressive sight (see Figure 3.8).

The site of Roman Canterbury's forum – the centre of civic life – has only been known for certain since 1984, as a result of observations and small-scale excavations in the High Street area, and little of its plan is apparent. In the *insula* immediately to the south-east, however, were the baths. They were originally discovered by Frere, but recently more of their lost splendour has been revealed, with evidence for colonnaded porticos on the main streets on both the north-west and south-west sides. Across the latter street lay the famous theatre. The plan of the earliest building is not entirely clear, but, like its better known successor, it was probably of classic semi-circular plan with banks of seating on the curved side and the stage on the chord, or straight side. In the later second century the theatre was rebuilt on a monumental scale. It measured 80m (262 ft) across and the seating was carried on great arched colonnades, in a manner which has no parallel in Britain, but it was similar to the great Gallic theatres which still stand at Lyon or at Orange where the walls are over 37m (121 ft) high.

The Canterbury theatre could have accommodated some 7,000 people, rather more than the likely urban population, and it must have been an amenity for the region. In addition to secular entertainments, the theatre was probably used for religious ceremonies, and immediately to the

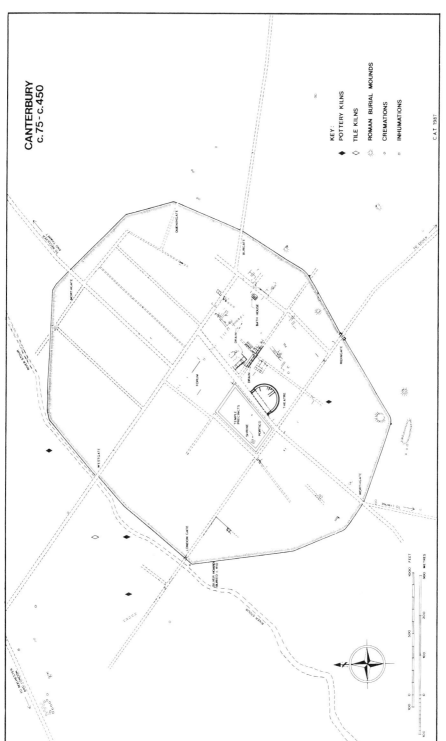

Figure 3.7 Plan of Roman Canterbury (Canterbury Archaeological Trust)

Figure 3.8 An imaginative reconstruction of Roman Canterbury in its heyday, looking west with the theatre in the centre, temple upper right and public baths lower right (drawn by J.A. Bowen, Canterbury Archaeological Trust)

north-west lay a large temple complex – this proximity is also found at Verulamium and is again reminiscent of Gaul. The temple was another major discovery which demonstrates the value of small-scale rescue work and observation in historic towns. A suggestion of some unusual structure had been made by Frere in the 1950s when he noted finds of imported marble veneers and spreads of rammed gravel suggestive of a courtyard in the Castle Street area. In 1977, work on the north-west side of the *insula*[69] produced similar finds, and in 1979 a site in the centre of the *insula* revealed more of the courtyard around two tanks probably connected with fountains.[70] Finally, in 1980 it became clear that the gravelled area was the courtyard of a great temple precinct surrounded on at least three sides by a double-colonnaded portico.[71] In this excavation also, the remains of a small shrine of Celtic type were found. The main temple building was probably of classical form, but its remains are likely to have been destroyed in the 1960s – the dark years of Canterbury's archaeology – during the construction of a hotel.

In conclusion, Canterbury has produced one of the most extensive suites of public buildings of any Romano-British town. Their physical proximity and architectural unity served to emphasise the Roman state's dominance over all aspects of public life. At the same time it may be inferred that the upper echelons of the population were sufficiently impressed with Roman values to wish to express their status with urban public works.[72] The wealth to do this presumably resulted from a growing productivity of agriculture in the region, stimulated in part, perhaps, by the demands of the army and the imperial tax gatherers.

A similar concern on the part of wealthy natives to display status, as they gradually integrated themselves into urban society, may be reflected in the development of dwellings in the *civitas* capitals.[73] Around the central *insulae* at Canterbury a typical range of houses has been found. The earlier examples appear to be of a relatively modest strip-type plan with, as elsewhere, walls built of timber or clay. During the second century stone was used more frequently and houses developed more elaborate plans, with additional wings arranged around courtyards. Luxurious appointments begin to appear including mosaics, and *in situ* examples can be seen in a museum in Butchery Lane.

Frere concluded from his excavations that: 'The purpose of the town ... was to provide a comfortable and civilised life for the Romanised upper and middle classes, rather than house a crowded working class as a modern industrial city does.'[74]

Although recent excavations have located an industrial suburb to the north-west of the town, where pottery and metalwork were made,[75] it remains the case that, until the later fourth century, one imagines Canterbury, and many of the other *civitas* capitals of Britain, to have been prosperous and spacious garden cities. At the same time, however, we must remember that the evidence we have largely reflects the tastes and incomes of a relatively small elite group in the population and that substantial numbers of less archaeologically visible artisans and slaves existed to serve them.

An opportunity to meet all social classes in the *civitas* capitals is provided by their cemeteries, and the town which probably has more to offer than any other is Winchester where over 1,500 Roman burials have been excavated in recent years.[76]

The location of Winchester, at a point where a north–south route along the Itchen valley meets an east–west route across the chalk downs, has made it a focus for human settlement from early pre-historic times. In the later first century BC a large enclosure, defined by a substantial ditch and bank, was established on the west side of the valley, from where, presumably, a local chieftain controlled communications in the area. When the Romans arrived soon after the conquest, on their westward sweep through southern England, Winchester's strategic position would seem to have demanded at least a temporary military presence. Curiously, however, no certain fort has been located, and the history of the area is a little unclear until the foundation of the *civitas* capital of the Belgae (*Venta Belgarum*) in the mid 70s AD. The town occupied c. 58ha (143 acres) and was surrounded by a bank and ditch. Excavations in the centre of the town suggest that growth of settlement was rapid in the late first and early second centuries.

The town cemeteries were located, according to Roman law, outside settled areas (see Figure 3.9). Archaeological work has focused in particular on the northern cemetery, ranged along the road to Cirencester, and on the eastern cemetery, on the road to London. Most of the burials belong to the later Roman period, but an important early group was found in the northern cemetery at Hyde Street, immediately outside the north gate in a triangular area between the road running north–west to Cirencester and the road north to Silchester (see Figure 3.9).[77]

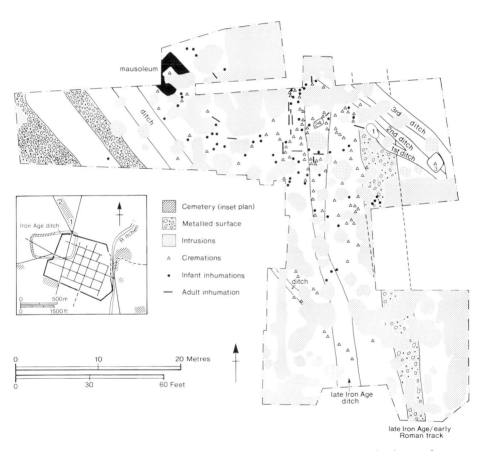

Figure 3.9 Winchester: the Hyde Street Roman cemetery site in the first and second centuries. *Inset*: simplified plan of the Winchester area showing the late Iron Age enclosure and the Roman town with principal cemetery areas (drawn by Glenys Boyles)

Key to inset: 1 Hyde Street; 2 Lankhills

As is so often the case on Roman urban sites, substantial damage had been done by medieval pits, but, in the c. 1,600 sq.m (1,900 sq. ft) examined, 189 graves, dated from c. 50 to c. 175, were found. We have here, therefore, the mortal remains of some of the very first inhabitants of Roman Winchester.

The layout of the cemetery was obviously constrained by the line of the main roads, but in its early years it was also influenced by the survival of a north–south trackway of late Iron Age date leading to the great enclosure. The trackway had a ditch running along its west side and as it silted up it became a favoured spot for burial. In the later first century a bank and ditch defined the east side of the cemetery and some form of ritual, as well as purely physical, protection is implied by a horse burial sited in the bank (see Figure 3.9, 1). This burial of an animal with powerful symbolic significance in British religion[78] is but one of several indications of the essentially native character of the cemetery.

One-hundred-and-one graves contained cremations. This was the principal rite for disposing of the bodies of adults in the early Roman period and it is frustrating for archaeologists, since little of the physical anthropology of the deceased can be studied from burnt bone. Nevertheless, other aspects of the graves were of great interest. The burning process had evidently been carried out away from the cemetery and the remains were then brought to it in a suitable container for burial. In fifty-seven graves this was a pottery urn, in four instances a wooden box, and in the others probably a bag, of which no trace survived. The graves themselves were shallow pits probably marked by low mounds. No grave markers were found and it is striking that Winchester, like a number of other *civitas* capitals, has produced no examples of the great stone funerary monuments which are such a feature of places like London and York, where Roman military and administrative personnel were based; presumably these people were a negligible element in the population of the native capitals.

Grave goods accompanied forty-seven of the Hyde Street cremations; among the items used, pots, principally bowls, flagons and jars, formed by far the largest group and may have served to symbolise a funeral meal shared by the dead and living. The same idea may have been behind the inclusion in a few graves of the skull of a pig, an animal frequently associated in Celtic mythology with feasting.[79] Less common grave goods were jewellery items such as armlets and rings, and toilet items including glass unguent phials and mirrors. The majority of the graves, however, were unfurnished or sparsely furnished; very few were richly furnished. It is not clear, however, if this is any kind of direct reflection of the social order. It is possible that the rich and powerful had their own cemetery elsewhere, but two graves stood out, both because of their contents and their distinctive location in the cemetery, which suggested that the deceased had some elevated status. One, dated to the 70s, was found in the centre of the Iron Age ditch and it contained twenty-two pottery vessels (see Figure 3.9, 2; Plate 3.6). In the other, dated to the mid-second-century, located on the eastern boundary of the cemetery (see Figure 3.9, 3), the cremated bone was contained in a box with bronze fittings and was accompanied by four pots, an ivory bracelet, two glass phials, and a bronze mirror.

Plate 3.6 Late-first-century cremation burial from Hyde Street, Winchester, with 22 pottery vessels (scale 0.50m/c. 1 ft 6 ins) (Photograph: Winchester Museums Service Archaeology Section)

The cremation graves at Hyde Street are broadly comparable to those in an early Roman cemetery at Chichester,[80] and to those at rural sites elsewhere in south-east England, of both Roman and immediate pre-Roman date, suggesting again that the people of the *civitas* capitals were natives who had been attracted by stick or carrot to urban living. Their burial customs probably continued more or less unchanged after the conquest, although artefacts in Roman style were used. Mention must also be made, however, of three anomalous cremations at Hyde Street which were amongst the earliest, dating to the mid-first century. The graves were unusual in containing distinctive imported pottery and spreads of charcoal. One of them, the only cremation grave to do so, contained a coin, as did the graves of two infants buried close by. These coins were further examples of the irregular issues of Claudius which we have already noted in Southwark. Since they are likely to have originated in army pay, we may be looking here at the graves of soldiers, or their families, based in Winchester's as yet undiscovered fort.

In addition to the cremations, seventeen of the graves at Hyde Street contained adult skeletons.[81] This may reflect another native tradition prevalent in areas west of Winchester,[82] but some of the skeletons were a little unusual. One was buried without a skull and three were buried prone; one of these, a female, had her legs crossed at the ankles suggesting that they had been tied together. One wonders if this group had been denied the usual rite of cremation because they were outcasts or criminals of some sort.

Sexing of cremated remains is very difficult, but it may be inferred that some of them were female because of the jewellery and toilet items buried in the grave. In five cases, however, a female cremation was implied by the burial alongside of a new-born infant (see Plate 3.7), graphically indicating that one of the principal causes of the death of Roman women was childbirth. Indeed one of the most striking aspects of the Hyde Street cemetery was the total of seventy-six infant burials, all of which were probably new-born, testifying to a very high infant mortality. To the archaeologist, these pathetic collections of fragile bones are a mute expression of heartache and disappointed hopes which can still touch us nearly 2,000 years after they were laid to rest.

Plate 3.7 Early-second-century cremation burial from Hyde Street, Winchester, with (top) an infant skeleton (scale 0.50m/c. 1 ft 6 ins) (Photograph: Winchester Museums Service Archaeology Section)

4

LATE ROMAN TOWNS

If one of the criteria for assessing the success of the Roman conquest of Britain is the extent to which the natives had accepted urban living, then by the end of the second century the imperial authorities might have reflected on some 150 years of considerable, if somewhat uneven, progress. Towns on something approaching the classical model were functioning in virtually all parts of the province. There were signs of a change in urban fortunes, however. London, the provincial capital, for example, and Verulamium both suffered setbacks after serious fires. In many other centres the growth of population had not been as rapid after the death of Hadrian (in 139) as it had been in the previous sixty years. Nevertheless, while the great surge to urbanisation was over, the second half of the second century witnessed one very significant development at the site of Rome's most northerly military headquarters at York.[1]

York – the last *colonia*

The city of York owes its origins to the Roman 9th legion which, under its commander Petilius Cerialis, marched north from Lincoln in AD 71, ostensibly to prevent a dispute between the native Queen Cartimandua of the Brigantes and her former consort, Venutius, affecting the safety of the Roman province.[2] On arriving in York, which the Romans knew as *Eboracum*, Cerialis constructed a fortress on slightly raised ground between two rivers, the Foss and the Ouse. Visible remains include a fine stretch of the late-third-century walls, incorporating the west corner, or 'multangular', tower in the Museum Gardens. One can also inspect parts of the legionary headquarters under York Minster where they were unearthed during underpinning work between 1968 and 1972.[3]

Although York was established as a military site, it is thought likely that a civilian settlement grew up around the fortress, especially on its south-east side, in the late first and early second century. This was probably known to the Romans as the *canabae legionis* which means literally 'booths of the legions', and would initially have existed as simple timber buildings housing local people trading with the army. Subsequently, more substantial stone structures were erected in this area[4] including a temple of Hercules, doubtless patronised extensively by the soldiers.

By the mid-second century a more substantial civilian settlement began to grow up on the south-west side of the River Ouse which, for perhaps fifty years in the later second / early third century, was the boom town of Roman Britain (see Figure 4.1). That this was the *colonia Eboracensis*, a town of the highest rank, equivalent to Colchester, Gloucester and Lincoln, was indicated by the discovery of the coffin of a *decurion*, Flavius Bellator, in a cemetery disturbed during the construction of the railway station in 1872. Other funerary monuments found on the Mount, alongside the main Roman road to the south-west, are witness to a population with Romanised tastes and cosmopolitan origins. The date at which York acquired *colonia* status is not known for certain, but it was clearly before AD 237, the date of a fine Pennine millstone-grit altar set up in Bordeaux by Marcus Aurelius Lunaris, a *sevir augustalis* (priest of the deified emperor) of the *coloniae* at both York and Lincoln, perhaps to give thanks for some successful business trip. One possibility is that the title was acquired when the British province was split in two and York assumed the role of capital of lower Britain (*Britannia Inferior*). This division probably occurred early in the reign of Emperor Caracalla whose father, Septimius Severus, had died in York in 211.

The extent of the area with *colonia* status also remains uncertain, but the principal urban site lay within the circuit of medieval walls south-west of the Ouse. One of the peculiarities of the medieval walls of York is that they were not built from ground level, but on top of a pre-existing rampart. North-east of the Ouse, excavation has shown that this rampart dates from the tenth to thirteenth centuries and covers the Roman fortress wall.[5] Although it has only been demonstrated in three places on the north-west side of the circuit, it is reasonable to assume that a Roman wall also exists under the rampart south-west of the Ouse.

In spite of the many discoveries in and around the presumed *colonia* area, it is remarkable that until the early 1970s little was known of the town in terms of either its history or layout. Not only the defences, but also the street plan, public buildings, houses and waterfront were virtually unexplored in controlled excavation. The conditions under which the student of Roman York usually worked until relatively recently can be summed up by the antiquary Charles Wellbeloved, who in 1842 wrote:

> But ordinary excavations [i.e. for building foundations, sewers, etc.] are of so limited an extent and carried on with such rapidity and heedlessness that it is generally impossible for the most sagacious and scrutinising antiquary to ascertain the character of the remains

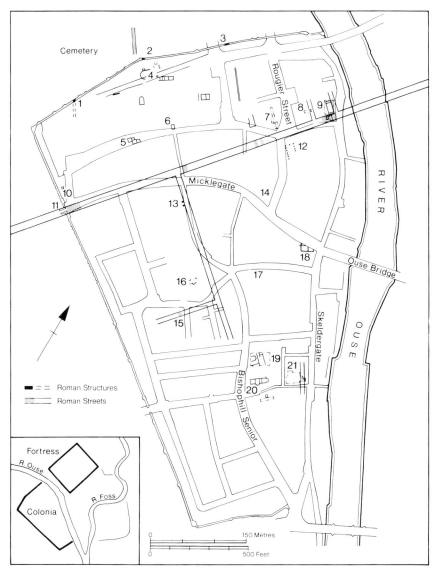

Figure 4.1 Roman York: principal excavation sites, structures and conjectured street lines in the *colonia* on the south-west bank of the Ouse (drawn by Glenys Boyles)

Key: 1–2 Old Station: Roman defences; 3 Old Station: Roman defences and mithraic relief; 4 Old Station: baths; 5 House with four seasons mosaic; 6 Temple of Serapis; 7 General Accident site, Tanner Row; 8 5 Rougier Street; 9 Wellington Row; 10 Bar Lane: mosaic; 11 Micklegate Bar (medieval gate); 12 George Hudson Street: column bases for ?forum basilica or temple; 13 Trinity Lane: columns for ?portico; 14 Mithraic relief; 15 Bishophill Senior; 16 St Mary Bishophill Junior; 17 Fetter Lane: bath house; 18 Queen's Hotel (1–9 Micklegate); 19 37 Bishophill Senior; 20 St Mary Bishophill Senior; 21 58–9 Skeldergate thus casually and partially brought to light or to form even a con-jecture as to the original superstructures.[6]

The *colonia* at York was, in short, not only the last major Roman town before the northern frontier, but the last to be explored archaeologically. In the 1950s and 1960s the pace of development in the city began to quicken and numerous opportunities for archaeological excavation were missed. A great deal was to rest on the shoulders of Mr Peter Wenham, head of history at St John's College, who did heroic work with a band of enthusiastic voluntary helpers on sites of Roman and other periods. Unfortunately Mr Wenham only had the resources for small-scale inves-tigations, and in the late 1960s, as elsewhere, the rescue archaeology crisis in York came to a head. One reason was that York was selected in 1966 by the Minister of Housing and Local Government for a detailed study to discover how to reconcile Britain's ancient towns with the twentieth century. For York the end product was Lord Esher's *York: A Study in Conservation* published in 1968. As a result of this an inner ring road was planned which would keep traffic from the historic core, but would involve cutting a swathe through archaeological deposits, often several metres deep, immediately outside the city walls. Thanks to the Yorkshire Philosophical Society and Council for British Archaeology, however, Peter Addyman, a young lecturer at Southampton University, but a York-shireman by birth and upbringing, was commissioned to produce a report on the archaeological implications of development, which appeared in 1971.[7] By April 1972, with funding from the DOE and premises from York University, the York Archaeological Trust (YAT) was established under Addyman as director, with a brief to conduct rescue excavations in the city.[8] Since 1972 research has continued on all aspects of York's archae-ology, but some of the most important discoveries have taken place in the Roman town on the south-west bank of the Ouse.

Work began in 1973 at 37 Bishophill Senior and 58–9 Skeldergate in the south-eastern part of the *colonia*[9] where, in confirmation of previous work at St Mary Bishophill Senior,[10] it was found that the steep natural slope up from the river Ouse had been terraced in the early third century, creating great artificial platforms for stone buildings, probably residences of the better-off members of the community. They may have included Lucius Viducius Placidus who is known from a commemorative inscrip-tion to have paid for an arch in York in 221.[11] He was a native of the Rouen area in northern France and a *negotiator* (merchant) by trade. An altar found at the mouth of a tributary of the Rhine, also apparently dedicated by the same Placidus, indicates that he was primarily engaged in trade across the North Sea with the cities of Roman Germany principally, perhaps, Cologne and Trier.

The Bishophill excavations illustrated one aspect of Roman urban development, but more important evidence for the process has come from sites in the heart of the *colonia* around the main Roman road to the south-west. It is now clear that this road was a primary feature of the landscape, and ran in a straight line down into the Ouse valley, from where medieval Micklegate Bar now stands, crossed the river and then entered the fortress through its main gate. Since the late first century the road has had a crucial influence on the topography of York, which we will look at again in the next chapter (see p. 131), but its exact course was only confirmed in 1988, when a cross-section was dug across it for the first time, on a site in Wellington Row (see Plate 4.1).[12]

Plate 4.1 The Roman A1: cross-section through second-century road surfaces at Wellington Row, York. At the bottom is the late-first-century flood silt; the mid-second-century limestone surface occurs at the level of the bottom of the upper shoring sheets (scale 1m/c. 3 ft 3 ins) (Photograph: York Archaeological Trust)

The road's earliest gravel surface, 10m (33 ft) wide, probably had a brief life, for it was covered with a deposit of silt deriving from a late-first-century flood, the first of the many floods which have regularly engulfed York since that time. To avoid further calamity the road was then built up on a mound of cobbles and gravel over 1m (3 ft) thick, forming a causeway leading, it is assumed, to a river bridge. Continual resurfacing through the Roman period led to a total build-up of Roman road of over 4m (13 ft).

Although most of the surfaces were of gravel or cobbles, a remarkable and unique crushed-limestone surface was found, dating to the mid-second century. Still smooth and hard when found, it does not seem to have been extensively used, but as a 'great white way' running up the hill from the bridge it must have been a splendid sight. At the same time the road was doubled in width and a stone-lined culvert containing a lead water pipe ran down the centre. One cannot help wondering whether these great works commemorated some significant event in the life of the town, even perhaps its formal foundation as a *colonia* over fifty years earlier than previously thought.

Until the mid-second century archaeological evidence for occupation on the south-west bank is sparse, but then there was a sudden increase in human activity. This was indicated first by drainage ditches, which soon became clogged with domestic refuse, and secondly by new buildings. One of these was excavated in 1988–9 at the Wellington Row site (see Plate 4.2).[13] The complete plan was revealed and the stone walls still stood 2m (6 ft 6 ins) high in places. The building had been erected at the time of the unusual limestone road surface, but subsequently had a long and varied history which may, in a way, be seen as a microcosm of the history of the *colonia* itself.

As originally constructed, the building measured 15.5m (55 ft) by 10.3m (35 ft); its roof, probably of sandstone slabs, had been supported in the centre on a row of four posts resting on stone pillars, one of which survived intact. There was a clay oven built against the south-west wall and the floor had clearly been timber, since joists and boards were found preserved by charring after a major fire early in the building's life. There is no suggestion that this was other than accidental and merely indicates an ever-present hazard in the densely built-up centres of early towns. Although badly damaged, reconstruction followed the fire and the opportunity was taken to extend the building 2m (6 ft 6 ins) to the north-west. The extension may, however, have been built on a much more massive scale than the original structure, since, although the upstanding walls did not survive, the clay and cobble footings were packed around a forest of massive timbers up to 3m (10 ft) long, employed to ensure stability in the damp ground. It is possible that this extra solid base supported a monumental addition to the original structure, perhaps surrounding a grand entrance.

Identifying the function of the Wellington Row building is a good example of the sort of problem archaeologists can face in dealing with the ambiguous nature of many of their discoveries. Although preservation of the remains was good, there were no diagnostic finds to suggest that this was, for example, a dwelling or a workshop. The plan, with its lack of internal partitions, and the prominent location near the main road and river bridge does, however, suggest a public building. Some support for

Plate 4.2 The Roman stone building at Wellington Row, York, looking south-east. Top right, within the walls, the surviving roof

this is provided by the original length to width ratio which at 3:2 conforms to that recommended for such structures by the Roman architect Vitruvius. The possibility of a temple has been raised,[14] not of Celtic type, but of a type providing accommodation for a congregation of worshippers. While some support for this idea may derive from the presence of pottery vessels buried in the floor, which perhaps served as offerings for gods worshipped there, it is at present safer simply to suggest the building was a place of 'public assembly'.

A little to the south-west of the Wellington Row site a small trench excavated at 5 Rougier Street in 1981[15] also revealed a burst of construction activity in the later second century. This included a small street running north-west–south-east at right angles to the main road, indicating for the first time that there was probably a regular street grid in this part of Roman York. Alongside the street were four massive stone pillars standing 1.50m (5 ft) high, which had probably supported the floor of a warehouse (see Figure 2.4).

Moving south-west again to the General Accident site in Tanner Row (a sponsor immortalised!),[16] urban development began with an artificially created level platform on which the remarkable remains of late-second-century timber structures were found (see Plate 4.3). In refuse tips around the buildings there were large quantities of artefacts suggesting intense industrial and craft activity, including iron and bronze working, and butchery on a commercial scale. Of particular interest, however, was the evidence for leatherworking. Amongst numerous offcuts were a variety of shoes and a complete panel from a leather tent of the type used by soldiers on campaign. A fragment of another tent bore a graffito inscription referring to one Sollius Iulianus,[17] a centurion of the 6th legion who is, remarkably, also known from an inscription on Hadrian's Wall where he and his men were engaged in construction work. A sword and some dress fittings of a type worn by soldiers were also found and it may be suggested that the workshops here derived much of their business from the army across the river.

A mass of organic refuse was well preserved at the General Accident site and its analysis has shown how an urban ecology develops and has cast a rather new light on the ambient conditions in a Roman town.[18] Rather than reflecting a regime of tidiness and order, with refuse put in pits or dumped away from settled areas, the evidence is for a filthy, smelly, unhygienic environment, at least in the later years of the second century. Work by the Environmental Archaeology Unit at York University has shown how the pleasant water meadows of the early second century were gradually affected by the presence of people, leading to the arrival of insects living on middens of rotting vegetable matter, animal dung and human faeces. Judging by the number of their bones, mice and rats were abundant. Amongst the food remains, however, there was evidence for

Plate 4.3 Late-second-century York: the remains of a timber building with well-preserved sill beam (centre), and (right) accompanying timber drain at the General Accident site, Tanner Row (scale 1m/c.3 ft 3 ins). Note the shoring brace, vital for

the unusual imports, such as crab from the Yorkshire coast, and figs and olives from further afield, which one would expect in a town with the wealth to reach beyond its immediate hinterland for sustenance.

In the early third century there appears to have been a change in site function at Tanner Row, as the timber structures were swept away and replaced by a substantial stone building. There was no further build-up of organic refuse as the more familiar Roman urban discipline prevailed.

As we have seen at Colchester, a town of *colonia* status would have been graced with major public buildings. At York we know there was a baths complex on the north-west side of the town, where evidence for temples has also been found, suggesting an area of recreation and religious observance similar to that in the Huggin Hill area on the south-west side of Roman London. Unfortunately these buildings were largely uncovered in the last century and not systematically excavated. In 1988, however, archaeologists had the opportunity to examine a monumental structure, presumably with a public function, on the Queen's Hotel site 200m (220 yds) south-east of the main road.[19] While some of the most spectacular remains ever found in York were revealed (see Plate 4.4), the site also received publicity of the wrong sort, showing that, as at Huggin Hill, development and archaeology remain difficult to reconcile in Britain's great historic cities.[20]

Since the illegal demolition in 1974 of the Grade 2-listed Georgian hotel, the site near Ouse Bridge in Micklegate had lain empty. Although there could be little doubt that redevelopment would take place in due course, no developer was willing to build a replica of the hotel as stipulated by the Secretary of State for the Environment. At the same time, in spite of the manifest archaeological potential of the site, English Heritage was unwilling to fund excavation in the absence of an imminent threat. In March 1988, however, a planning application was submitted and YAT notified English Heritage and the City Council of its wish to excavate. No grant aid was forthcoming, but English Heritage expressed the view that, in the course of the Minister's review of the planning application, provision for archaeology would be ensured. The planning application was, however, approved by the Minister without reference to archaeology. The developer was unwilling to make funds available and York City Council felt unable to insist on excavation in giving planning consent because in its view archaeology was already catered for by the AAI legislation (see p. 14).

As the statutory four-and-a-half months for access under the 1979 Act moved to a close, YAT observed nine contractor's test pits which revealed up to 5.5m (18 ft) of archaeology, with organic remains of the Anglo-Scandinavian period overlying Roman buildings. English Heritage deferred consideration of an urgent request for funds until the first week in November, when the contractor's works were due to begin. In the

Plate 4.4 The Queen's Hotel site, York. Wall of a major late-third-century Roman public building (vertical scale 1m/c. 3 ft 3 ins) (Photograph: York Archaeological Trust)

meantime (September) a further planning application had been submitted which would involve removal of 2.6m (8 ft 6 ins) of deposits over most of the site for a basement car park. After some work on this removal had begun before consent was formally granted, it was stopped by the City Council and £2,000 was given to YAT by the developer for a watching brief while work for which permission had been given proceeded. The watching brief began on 21 November, with a deadline of 12 December. In the course of this work it became clear that Viking Age and Roman buildings survived in very good condition on the site, and after a tip-off the *Yorkshire Evening Press* of 16 December, under a headline, 'Parliamentary probe call on dig site's destruction', recorded that:

> Bulldozers moved onto the Micklegate site today to begin work which will destroy eleventh century medieval buildings and shop fronts of national archaeological importance. Developers will soon drive 56 piles through the Viking and Roman remains – a process

compared by a York Labour Party spokesman, Mr Hugh Bayley, to 'hammering blunt nails through the Leonardo Cartoon'.

At this point a delay to the contractor's work was secured, and with £18,000 from the developers and £20,000 from English Heritage archaeology continued, with a 10 February 1989 deadline, the main aim being to excavate three of the 3m (9 ft 6 ins) square pile holes. At the same time, however, media interest took off, led by the *Yorkshire Evening Press* who, to their eternal credit, kept the issue in the public eye under their 'Fight for Roman York' banner. In one of the trial holes, meanwhile, a substantial Roman wall, 1.8m (6 ft) wide and standing over 2m (6 ft 6 ins) high, was found which had clearly formed part of a major building. The heat of controversy was raised when, on the 1st of January, Professor Jones of Manchester University suggested that the building could have been the *domus palatina*, or palace, referred to in a contemporary source as the residence of the Emperor Septimius Severus on his visit to York in 209–11. At the same time there was talk, on the one hand, of the tourism potential of the site, if properly displayed in the manner of the Jorvik Viking Centre, and the jobs that would be created, but, on the other, of jobs that might be lost if developers were scared away from York by archaeological problems.[21]

In the event the second planning application was called in for review by the DOE, the developers sold the site to a new concern and a breathing space was gained. Excavation was resumed for a two-month period in the summer of 1989 and the promise of the trial pits was realised. A large stone building of the early third century had evidently been replaced by a monumental structure of the later third – too late to be a Severan palace. Close to the Micklegate frontage, a stretch of wall was found running north-west–south-east – but on a slightly different alignment from the main Roman road – and still standing some 4m (13 ft) high. Because the excavation area was relatively small it was not possible to identify what the walls uncovered had formed part of, although the proximity of the river suggests that one option is a second public bath house.

The walls discovered at Queen's Hotel were clearly candidates for preservation *in situ*, especially because, as in London, there is nothing to be seen today of the Roman town – as opposed to the fortress – at York. English Heritage again took the view that scheduling was inappropriate given their potential liability for large compensation payments. YAT made representations to the developers urging the adjustment of footing plans to preserve the walls, but in vain, and most of the masonry was reduced to rubble in January 1990, an event recorded by the *Evening Press* on the 20th under the oddly gory headline 'MP acts over Roman site carnage'. As a result of the Queen's Hotel affair, the city has appointed its own archaeologist, who in accordance with the DOE's advice[22] insists on full evaluation of development sites before planning consent is given. In addition, under the terms of a recently published document, *Draft Conservation Policies for York's Archaeology*, the city is proposing to insist that developers should make every effort to employ a construction design which will preserve 95 per cent of archaeological deposits on their sites.

By way of a conclusion to our survey of Roman York we may, for a moment, accompany the Emperor Severus, the Empress Julia Domna, their son Caracalla and a vast retinue on their arrival in York in AD 209 to prepare for campaigns in the north.[23] All recent excavations have shown that we would probably have found a town in the middle of a golden age of growth and prosperity, although no doubt it appeared as something of a one-horse, or one-chariot, town to the imperial party. We can, however, imagine the emperor borne in his litter, due to ill health and advancing age (he was 65 in 210), pausing where medieval Micklegate Bar now stands, perhaps to admire a Roman gateway on much the same site and, close by, a statue to the spirit of *Britannia* erected by one Nikomedes, a freedman from Greece.[24] On either side there would have been elegant houses and others, perhaps, were just hidden from view away to the right where they were laid out on great terraces sweeping down to the river.

As the party moved slowly down the great main street, greeted by awe-inspired crowds, largely of Britons, but with a fair sprinkling of people from far and wide in the empire, Severus might have appreciated a tidy grid of streets and the solid, if not extravagant, public buildings showing that Roman civic values survived even in this remote outpost. There might be nothing here to rival the splendour of the emperor's home at Lepcis Magna (now in Libya), let alone Rome itself, but once blessed by the imperial presence who could deny that more glorious achievements were just around the corner. As someone who, like his empress, a priest's daughter, was deeply interested in religious matters, Severus must have been particularly pleased to hear of the small temple of Serapis, associated with the mysterious Egyptian death-and-rebirth cult of Isis, and the temple of Mithras, the 'lord of light', whose harsh and savage rituals had been spread by soldiers from the east. After crossing the River Ouse, after some suitable sacrifice to local spirits perhaps, the imperial party would have entered the fortress of the 6th legion, where the emperor and empress probably took up residence in the legionary commander's house rather than a purpose-built palace.

During the next year or so while Severus used York as his base for military operations and, equally important, for governing the empire, his presence must have provided a substantial boost to the local economy, although the billeting of officials and extra soldiers on the townsfolk may have eventually become too much of a good thing. When Severus died in York on 4 February 211, the sudden departure of Caracalla and the empress must have been a blow to the local merchants and craftsmen. In one sense we may see it as a blow from which York never recovered, for if there had been plans for a great imperial city in the north, they were never fulfilled.

A striking feature of the *colonia* is that the area traditionally ascribed to it is small, only c. 27ha (67 acres), as opposed to the walled area of Roman London which is over 140ha (346 acres). Even if the settled areas around the fortress on the north-east bank of the Ouse also enjoyed *colonia* status, we still have one of Roman Britain's smaller towns. The imperial authorities may, in other words, have looked on their last major town foundation as both a success and, in due course, an admission of restricted urban ambitions at a time when economic and political changes in the western empire were beginning to render the future of a town-based economy less certain.

Town defences – a province under threat?

Another indication of change in the urban order in the late second century can be found in the erection of defences around many of the towns of Roman Britain. Understanding these defences is important not only because they are usually the most visible reminders today of a town's Roman past, but also because they are one of the principal determinants of subsequent topographical developments, since the Roman work was adopted wholesale, or in good part, in Anglo-Saxon and medieval times. In recent years the study of the architecture, dating and function of Roman town defences has been a major theme in urban archaeology and a subject of lively debate.[25]

Town defences were, of course, not unknown in Britain before the later second century. Verulamium was defended shortly after the Roman conquest[26] and Colchester was probably walled in the aftermath of the Boudiccan revolt. Nervousness at this time may also explain the banks and ditches surrounding Silchester and Winchester. The *coloniae* at Gloucester and Lincoln,[27] and *civitas* capital at Exeter (see Figure 4.2), inherited the defences of the former legionary fortresses on their sites. As befitted their status, the earth and timber ramparts at Gloucester and Lincoln were fronted with a stone wall early in the second century. A concerted effort to defend most of the other towns, however, including the *civitas* capitals at Chichester and Cirencester,[28] had to wait until shortly before 200.

In the majority of cases the first phase of construction involved a ditch, earthen bank and timber gates, except at Cirencester and Verulamium where stone gates were built. At some subsequent date towns acquired a stone wall placed in front of the bank. At Exeter recent work[29] suggests that this occurred after only a short space of time, whereas at Silchester[30] and Verulamium a date in the 270s is indicated. At London, however, it appears that the wall, dated to c. 200, was not preceded by earlier defences,

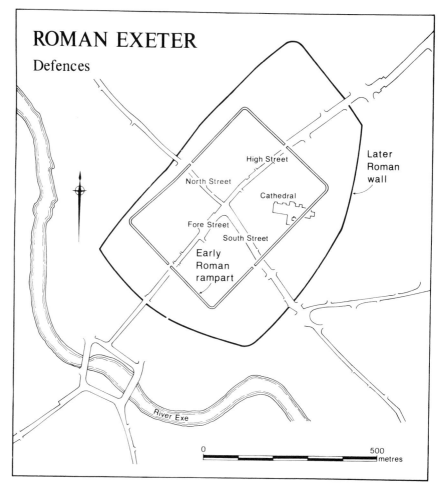

Figure 4.2 Defences and urban ambition: Roman Exeter showing the line of the early Roman fortress and town defences in relation to the town wall of c. AD 180–200 (length of later circuit 2.35km / 1.45 miles) (Exeter Museums Archaeological Field Unit)

although there has been some speculation on the subject of an earlier rampart, possibly on a different line.[31]

The construction of defences would not have been entered into lightly. Apart from the expense involved, the work required the emperor's explicit approval. A concerted programme in Britain might, therefore, suggest a co-ordinated response to some specific threat. Given the length of the circuits, however, they would have been difficult to defend without considerable manpower, although it is unlikely that any force other than the

Roman army was capable of sustaining a siege. At Exeter and Verulamium, moreover, the new ramparts encompassed areas up to 50 per cent larger than the original circuit (see Figure 4.2). The British town defences may at this time, therefore, have been only partly a defensive obstacle and partly a means to define the area within which inhabitants had privileges attendant on urban residence; the gates would have served as places to collect tolls and taxes. The apparent similarity in date and in form of urban defences may reflect competition between towns striving to emulate their neighbours.[32]

As a good example of the way Roman urban defences can be interpreted in terms of the changing status of the town itself, we may return to Lincoln where there has been an extensive examination of the circuit around both the upper town, the original *colonia*, and the lower town, the settlement which grew up alongside Ermine Street on the steep scarp of the Lincoln edge above the River Witham (see Figure 4.3).[33] Lincoln is, moreover, singularly blessed with visible remains of its Roman defences. In the upper town, for example, the north gate or Newport Arch, probably of the early third century, is, apart from the Balkerne Gate in Colchester (see Plate 3.2), the only surviving Roman town gate in Britain with an intact arch, and the excavated remains of the east gate of similar date can also be seen. In the lower town an important stretch of the defences is visible at The Park on the west side of the enclosure.

It is clear that a great deal more of the Roman walls survived until at least the later eighteenth century, including more of the Newport Arch and the south gate of the upper town. In such surroundings it is not surprising that interest in Lincoln's antiquities has a long history; indeed William Stukeley, a native of Lincolnshire, wrote in 1724: 'I never saw such a fund of antique speculation in any town in England. I heard continually of coyns and urns.'

There was no full-time archaeologist in Lincoln, however, until 1972 when Christina Colyer was appointed director of the Lincoln Archaeological Trust. Her first project was the excavation of the defences at The Park and West Parade, where in 1970–2 some 56m (184 ft) was excavated, providing what is probably an unrepeatable opportunity to study their history (see Plate 4.5).[34] The site showed that in c. 200, when the defences of the upper town were modified with a wider rampart and heightened wall, work also began on defending the lower town. At The Park the rampart and wall in front of it were contemporary, the former heaped up while the latter was constructed. The occasion for this work and the reason there was, unusually, a wall from the outset could be connected with the extension of *colonia* status to the lower town (see Plate 4.6).

It was thought until recently that the wall found at The Park was continued the length of the complete 1.5km (0.93 miles) circuit around the lower town, although excavations at Silver Street on the east side sug-

Plate 4.5 The Park, Lincoln: the west gate of the Roman lower town looking west. Left and right foreground, bases of the mid-

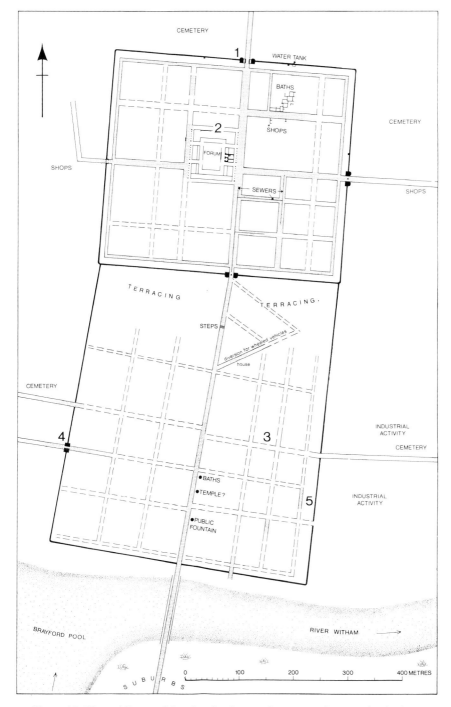

Figure 4.3 Plan of Roman Lincoln: the former fortress and original *colonia*, or upper town, is at the top, the lower town is at the bottom (City of Lincoln Archaeological Unit)

Key: 1 Newport Arch; 2 Mint Wall; 3 Flaxengate excavation; 4 The Park; 5 Silver Street

Plate 4.6 A *colonia* as a centre of Romanised tastes: a relief thought to be of Venus and Adonis in provincial style from the Hungate site, Lincoln (Photograph: City of Lincoln Archaeological Unit)

gested that the rampart here pre-dated the wall.[35] Recent re-examination of pottery, however, suggests that the Silver Street rampart was mid- to late-third-century and the wall was roughly contemporary. It is likely, therefore, that the initial work on the west side of the defences went unfinished, perhaps due to lack of funds, and was only completed fifty years or more later. Towers were apparently integral to the second stage of wall construction and were added to the earlier wall on the west as was seen at The Park.

In the reign of the Emperor Diocletian (284–305) Britain was divided into four provinces and Lincoln probably became a provincial capital. This new status may have been the inspiration for a further stage of work on the defences of the upper town which involved digging a wider ditch, and thickening and heightening the wall so that it stood some 7m (23 ft) or more high, a formidable obstacle. A surviving stretch of this late wall can be seen at the Eastgate Hotel. In the lower town at The Park the excavations showed that the tower was replaced by a new and hitherto unsuspected gateway. It initially consisted of flanking walls to retain the rampart and probably had a simple arch. As we shall see (pp. 110–11), the gate was remodelled when another episode of construction on the lower town defences took place in the mid-fourth century.

Later Roman London – within these walls

Work on town defences in the later third century may have had a particular urgency in areas of the south-east of England within striking distance of the coast, as sea-borne barbarian incursions became an unchecked hazard during long periods of political and military difficulty. These include events surrounding Britain's secession from Rome, first as part of a break-away Gallic empire from 259 to 273 and, second, in 285 as part of the area, also including northern Gaul, under the former naval commander Carausius and his assassin and successor Allectus. A long period of uncertainty for Britain was only brought to an end when Allectus was defeated in 294 by the legitimate emperor in the west, Constantius I.

During the third century emperors, legitimate and otherwise, put together a system of coastal defences in southern and eastern England based on forts known to us as the Saxon Shore forts. The upgrading of defences at towns such as Canterbury, previously undefended, but walled in the 270s,[36] was probably an integral part of the system. We can also suggest that another element was the riverside wall of London whose existence was finally demonstrated as recently as 1974.

The presence of the wall had been hinted at in William Fitzstephen's twelfth-century description of London:

> London was once walled and towered in like fashion [to the landward wall] but the Thames ... which runs on that side with the sea's ebb and flow, has in course of time washed away these bulwarks, undermined and cast them down.

Scholars, apart from Roach Smith, had usually dismissed this passage as a product of Fitzstephen's imagination, but in 1972 a large section of wall core was found on the Baynard's Castle site at the south-west corner of the Roman town. When, on a nearby site, the realignment of Upper Thames Street in 1974–6 made possible the first archaeological excavation across the river frontage, foreshore and the land behind, the river wall's existence was confirmed.[37] Seven discrete stretches are now known, showing that it ran the complete length of the waterfront. Dendro-chronology of timber piles under the wall at the New Fresh Wharf site suggests a date of construction of 255–70, that is during the Gallic empire or immediately after its collapse.[38]

The wall is reckoned to have stood over 7m (23 ft) high and was largely ragstone (a limestone from Kent), much of it probably re-used from other buildings. Also found incorporated in the fabric on the 1974–6 site was a collection of re-used sculpted stones which form one of the most remarkable archaeological discoveries in Roman London this century. There was a series of relief carvings of gods and goddesses, now in the Museum of London, which probably formed part of a monumental screen and arch, and two altars, one dedicated to the goddess Isis and the other probably to Jupiter. These sculptures give some hint of the grandeur of the suggested public assembly and recreation area in the south-western part of Roman London. The fact that parts of its major buildings could be sacrificed to the needs of defence, however, indicates a radical re-ordering of priorities in the later Roman urban community. It is equally significant in this context that the wall would have severely restricted access to the riverside quays.

The final advance of the north bank of the Thames took place in the early third century. The latest quay, again employing tiers of massive horizontal timbers, is now known to have extended from the recently excavated Vintry House and Thames Exchange sites beyond the Walbrook in the west as far as Old Custom House in the east, with particularly well-preserved stretches at New Fresh Wharf[39] and Billingsgate Lorry Park.[40] It was clearly a massive undertaking and no permanent decline in London's fortunes as a trading centre can have been envisaged when the investment was made. No further advance of the waterfront has, however, been found and there are relatively few finds datable after the mid-third century from riverside sites. The implication is that London had, after perhaps a quite short, but sharp, period of decline, ceased to be a major centre for riverborne trade, a situation apparently confirmed by the construction of the riverside wall. A further contributory factor may have been a drop in river level which moved the tidal head, required by larger ships, further to the east.

In view of this major change in London's economic role, we may ask what sort of town this now hermetically-closed circuit of walls served to protect. As far as the forum is concerned, the Leadenhall Court excavations of 1984–6 suggest that final refurbishment of the basilica took place in the late third century, but that disuse and some deliberate demolition, perhaps to supply stone for the river wall, followed shortly afterwards.[41] On the subject of public buildings, however, we may also note a discovery made on a site at St Peter's Hill, west of the Walbrook. Here excavations have shown that the ground sloping up from the Thames had been terraced for the construction of massive stone buildings. Dendrochronology of the timber piles below some of the walls gave an unusually exact date of 294, which has prompted identification of the site as the palace of the ill-fated 'British emperor' Allectus.[42]

Elsewhere in London and Southwark the remains of numerous large stone buildings of the later third and fourth centuries have been found[43] and it is suggested that they were associated with government and administration. After Diocletian's reforms London became capital of the British diocese, a new tier in the administrative structure between the four provinces and the capital of the western empire in Trier. The added bureaucracy this involved presumably brought more civil servants to London, reinforcing the ranks of one of the city's oldest professions. The upper echelons, no doubt, found ways of feathering their nests and a splendid suite of sculptures found in a fourth-century well under Southwark Cathedral, including the statue of a hunter god and a stone tomb cover bearing a female figure, has been identified as the property of a wealthy official family living in the area.[44] What is largely lacking in later Roman London, however, are the strip buildings for artisans which were so characteristic of the first and second centuries.

Later Roman towns – the *coloniae* and *civitas* capitals

One of the problems archaeologists have in determining the state of urban fortunes in the mid to later third century is the relative lack of deposits containing diagnostic pottery and other finds. This may mean lower levels of population and economic activity or, alternatively, that buildings were kept scrupulously tidy by prosperous and orderly urban communities. It would appear, however, that there was usually no further expansion of the area they occupied and in many cases some contraction. At Exeter, for example, the recent excavations in peripheral areas within the defences have shown that the enlarged circuit was not crammed with buildings as was previously thought.[45] One reason for stagnation may be the disruption to interprovincial trade routes caused by political turmoil and piracy, so that one of the traditional roles of towns as centres for the distribution of imported goods came to an end. This would have left the only substantial source of wealth as land ownership. It has been suggested, therefore, that as a result of diminished opportunities in Romano-British towns, many of the native aristocracy moved back into the countryside and developed their villas, leaving the primary function of late Roman towns as administration and tax collection.[46]

In addition to their decline as trade centres, later Roman towns may also have had a less important role in manufacturing as villas became increasingly self-sufficient in the production of woodwork, iron tools and other humble artefacts. The industrial suburb at Canterbury, for example, disappeared in the third century. There were probably some exceptions to this picture, however; Water Newton, for example, appears to have enjoyed its greatest growth in the third and fourth centuries, thanks to the success of the local pottery industry, and may have been promoted to *civitas* capital.[47] There may, moreover, have been a particular role for towns in the production of luxury goods which required groups of specialist craftsmen. Cirencester (*Corinium*)[48] was one of several towns which were centres for mosaic production and also, it is suggested, possessed a school of sculptors. In addition, Cirencester was important as a centre for administration, especially after it became the capital of the province of *Britannia Prima* in Diocletian's reforms. There is no evidence, however, that the later Roman town was densely populated and indeed an atmosphere of '*rus in urbe*' is conjured up by the villa-type establishments excavated on the immediate outskirts of the town in the Beeches Road area. The principal buildings produced a remarkable group of mosaics showing that the town's workshop was still operating in the 360s.

Administrators in both the civilian and military spheres are also likely to have been prominent among the inhabitants of later Roman York. In 306 Constantius I died in York and his son, Constantine I, was acclaimed emperor there. It was probably during his reign that York became the seat of the *Dux Britanniarum*, a military commander responsible for the whole of the north including Hadrian's Wall. During the third century York's status had been enhanced by reconstruction of the fortress defences, in particular on the south-west front facing the river, where a stupendous scheme of polygonal corner and interval towers was doubtless intended as much to impress the civilians on the opposite bank as to add to defensive capabilities.[49] Not to be outdone, the townspeople themselves were also engaged in construction work on, for example, the remarkable late-third-century public building at Queen's Hotel. In the Bishophill area evidence has been found for the erection of new houses and extension of old ones at much the same time.[50] Two mosaics in the *colonia* may be dated to the fourth century, and immediately to the south-west of its presumed defences a large early-fourth-century villa-type house with a mosaic floor was found at the Clementhorpe site.[51]

On the north-east bank of the Ouse at the Ebor Brewery site, near the east corner of the fortress, a mosaic was found featuring a central roundel with a woman's face (see Figure 6.12).[52] This had presumably decorated another large town house, but acquires additional interest because immediately above it was a small medieval church dedicated to St Helen (see pp. 201–2), mother of Constantine, who, like her son, became a Christian convert and is supposed to have unearthed the true cross in Jerusalem (perhaps Helen should be the patron saint of archaeologists!). The location of the mosaic and church must, however, be fortuitous, as the excavations showed that it was unlikely that the church builders had seen the mosaic and, mindful of Christian tradition, mistaken the figure for Helen.

In addition to looking at defences and the buildings within them, another way of assessing the state of later Roman urban fortunes is to study the centres of local government – the fora – to see if they continued to function as centres of political and administrative authority in the traditional manner.[53] In most cases the archaeological evidence is equivocal since only small areas have been examined, although at London, as we have seen, demolition probably took place before 300. Elsewhere there is as yet little evidence for demolition, but important evidence for a change in character has come from the recent excavations in the forum basilica at Silchester.[54] The Victorian excavations were found to have been less destructive than had been feared and a fascinating sequence has emerged. In origin the basilica had been a simple timber building which was replaced by a fine stone structure in the early second century, elaborately decorated with marbles from the Mediterranean. Surprisingly, however, rubbish pits of the late second/early third century were found dug into the floor, and in the late third century the main hall had been partitioned into small enclosures where metalworking had taken place until c. 330. The partitions were then removed and the building was used for ironworking. The evidence is, therefore, for a change in the basilica's role in the late Roman period, but this need not mean that civic life had collapsed. It is possible that the local *ordo* had taken to meeting elsewhere while continuing to exercise control over the organisation of the basilica and perhaps deriving a lucrative rent from the metalworkers.

Contributing to the changing character of later Roman towns are new forms of religious observance, in particular the adoption of Christianity. Until its acceptance by Constantine and his successors as an official religion of the Roman empire, however, Christianity was just one of a number of similar cults, also including, as we have seen at York, the worship of Isis and Mithras, which swept through the empire from the east carried by the army and travelling merchants. The theology of these cults usually involved a death-and-rebirth myth and their adherents were promised revelations of the secret of eternal life. Initiation into the body of believers might be a simple baptism, but in some cases was more elaborate, involving incarceration or other ordeals. For such ceremonies, the cults required a different sort of building from the classical or Celtic temples because they involved the assembly and participation of a congregation. We therefore find the traditional Roman aisled basilica newly adopted for religious purposes.

The evidence for Christianity in Roman Britain[55] in, for example, the form of hoards of church silver, and mosaics or wall paintings on Christian themes, comes largely from urban or villa settings. This appears to indicate a religion, in the first instance, of the townsmen or upper classes with urban connections rather than of the mass of the rural poor or *pagani* (hence our word pagan – an unbeliever) living remote from the influence of new ideas.

Early British Christians often assembled in each others' houses, and churches have proved elusive. There is a possible example at Silchester which was located in the forum *insula*,[56] but a more convincing church, in this case within the forum courtyard, has recently been discovered at Lincoln on the St Paul-in-the-Bail site.[57] The lines of the building's timber walls, erected c. 390, have now been picked out in stone setts in a pleasant open area north-east of the castle. With the Mint Wall and Bailgate colonnade nearby (see pp. 51–3), one can easily appreciate the church's location in the heart of the Roman town which thus serves to confirm the acceptance of Christianity by the state. Although small, this was probably the seat of the Roman bishops of Lincoln, the first of whom, it is believed, was one of the three British bishops (the other two were from London and York) summoned by Constantine to the Council of Arles in 314. The Lincoln church had probably disappeared by the mid-fifth century when radiocarbon dating suggests burials were cut into the empty wall trenches. There seems to be no question of the church forming a focus for continuity of settlement in Lincoln in the later fifth and sixth centuries as is apparent in towns elsewhere in western Europe.

Another potential source of information on the extent of Christianity in late Roman Britain is burials. In theory the Christian emphasis on the idea of resurrection appears to require burial of a body on an east–west line with its head at the west end of the grave. The deceased would therefore arise to face east on hearing the 'Last Trump', usually expected to issue from the Holy Land. Furthermore, an emphasis on spiritual over material values would seem to preclude grave furnishings of traditional Roman type. In view of the theological considerations, it might seem, at first sight, that the large number of unfurnished east–west inhumation burials now known from late Roman contexts in Britain are evidence for mass Christianity, while the relatively smaller number of furnished burials, often on other alignments, are evidence for lingering paganism. Unfortunately this is a great oversimplification, as mode of burial may relate to a wide range of cultural and social factors. East–west burial could, for example, be related to the worship of a sun deity or to the simple convenience of using the position of sunrise to guide grave-digging in an ordered cemetery. Lack of grave furnishing may relate to an unwillingness to part with material possessions in straitened economic circumstances.

In spite of the problems, good evidence for a marked change in burial practice at about the time the empire became officially Christian, which may suggest adoption of the new faith, comes from the Colchester Butt Road cemetery.[58] It lay close to the south gate of the *colonia* and produced over 700 burials. The sixty-five graves in the first cemetery were third-century and were aligned north–south. Offerings, in the form of pots, glass vessels and jewellery, were frequent. This cemetery was cut into by a second whose use began in c. 320–40, continuing until the early fifth century. The graves were laid out east–west and offerings were confined to children. On the west side of the site graves came to within 1m (3 ft 3 ins) of a stone-and-brick building measuring 24m (79 ft) by 7m (23 ft) with an apsed east end (see Figure 4.4). This is interpreted as a cemetery church.[59] The consolidated remains can be seen today, as the new police station on the site was redesigned to avoid destroying this remarkable memorial to the antiquity of British Christianity.

Figure 4.4 Imaginative reconstruction of the Colchester Roman church (drawn by Peter Froste)

Among the 444 inhumation graves in the Lankhills cemetery at Winchester (see Figure 3.9), unfurnished inhumations also occurred in some numbers, but there was, again, no conclusive evidence for Christianity.[60] Lankhills is, however, one of very few systematically excavated late Roman cemeteries and has yielded a great deal of information on burial customs and urban society in the fourth century. What is, perhaps, immediately striking about the site is how wide-ranging these customs were, not only in the provision of grave goods, but also in the shape and size of the grave pit, the position of the body and so forth. This may relate to the diverse and rapidly changing ideas on burial and spiritual matters generally among townsfolk, and appears to contrast with the relatively uniform and simple mode of burial in rural cemeteries of the period.

The Lankhills site is c. 500m (550 yds) from the north gate of Roman Winchester and, since the graves date from c. 310–410, it forms the latest extension of the great northern cemetery of which the Hyde Street site (see pp. 77–80) is the earliest part. In terms of organisation, a strictly disciplined approach to cemetery management prevailed, with graves arranged in rows with little intercutting of one by another. The principal determinant of the layout of the graves was probably the Cirencester road in relation to which they were dug at an angle of roughly 90 degrees. Discipline only began to break down at the end of the fourth century when grave pits became shallow and were dug on a variety of alignments. At the same time grave furnishing became much less frequent, evidence, perhaps, for poverty in troubled times. These developments would seem to echo, as we shall see, other evidence for changes in the urban order at Winchester and elsewhere.

Particular interest at Lankhills attaches to two groups of burials taken to indicate the presence of new ethnic elements in late Roman Winchester. This is of great importance because of the debate about the extent to which people from outside the Roman empire had settled within it during the fourth century, either compulsorily, to prevent them causing trouble, or by invitation, as so-called *foederati*, to strengthen the army. One group of sixteen burials dated c. 350 contained distinctive grave goods including, for males, the fittings for official-issue belts at the waist. It is suggested, first, that these people came from a part of what is now Hungary, on the fringes of the empire, and second, because they were buried in what were thought to be prominent and desirable locations in the cemetery, that they had a distinct status conferred on them by the Roman authorities, although as what is uncertain.

The second unusual group of graves from Lankhills, six in number, date to perhaps the last decade of the fourth century. They were not particularly similar to one another, but, it is suggested, they all had affinities with contemporary Germanic burials in areas outside the empire and with fifth-century Anglo-Saxon burials in this country. The most striking grave contained fittings from a double-strap belt, again of a type recognised as part of the equipment of late Roman officials. The interpretation of these graves is that they are rare evidence for deliberate import of aliens, Germanic in this case, by the imperial administration to bolster the defences of Britain.

The human remains from Lankhills have not yet been published, but a thorough survey of the physical anthropology of a late Roman urban population comes from the Bathgate cemetery on the south-west side of Roman Cirencester.[61] In the principal group of 362 skeletons studied, one of the most surprising conclusions is that males outnumbered females by two to one. This may be an accident of sampling, but is not unprecedented since in a largely third-century cemetery at York males were four times more common than females.[62] At York the figures may reflect the presence of a large military element in the population, but at Cirencester an explanation is less easy to find, although the human bone specialist Calvin Wells offered the curiously sexist comment that:

> Cirencester like York was largely given over to retired legionaries and to various Roman officials, many of whom lacked regular wives and whose sexual partners, if any, were probably drawn from the professional prostitutes who were no doubt an abundant and pleasant amenity of the town.[63]

Once out of childhood the average life expectancy for the people of Cirencester was c. 40 years, with a tendency for males to outlive females. This is a rather different situation from today when, on average, women live longer, but reflects, perhaps, the hazards of childbirth. Even in the days of rudimentary obstetrics, however, some women could achieve a great age and the tombstone in Lincoln of the egregious Claudia Crysis records her death at 90 years. Assessment of stature at Cirencester shows that men were between 1.6m (5 ft 3 ins) and 1.82m (6 ft) with an average of 1.7m (5 ft 7 ins), and women between 1.45m (4 ft 8 ins) and 1.7m (5 ft 7 ins) with an average of 1.58m (5 ft 2 ins).

There was a good deal of evidence for osteoarthritis and fractures were also quite common, occurring in 20 per cent of skeletons, most frequently on the ribs, fibulae (leg) and forearm. Some were no doubt accidental, but others are thought to derive from aggression, especially between men amongst whom fractures were much more common. Interpersonal violence was also suggested by a number of incised wounds from sharp instruments on skulls and limbs, leading Wells to conclude 'beyond reasonable doubt that fighting – in battle, arena or "pub" – was a commonplace event with these people'.[64] A more formal type of violence to the person is indicated by six decapitations effected by a blow on the back of the neck. We may have evidence for the execution of malefactors here, but at Lankhills there were seven graves of decapitated individuals, whose skulls, buried at their feet, had in each case been removed by careful cutting from the front. Some sort of ritual, reminiscent of the burial of skulls in London's Walbrook (see p. 63), is thought more likely here than execution.

The end of the Roman town – not a bang but a whimper?

While vigorous debate continues on the role and fortunes of Britain's Roman towns in the third and early fourth centuries, there is fairly general agreement that the last twenty to thirty years of the fourth century were a time of marked change in the urban order. Fewer buildings were occupied, and those which were, like the streets around them, experienced declining standards of maintenance. These developments occurred against a background of renewed economic dislocation, with inflation rampant, and a breakdown of imperial authority in the western Empire. As far as this country was concerned one of the most catastrophic episodes was the 'Barbarian Conspiracy' of 367 when, as we are told by the contemporary historian Ammianus Marcellinus, some unlucky chance led hostile forces from across the North Sea, and from Ireland and Scotland, to attack at the same time. Finding the Roman army unable to repel them, they 'reduced the provinces of Britain to the verge of ruin'.[65]

The archaeology of London (Augusta as it was now known) suggests that the diocesan capital witnessed no major new building after c. 300, except on the defences. At some time between 351 and 375 a series of semi-circular projecting bastions was added to the landward wall on its eastern side,[66] presumably indicating that the likely direction of an attack was from up the Thames. Beyond the wall the ditch was widened to create a more substantial obstacle to any hostile forces. Another late Roman defensive work was discovered during excavations at the Tower of London in the south-east corner of the Roman town. Found running east–west inside the line of the late-third-century riverside wall was another wall (now on permanent display) thought to date to the 390s.[67] Its function is unclear, but it was probably part of a final attempt to strengthen the defences of London, perhaps to create a stronghold for the diocesan treasury. The location of this establishment at London is specifically mentioned in the *Notitia Dignitatum* and is also suggested by the discovery at the Tower, in 1777 and 1898, of silver ingots and gold coins dated to c. 395.

Although some remnants of both governing and other classes were presumably to be found in London around the year 400, the nature of occupation within the walls at this time is poorly understood, partly, at least, because later Roman deposits are vulnerable to destruction by modern cellars. The only site in London, as yet excavated, where it can confidently be suggested that some sort of occupation took place in the immediate post-Roman period is the bath house of a large building near the river at Billingsgate. An early Anglo-Saxon brooch was found in the ruins indicating fifth-century visitors if not actual residents.

Away from the capital the picture of gradual decline is similar, with the evidence of building in stone in the mid to late fourth century largely confined to the strengthening of defences, perhaps to create strong points, similar to forts, in an otherwise vulnerable province. In addition to London, external bastions are known elsewhere including Caerwent, where good examples can be seen today. A comparable motive may lie behind the thickening and heightening of the walls and the digging of a new wider ditch around the lower town at Lincoln, in a manner comparable to the works in the upper town at the beginning of the century. In addition, the gateway at The Park was remodelled with two projecting gate towers, of which parts of the guard chambers survive. The base of their walls incorporate very large blocks of limestone including carved pieces from a building of some architectural pretension, possibly a pagan temple demolished by the triumphant Christians of Roman Lincoln.

In a formal sense, the Roman period is often taken to end in c. 410 with an imperial edict known as the 'Rescript of Honorius', supposedly a response to an appeal for help from the British cities which instructed them to look to their own defences. Some doubt has recently been cast on the translation of the source and it may not refer to Britain at all,[68] but the date is still a convenient one to use when assessing the decline of town life in Roman Britain and the fate of town sites in the post-Roman period.

One of the problems of understanding these topics is the peculiarly equivocal nature of the evidence. First of all, late Roman layers have often been severely truncated by medieval pits, modern basements, etc. Secondly, even where the deposits survive, they have, until recently, often been summarily removed by archaeologists looking for stone structures, unaware that the latest Roman buildings were often built of timber and have therefore only survived as very insubstantial remains. Thirdly, while late Roman layers are often very productive of finds, compared to those of earlier periods, this does not necessarily indicate intense occupation, but rather that the standards and organisation of the disposal of refuse had changed; instead of being taken out of town it was dumped on vacant ground or unused streets near the remaining dwellings. Finally, because there are few artefacts that are identifiably early-fifth-century, some of the deposits which apparently contain only Roman material may well be later than 410, but this cannot be proved. While new coinage did not reach Britain after c. 402, implying an end to the imperial tax system, coinage already in circulation may have continued in use for some years. Pottery in Roman style may have been made until, perhaps, 420 or 430.

The problem of the late and early post-Roman periods has been addressed archaeologically at a number of towns, including Verulamium. An important building sequence in one of the *insulae* excavated by Frere probably takes occupation well into the fifth century, providing a context for the documented visit of St Germanus in 429.[69] Some of the most interesting recent results, however, come from Canterbury, Winchester and York.

At Canterbury town life is thought to have continued relatively unaffected by the troubles of the empire until the last quarter of the fourth century. A bath house in St George's Street, for example, was evidently renovated in 355–60, but it was damaged by fire soon after and, instead of being rebuilt, was allowed to fall into disrepair.[70] The public baths in St Margaret Street appear to have decayed after 350 and there was an accumulation of silty material over the floors, the result, perhaps, of blocked drains. Another indication of a change in the traditional urban order was the appearance in the portico on the street to the south-west, of a row of timber buildings which had extended out on to the latest street surface. At the Riding Gate the southern carriage way was blocked indicating, perhaps, both declining traffic and increased concern for security.[71]

Of particular interest at Canterbury was a grave found cut into the latest surface of the temple courtyard (see Figure 4.5).[72] Since burial, except of infants, was strictly forbidden inside the settled areas of Roman towns, this again indicates a breakdown of civic authority. The grave contained a family group with an adult male and female, two young girls and a dog. The women's jewellery is the only distinctive artefact and probably dates to c. 400. The circumstances in which these individuals met their end are clearly intriguing and it is likely that they were amongst the last inhabitants of the Roman town. At much the same time a remarkable hoard of silver objects, including a spoon which had the Christian chi-rho monogram, was buried just outside the London gate.[73] This must also be evidence of troubled times and anxious citizens. A human presence in late-fifth-century Canterbury is, however, attested by the find at the Marlowe Theatre site of one of the earliest post-Roman coins from Britain, a Visigothic gold *tremiss* dated to 480.[74] By this time the walled area can probably be envisaged as an overgrown ruin in which decaying vegetation made its contribution to a 'dark earth' layer.

The length of time over which this deposit accumulated in Canterbury is not known exactly, but it was cut into by small structures, no more than huts in modern terms. Some of them may be as early as the late fifth century, but they are largely of the sixth and seventh centuries (see Plate 4.7). The first structures were found by Sheppard Frere and, as Andrew Selkirk wrote in *Current Archaeology*,[75] they became: 'a major part of archaeological mythology for it was assumed they were the huts of the *foederati* and the Anglo-Saxon settlers arriving with Hengist and Horsa'. Some forty 'huts' are now known, but recent excavations at the Marlowe Theatre site have shown that there was no continuity of occupation from the Roman to Anglo-Saxon periods. Canterbury need not have been abandoned for more than twenty-five years or so, however, and the occurrence of early Anglo-Saxon burials in the immediate vicinity of the town suggests that its role as a focus for settlement and as a centre from which authority in Kent was traditionally exercised remained unbroken into the post-Roman period.[76] It is even possible that the great Roman amphitheatre was used for the relevant ceremonial functions.[77]

The inhabitants of the 'huts' in sixth–seventh-century Canterbury may have been the retainers of the early kings of Kent. They included Aethelberht who married a Christian Frankish princess, Bertha, and sponsored the mission of Augustine to the English in 597. According to Bede,[78] Bertha worshipped at St Martin's Church which can be found

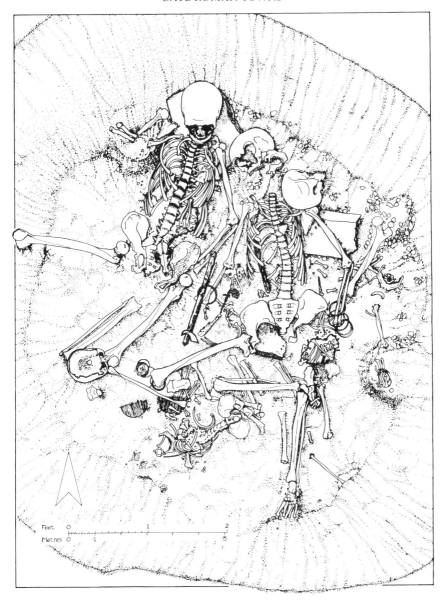

Figure 4.5 The last of Roman Canterbury: a family burial of c. 400 in the temple precinct

on the east side of Canterbury outside the walls. In origin St Martin's was a very small, rectangular, brick structure possibly of Roman date,[79] but it is thought to have been extended in the seventh century and

Plate 4.7 The beginnings of Anglo-Saxon Canterbury: remains of two sunken-floored buildings from the Marlowe Theatre site. Originally they were probably low tent-like structures supported on posts set in the holes showing clearly at the sides and corners of the left-hand building (scale 2m/c. 6 ft 6 ins) (Photograph: Canterbury Archaeological Trust)

remains one of our most evocative monuments to the revival of the Christian faith.

At Winchester excavations have shown that after c. 350 the character of the town changed radically.[80] All the town houses of which anything is known went out of use and in most cases they were demolished. Dark earth occurs widely, but there is also evidence for the construction of new timber buildings on the streets and for industrial activity. Biddle has argued that Winchester was the Venta named in the *Notitia Dignitatum* as the location of an imperial *gynaceum* or textile factory. Biddle also argues that it is difficult to claim major depopulation until perhaps the early fifth

114

century, given the large number of late-fourth-century burials at Lankhills and other cemeteries. It is possible, however, that many of the people buried at Winchester lived in the surrounding countryside and for some reason, perhaps related to the town's role as a centre for Christian worship, preferred to be buried in its cemeteries. In any event, it is clear that Winchester had a significant role in its region well into the fifth century and beyond.

Crucial evidence comes from excavations at the South Gate which showed that at some stage in the fifth or sixth century the gate and an adjacent bastion on the town wall probably collapsed, but that traffic continued over the rubble until perhaps the seventh century when the opening was blocked off by a ditch.[81] Recent analysis has shown that an appreciable quantity of early Anglo-Saxon pottery has been found within the walls, which presumably indicates that some sort of occupation, if only on an intermittent basis, took place in Winchester in the fifth–sixth centuries. Biddle suggests that, like Canterbury, Winchester remained a centre of authority in the early Anglo-Saxon period and that this accounts for its re-emergence in the seventh century, as a bishopric, and a political and economic centre (see p. 126).[82]

At York there is evidence for radical changes in both the military and urban order after c. 360. In the fortress dark-earth deposits containing domestic and industrial debris have been found on floor and street surfaces.[83] Immediately outside the fortress on its south-east side a small cemetery of inhumations was found at 16–22 Coppergate in a previously settled area, indicating a contraction of population or, as at Canterbury, a contravention of Roman rules on burial. The most striking evidence for the end of Roman York has, however, come from the Wellington Row site in the *colonia*. At some stage in the fourth century the main road from the south-west was narrowed by the construction of timber buildings on part of its surface, and the remainder was poorly maintained. The date at which this road and the attendant River Ouse crossing finally ceased to function is unknown, although it may not have been entirely abandoned until the ninth century (see p. 148).

The latest floor in the stone building by the main road at Wellington Row was a very rough cobble and earthen surface which can be dated to c. 360–80. Subsequently the building started to fall into disrepair and the mortar between the stones in the wall eroded away, probably due to exposure to the wind and rain. Most remarkable, however, was the discovery of nearly 1,000 small late Roman bronze coins scattered on the floor, within c. 2m (6 ft 6 ins) of the still-surviving north-eastern roof-support pillar. The grave of a lamb and a number of deliberately buried pots, one of which contained the bones of a puppy wrapped in a woollen bag, were found in the same area. These items may have been deposited as forms of votive offering, but it is also clear that the building was used as a refuse tip. There is, therefore, the suggestion of some form of cult observance, perhaps in a building with pagan associations, but now no longer usable because of official Christian interdict.

After c. 390 dark earth built up on the floor to a depth in places of almost 0.80m (2 ft 6 ins), but how long this took is hard to estimate. On the surface of the dark earth, however, a timber building was erected within the shell of the former stone building and re-using parts of its structure. It cannot be dated exactly, but was presumably very late Roman or early post-Roman and is the first glimpse at York into what is a very obscure period of the city's past. By the mid-fifth century archaeology would suggest that the population of York on both sides of the River Ouse was minimal: the military were long gone and the economic system supporting town life had collapsed, but clearly the Roman defences remained reasonably intact as did many buildings, including the basilica of the fortress headquarters which the excavations under the Minster suggest may have remained intermittently in use until the ninth century.[84]

The later fifth and sixth centuries are a virtual blank in the immediate York area. The only evidence for a human presence is two Anglian cemeteries, one at Heworth to the north-east of the city centre, and the other on the Mount to the south-west, significantly, if one is searching for signs of continuity, in an area of a Roman cemetery adjacent to the main Roman road, but it is too early to say that York remained a focus for settlement and authority in the early post-Roman period. The value of the defences cannot, however, have been lost on the early kings of Northumbria and this appears to be confirmed by Bede's record that York was the site of the baptism of King Edwin in 627.[85]

The only Roman town where extensive buildings which seem certain to be of the fifth century and later have been found is Wroxeter (*Viroconium*),[86] although it must be stressed that not a single fifth–seventh-century artefact has been found in the excavations. Dating has had to rely almost exclusively on estimates of the amount of time the superimposed buildings remained in use between construction and demolition episodes.

Phillip Barker's recent excavations in the *palaestra*, or exercise hall, of the public baths are of great importance for the history of Romano-British towns and for the development of excavation techniques, since it is only by the meticulous examination of large open areas, with every stone recorded, that the complex history of the site in the late and post-Roman period has emerged. The *palaestra* was originally a huge aisled building as big as a medium-sized cathedral, and a part of the south wall still survives as the so-called Old Work (see Figure 4.6). The current interpretation[87] is that the *palaestra* was kept in good repair until the end of the

Plate 4.8 Figure in relief from a jet plaque found in a late-fourth-century context at Wellington Row, York (height 45mm/c. $1\frac{1}{2}$ ins) (Photograph: York Archaeological Trust)

fourth century, but early in the fifth century it was deliberately demolished and the site was cleared. After a period of desertion, extensive rubble platforms were imported to form the foundation of a massive Roman-style timber structure and a series of subsidiary structures. One of these may have been a church into whose structure the Old Work was incorporated and this might explain the wall's unusual survival.

Although there is no evidence that Wroxeter was truly urban at the time of the timber buildings, the degree of organisation involved in their construction suggests it was the headquarters of some powerful British chieftain and his retinue. In the later fifth century this may have included one Cunorix, a man of possible Irish origins, whose tombstone was found just outside the defences. After several phases of reconstruction the buildings appear to have been deliberately dismantled. The date at which settlement in Wroxeter finally came to an end is uncertain, although the latest structures were post-dated by a burial dated by radiocarbon to c. 610.

In conclusion, the early fifth century brings Britain's first experience of urbanism to an end. While the physical fabric of Roman towns may have survived, it seems unlikely that they functioned as towns for long after c. 410 and in many cases may have ceased to do so some time before this.[88]

In the nineteenth century many scholars looked for an apocalyptic end to the towns of Roman Britain, envisaging some sort of twilight of the gods as the barbarous Anglo-Saxons rushed in. At Wroxeter, for example, Wright concluded:

> Our excavations have proved beyond a doubt that the town was taken by force, that a frightful massacre of the inhabitants followed and that it was then plundered and burnt. Remains of men, women and children are found everywhere scattered among the ruins, and the traces of burning are not only met with in all parts of them, but the whole of the soil within the walls of the ancient city is blackened by it to such a degree as to present a very marked contrast to the lighter colour of the earth outside.[89]

It is now thought likely that what Wright found was part of a post-Roman cemetery on the site of the decaying baths, belonging, perhaps, to a community on the site of present-day Wroxeter village.[90]

Figure 4.6 The Old Work at Wroxeter c. 1860

The evidence as it appears to us today is not so much for a violent bang, but rather for a feeble whimper as the urban economy expired and townsfolk drifted away to the countryside to become subsistence farmers. Are we, therefore, to judge the Romano-British urban experiment a failure? On the one hand, of course, it was, since town life did not survive the end of empire, but, on the other, the vast majority of places selected by the Romans in the late first and second centuries as suitable centres for a town-based economy and society became towns again during the great surge of late Anglo-Saxon urbanisation. The Anglo-Saxon towns usually re-used the defences of the Romans and, although street plans did not survive, the grid idea pioneered by the Romans was put to good use once more. It is arguable, furthermore, that many of the ideas on religion and the arts which were to enrich the Anglo-Saxon era stem directly from the cultural environment of the Roman town.

5

ANGLO-SAXON TOWNS

The middle-Saxon wics – towns or trading centres?

To a student of the achievements of English royalty, those of King Ine of
Wessex (688–726) do not immediately appear in the first rank; indeed as Sir
Frank Stenton commented: 'the course of events in his reign is remarkably
obscure'.[1] Some indication of the calibre of the man is, none the less, to be
found in Ine's code of West Saxon law, later adapted by King Alfred, his
more famous successor, for the code with which our modern legal tradition
begins. The written sources give little clue, however, to Ine's key role in
the revival of urbanism in England in the post-Roman period, although
this has been graphically demonstrated by archaeological excavations at
Southampton, in the heart of Ine's kingdom. Today Southampton is a
modern port city of a quarter of a million inhabitants, but its origins lie
on the narrow spit of land between the rivers Test and Itchen, just above
the point where they join to form the Solent estuary (see Figure 5.1). A
Roman fort, often known as *Clausentum*, lay on the east side of the Itchen,
but there seems to be no direct continuity with the middle Anglo-Saxon
site on the west bank. It is now clear from artefactual and dendrochronological evidence that a settlement of quite distinct character was
deliberately founded here in the early years of the eighth century, a little
before 721 when St Willibald departed from nearby Hamblemouth on his
mission to Germany. The record of this event, dated to 778, is the earliest
written source to refer to middle Anglo-Saxon Southampton and gives its
name as Hamwih, but this spelling is now thought to be an error and the
site is known today as Hamwic.[2] The *wic* element in the name is shared
by a small group of seventh–ninth-century sites in southern and eastern
England, but also including Quentovic in northern France, and is thought
to mean a specialist trading centre.[3]

Although it was largely abandoned by c. 900, knowledge of the site of
Hamwic has never been completely lost; a tradition of its location survived
to the time of the Tudor antiquary John Leland and the seventeenth-
century geographer and historian William Camden, but investigation of
buried remains has its origin in the second quarter of the nineteenth

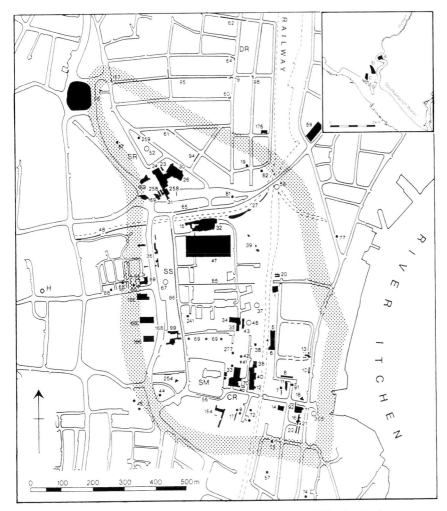

Figure 5.1 Plan of archaeological sites in Hamwic (middle-Anglo-Saxon Southampton) with the probable boundary of the settlement shown toned (Southampton City Museums). *Inset*: the three principal settlements at Southampton: (a) The Roman fort at Bitterne (?Clausentum); (b) Hamwic; (c) the late Anglo-Saxon and medieval walled town
Key: CR Chapel Road; SM St Mary's Church; SS St Mary's Street; The Six Dials Site is numbered 23–6 and 30–1

century. During commercial digging for brickearth, pits were noted by several local antiquaries, in particular the Reverend Edmund Kell who, between 1853 and 1874, in the best traditions of the day, communicated his findings regularly to the British Archaeological Association and to his local paper *The Hampshire Independent*. It was not until the 1940s, however, that the real significance and date of the site became apparent when, as elsewhere, enemy bombing had the side-effect of clearing sites for archaeological excavation. Between 1946 and 1953 work was undertaken by Maitland Muller for the Southampton Excavations Committee, although resources only allowed investigation of small sites.[4]

A major landmark in the study of Hamwic was a review of the evidence in 1969 by Peter Addyman and David Hill, the former then a lecturer at the university before his move to York.[5] The pair had previously excavated at Bevois Street North (Site 32, Figure 5.1) where a road and pits were found, providing the first suggestion of deliberate settlement planning of urban character. This could, however, only be tested by large-scale excavation for which circumstances did not seem favourable and Addyman and Hill were led to conclude:

> The remaining archaeological evidence is now imminently threat-
> ened as redevelopment of the St Mary's area gains momentum. We
> can foresee, in the next few years, the final loss of a town story which
> cannot be written anywhere else unless appropriate action, on a scale
> commensurate with the importance of the site, and the magnitude
> of the destruction, is taken.[6]

Fortunately this appeal led to the foundation of the Southampton Archaeological Research Committee in 1972. After eight years of independence, characterised by periods of financial uncertainty similar to those afflicting many other urban units in their 'heroic' early days,[7] the responsibility for archaeology passed to the City Council, where it continues to flourish. A simple indication of the rapid growth of knowledge about Hamwic since 1972 may be found in the regular revisions of its estimated extent. In 1969 Addyman and Hill claimed 30ha (74 acres),[8] in 1980 this had crept up to 33ha (82 acres),[9] by 1984 it was 37ha (91 acres)[10] and by 1988 45ha (111 acres)[11] – an overall increase of 50 per cent in less than twenty years!

Within Hamwic the picture which has emerged from excavation is of a densely occupied settlement around the framework of a grid of gravel streets (see Figure 5.2). The line of the principal north–south street survives as St Mary's Street, which at the south end joined an east–west street on the line of Chapel Road. On its east side Hamwic was bounded by the Itchen and elsewhere by a ditch. This has only been excavated on the north-west and south-west corners of the circuit, but its course seems clear. Although only c. 3 per cent of the settlement has been investigated archaeologically, most areas, except the riverfront, have been sampled. While the intensity of occupation varies somewhat from site to site, the latest estimate of maximum population is 2,000–3,000.[12]

Today's visitor to the St Mary's area, with its Victorian and later street-scapes, will know that nothing remotely ancient survives above ground. Below ground level, however, the remains of Hamwic are abundant and

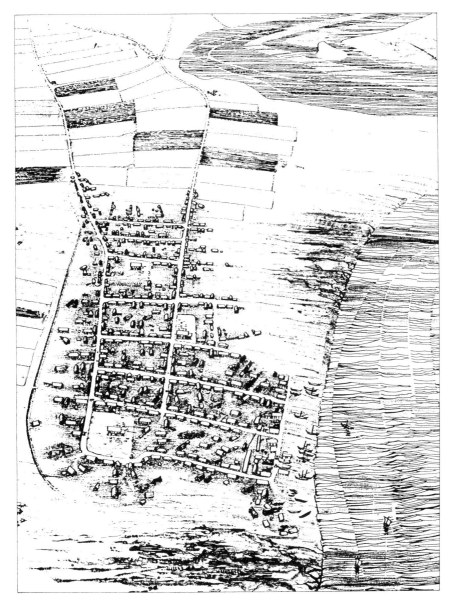

Figure 5.2 An imaginative reconstruction of Hamwic (drawn by John Hodgson)

exist for the most part as pits and wells, and traces of buildings, surviving as post-holes and slots for ground beams, cut into the natural brickearth (see Plate 5.1). Anyone who has seen a Hamwic site will be familiar with the perforated landscape created as a result of the excavations. The

Plate 5.1 Hamwic revealed: pits and post-holes from the Six Dials site
(Photograph: Southampton City Museums)

survival of horizontal strata above natural is rare, but has been found in
places consisting largely of street surfaces and building floors, which are
sometimes preserved by having collapsed into the top of earlier pits. In
view of the relatively ephemeral nature of the remains, excavation of
Hamwic sites calls for very special skills, especially in the summer months
when the brickearth can become extremely hard.

In their 1969 review Addyman and Hill commented on the virtual
absence of evidence for structures in Hamwic to set beside the abundant
pits, but since then the buildings have emerged, especially at the Six Dials
site.[13] In Hamwic's largest excavation 4,000 sq. m (4784 sq. yds) were
examined between 1977 and 1985. A main north–south street was found,
continuing the line of St Mary's Street, and it was crossed by two minor
streets. There were also the traces of over sixty buildings. Nothing of their
superstructure, of course, survived *in situ*, but it is clear that they employed
earth-fast posts, between which the walls were probably of wicker coated
with clay; roofs were presumably thatch. The principal buildings seem
very uniform in size, and were probably used for both domestic occupation and craft purposes. In addition three specialist smithies were
identified on the basis of abundant deposits of slag. The buildings were
sited on plots of land which were probably marked out at the foundation
of the settlement, although subject to some subdivision as population

124

increased. The boundaries were usually indicated by pits which had clearly been shared by neighbours.

In contrast to contemporary villages, there must have been numerous inhabitants whose involvement in agriculture was minimal, since it is clear from the prodigious quantity of objects and debris in the pits and wells that the manufacturing of a wide range of materials, including iron, copper, bone and antler, was taking place throughout the settlement. The quality of its products suggests that Hamwic forms an important landmark in the growth of craft specialisation. Metallographic examination of the ironwork[14] has, for example, shown that knives were consistently well made. They exhibit good steel cutting edges and sophisticated welding techniques which make them markedly superior to the knives of earlier Anglo-Saxon times.

While manufacturing formed a vital part of its economy, the principal reason for the establishment of Hamwic may have been to concentrate growing coastal and sea-going trade under royal control. International trade in northern Europe had been at a low ebb in the fifth–seventh centuries, but in the eighth century a revival is indicated by both archaeology and such written sources as the correspondence between Charlemagne and King Offa of Mercia concerning trade in querns and textiles.[15] The goods traded at Hamwic are not known, but exports may have included cloth, wool and other surplus agricultural products from the estates of the king and aristocracy. Imports may have included items such as wine and gold to cater to their taste for luxuries. That at least part of the trade was in the hands of foreign merchants is suggested by the fact that some 18 per cent of pottery sherds were imported.[16] Pottery was not necessarily a component of trade, however, since the foreign vessels are not containers and local potters made no attempt to copy them, as one might expect if they were suffering from competition in a free market. The imported vessels were probably merchants' personal possessions and, significantly, a higher concentration of imported sherds has been found near the waterfront, suggesting a foreigners' quarter.

Another feature of the finds from Hamwic, with a bearing on trade, is some 150 small silver coins known as *sceattas* (see Plate 5.2).[17] More eighth- and early-ninth-century coins have been found as single finds in archaeological layers, as opposed to hoards, at Hamwic than on any other site of the period in Britain, and they present a unique opportunity to measure the amount and use of money in a settlement of this date. It has been calculated that the mint functioning at Hamwic, principally, perhaps, in the reign of King Cynewulf (757–86), produced over 5 million coins, forming evidence for a vast number of transactions and a highly developed money-using economy. A curious feature of the Hamwic coinage, however, is that it is virtually unknown elsewhere, which is surprising if Hamwic was part of a free-market trading network fully integrated with

Plate 5.2 Typical Hamwic coins (*sceattas*) with pecking bird motif (scale 2:1)
(Photograph: Ashmolean Museum)

its hinterland. It looks as if its coins were primarily for use in the settlement itself, and they appear to be good evidence for restrictions on the inhabitants' freedom of choice in commercial activity.

When the evidence for the street plan, the regularity of the internal land division, the buildings of standard size and the restrictions on commerce is taken together, it appears to confirm the theory that substantial control over the settlement was exercised by the royal house. While it is likely that the king had a seat in Hamwic,[18] royalty at this time was usually peripatetic, and in any search for sites favoured by Ine and his successors we must also examine developments at Winchester 12km (7.5 miles) to the north. Within the surviving Roman walls and amongst numerous decaying Roman buildings, the seventh century saw the beginnings of new life which was to lead to Winchester becoming the principal town in Wessex, and, subsequently, capital of England itself.

The first church in Winchester, known as the Old Minster after c. 901, was founded by King Cenwalh of Wessex c. 648 as a royal chapel and became a cathedral c. 662.[19] In later times the building achieved great architectural splendour, but initially it was a simple structure some 29m (95 ft) long. The significance of the Old Minster's location on the site of the Roman forum has been stressed by Martin Biddle in support of his theory that Winchester retained its role as a centre of authority, if not of population, in the early Anglo-Saxon era after the demise of Roman *Venta Belgarum*.[20] Immediately to the west of the Old Minster, on the site of the Roman forum basilica, Biddle has identified the site of the royal palace. The nature of this building can only be guessed at, but initially, perhaps, it was comparable to the great 30m (100 ft) long eighth-century timber hall recently identified as a palace in excavations at Northampton.[21]

Away from the royal and ecclesiastical centre, excavations suggest that eighth- to early-ninth-century Winchester was occupied by a number of estates consisting of aristocratic dwellings serviced by a small craftsman community based on the High Street. One of these estates was excavated at the Lower Brook Street site where a small stone building, used, perhaps, for goldworking, was found. Two burials were also found, one of a female wearing a necklace of gold pendants and silver rings, which had lain in a private cemetery of the later seventh century.[22]

Reviewing the evidence for both Hamwic and Winchester, Biddle has suggested that in the eighth and early ninth centuries they were twin settlements complementing one another: Hamwic the manufacturing and trading site with a mint, and Winchester the site of religious and political authority, secure within its Roman walls.[23] In 840, however, the relationship was probably dealt a mortal blow when the Vikings raided Hamwic, even though, according to the Anglo-Saxon Chronicle, the Ealdorman Wulfheard managed to defeat thirty-three ships' companies of invading Norsemen. After 840 Hamwic declined rapidly and Winchester began to assume many of its economic functions. Sustained urban development at Southampton only began again in the mid-tenth century, on a new site west of Hamwic, on the banks of the Test, which eventually became the walled medieval town and modern centre.

Although Hamwic is perhaps the most extensively explored, it has become clear during the 1970s and 1980s that some of the other English *wic* sites shared many of its attributes, including a previously unoccupied site on a major river or estuary. In addition evidence has in each case been found for considerable industrial and craft activity, and, principally in the form of imported pottery, for long-distance trade.

The middle Anglo-Saxon origins of Ipswich, near the mouth of the River Orwell in Suffolk, were originally revealed through the discovery in the late 1950s that it was the manufacturing centre of a type of wheel-made pottery known as Ipswich ware which was made in large quantities from c. 650 to c. 850.[24] As the most sophisticated pottery around, it was exported to many places in eastern England. By plotting the occurrence of Ipswich ware in the town itself and by selective excavation, the outlines of a 50ha (124 acres) middle Anglo-Saxon settlement are beginning to emerge, based on a framework of streets whose lines have survived to the present day.

More recently, evidence has come to light for the *wic* in London.[25] Although it remains the case that the fifth and sixth centuries are a blank in the capital's history, archaeological evidence is now emerging to illustrate Bede's description of London in 731–2 as 'an emporium of many people coming by land and sea'[26] and give a context to the seventh–ninth-century references to a place named *Lundenwic*. Until recently, however, the middle Anglo-Saxon settlement seemed to have disappeared without trace, since little evidence had been found, where it was expected, within the Roman walls. In 1984, however, Martin Biddle and Alan Vince of the Museum of London, working independently, identified an area west of the walled city as the likely location of the *wic*.[27] All the finds of the period as were then known, principally coins and pottery, were plotted, and the distribution map showed that the vast majority fell within an area some 2km (1.2 miles) long and 500m (550 yds) wide, west of Aldwych – the old *wic* – and on the line of a former Roman road now followed by Fleet Street and the Strand.

In 1985 a major excavation on the Jubilee Hall site near Covent Garden Market produced more pottery of middle Anglo-Saxon date than had been recovered hitherto in the entire London area, and imports accounted for c. 15 per cent of the sherds. As at Hamwic evidence for crafts and industries was found in the numerous pits. Subsequently some twenty further sites with similar finds have been examined and, at sites in York Buildings and Northumberland Avenue – a little to the north and south of Charing Cross station respectively – the sandy foreshore, or 'strand' (hence the modern street name), where the ships were drawn up, was found with evidence for consolidation, with brushwood and timber revetments dated by dendrochronology to between 665 and 710.[28]

It is now suggested that the core area of the *wic* was c. 60ha (148 acres) and extended from the Aldwych in the east to Trafalgar Square in the west. Although much remains uncertain about the character and layout of the settlement, its role was probably comparable to that of Hamwic and it would have served as a trading centre and mint for the Mercian kingdom which controlled London at this time. It is now apparent that middle Anglo-Saxon London was a twin settlement. *Lundenwic* lay outside the Roman walled enclosure; within the walls, and known as *Lundenburh* from the mid-ninth century, was the ecclesiastical centre at St Paul's, originally founded in 604, and, perhaps, a royal or aristocratic residence in the old Roman fort at Cripplegate, where the modern street name Aldermanbury is thought to indicate the area's former status.

At the same time as the discovery of the *wic* at London came a comparable find at York,[29] where archaeologists also had the problem of a place name, in this case *Eoforwic* (for sites in Anglian York see Figure 5.9). There was no archaeological evidence for an accompanying emporium and no context, therefore, in which to set the reference to Frisian merchants at York in the eighth century contained in Altfrid's life of St Luidgar.[30] It was known, however, that York was a royal and ecclesiastical centre from the time of Edwin's baptism in 627, and during the seventh and eighth centuries, when Northumbria was the dominant kingdom in England, it was also a centre of European culture. York's most famous son of the period, the monk and scholar Alcuin (c. 732–804) even wrote a description of his birthplace.

> My heart is set to praise my home
> And briefly tell the ancient cradling
> Of York's famed city through the charms of verse.
> It was a Roman army built it first,
> High-walled and towered, and made the native tribes
> Of Britain allied to partners in the task –
> For then a prosperous Britain rightly bore
> The rule of Rome whose sceptre ruled the world –
> To be a merchant-town of land and sea,
> A mighty stronghold for their governors,
> An Empire's pride and terror to its foes,
> A haven for the ships from distant ports
> Across the ocean, where the sailor hastes
> To cast his rope ashore and stay to rest.
> The city is watered by the fish-rich Ouse
> Which flows past flowery plains on every side.[31]

These lines seem to imply that the former Roman fortress was a centre of settlement, but archaeological discoveries of the Anglian period within its defences are few, although the excavations at York Minster may, as we noted (see p. 116), indicate the survival of the headquarters basilica as an inhabited structure in the post-Roman period. The building may, perhaps, have formed part of the palace of Edwin and his successors, and his church may have been close by. As yet we do not know and probably never will while the present Minster stands.

Striking testimony to Anglian York as a centre of artistic and craft excellence is a recent find made immediately outside the south-east defences of the fortress. During work on the Coppergate development, after the formal excavation at 16–22 Coppergate, a watching brief was kept on the removal of material from unexcavated areas. One day the driver of a large mechanical excavator spotted something glinting in the ground beneath his cab and having received some archaeological training knew he had to stop and investigate. What he saw made him summon the archaeologist on duty, who was working elsewhere on the site, with the immortal words 'I've found a helmet with writing on it!' After initially telling the driver 'to pull the other one', the archaeologist went to look and did indeed find a helmet with writing on it (see Plate 5.3).

The main body of what is now known as the Coppergate helmet[32] is composed of eight iron plates riveted together; it also has two hinged cheek pieces and the wearer's neck was protected by a curtain of chain mail. It is edged and decorated with strips of brass and the nose protector with its relief pair of confronted animals whose rear parts develop into

Plate 5.3 'A helmet with writing on it': the eighth-century Coppergate helmet from York (Photograph: York Archaeological Trust)

interlace is particularly striking. At the junction of the eye sockets is an animal head serving as a terminal to a strip running across the crown of the helmet and a second strip runs from ear to ear. Both strips have the identical inscription in retrograde:

IN NOMINE DNI NOSTRI IHV SCS SPS DI ET OMNIBUS DECEMUS AMEN OSHERE XPI

The style of lettering and decoration date the helmet to the later eighth century.

The meaning of the inscription is somewhat obscure, but a recent translation provides a plausible hypothesis to link it to the spot where it was found.[33] The wording proposed is:

In the name of our Lord Jesus Christ and of the Spirit of God, let us offer up Oshere to All Saints. Amen

It is suggested that the reference to All Saints concerns the church of All

Saints, Pavement near the site, which is known to have existed in the Anglo-Scandinavian period, but may, perhaps, have begun life as an Anglian church outside the royal enclosure in the old Roman fortress. If this is so, runs the theory, then the helmet bore a religious invocation to his local church for the protection of the wearer Oshere.

Aside from its art-historical and technological aspects the circumstances in which the helmet was deposited in a humble wood-lined pit, probably of the ninth–tenth century, present an intriguing problem. It appears that a start had been made on dismantling it, but can it have been simply dumped as scrap, the redundant technology of a bygone era?

On the south-west bank of the Ouse it is likely that the main Roman road from the south-west and the Roman crossing over the Ouse remained in use in the Anglian period, although excavation on the Wellington Row site, where the road was found, gave no proof of this. Evidence for Anglian occupation in the former Roman *colonia* is sparse, but it may have been the centre of a major monastic establishment complementing the bishop's seat on the north-east bank of the Ouse within the former fortress.[34] It has been suggested that after the Norman Conquest the site of the monastery became Holy Trinity Priory of which the church of Holy Trinity, Micklegate is the survivor. Within the Anglian monastic precinct, it is thought, lay the church of Holy Wisdom whose consecration is referred to by Alcuin and can be dated to c. 780. Excavation at Holy Trinity would be needed to prove this, but there are two other churches close to it which may be contemporary in origin and related to the complex.

One of these churches is St Mary Bishophill Junior. Its earliest extant part is the tower of c. 1000, but it is also the source of early-ninth-century (i.e. Anglian) sculpture.[35] Equally significant is that the church's alignment respects both the main Roman road and a nearby Roman building known from excavation (see Figure 4.1, 16). All other extant medieval churches in the former *colonia* take their alignment from Anglo-Scandinavian Micklegate, although the church of St Mary Bishophill Senior, demolished in 1962, adopted the alignment of a Roman building below it. Another church on the Roman line may have been St Gregory's. No trace now remains, but it lay north-east of Holy Trinity. A remarkable newspaper report of the discovery of the main Roman road in a property on Micklegate during building work in 1821 also referred to skeletons in a later layer, presumably in St Gregory's churchyard, on the same alignment as the road.[36] The road cannot have been visible at the time of grave-digging, but, since burials frequently take their alignment from the associated church, it is possible that the church itself had adopted a north-east/south-west line when the road was visible and before the changes of the Anglo-Scandinavian period.

The commercial centre of Anglian York, the *wic* itself, was to remain elusive until the excavation in 1985–6 of the site at 46–54 Fishergate on the north-east bank of the Foss near the junction with the Ouse. It is in a position analogous to that of the *wic* at London, being nearly 1km (0.6 miles) south-east of the Roman fortress with which it was probably linked by a road along an old Roman line. Although a few Anglian finds had been recorded in the area, there was no inkling of what was to come when an excavation was planned to investigate the remains of the thirteenth-century Gilbertine Priory of St Andrew, for below the medieval buildings was a site which would not have been unfamiliar to the archaeologists of Hamwic. West of a north–south boundary ditch there were the remains of some 3–4 post-built timber halls, up to 15m (49 ft) long, set in discrete plots, the layout probably indicating some form of deliberate planning. The ubiquitous pits contained imported pottery from northern France and the Rhineland, which suggests that the site was part of the international trading network of the period, presumably serving as an emporium for the Northumbrian royal house. The pits also produced substantial quantities of animal bone[37] and when compared to the tenth-century assemblage from York (see pp. 153–4), it is striking that the Anglian site had a narrower subsistence base. There was much less evidence for the consumption of pigs, fish, fowl and geese, suggesting constraints on the inhabitants' ability to exploit the resources of their environment by trade, hunting or backyard husbandry.

Important as the Fishergate excavation is, there is as yet no indication of how large a settlement it is part of; three or four buildings do not make a Hamwic. Nevertheless a fairly extensive site is implied. We may now see Anglian York as a whole covering a relatively large area, comparable to, if not larger than, Roman York, yet with a diffuse population in several locations at each of which a distinct function was performed.

A good analogue for Anglian York and middle Anglo-Saxon London is, perhaps, the late Iron Age oppidum at Gosbecks/Sheepen near Colchester (see pp. 47–9) with its distinct functional areas. This prompts us to question whether the eighth-century *wic* sites are towns in the fullest sense. While there were areas of dense population with craft specialists, the complete set of urban functions was not clustered together in one place as they would be in late Anglo-Saxon London or Anglo-Scandinavian York. The spatial separation of functions requiring the use of new, previously unoccupied sites for the trading operations implies strict central control by the royal house, which for political reasons may actively have sought to prevent the agglomeration of population and the social and economic activities which would characterise later towns, but which would also, on occasions, make them centres of unrest and rebellion. In addition the artefactual evidence suggests an unusual if not overwhelming reliance on international trade and does not suggest a market economy with free interplay between buyers and sellers in all commodities and full integration with the surrounding hinterland.

Later Anglo-Saxon towns

'Felix Urbs Winthonia'[38]

If we compare the circumstances surrounding the origin of towns in Roman Britain with those surrounding their rebirth in the Anglo-Saxon period, we find that the crucial kick-start to establish these new and distinctive settlements came from, respectively, the imperial or royal authorities. In the first century towns were imposed on Britain as a result of conquest by a state which required convenient centres from which to conduct government and administration, including the raising of taxes, and in which a suitable setting could be created for the ceremonial that bestowed legitimacy on the new regime. Growth in the urban population and promotion of its well-being were not particular concerns of the Roman state, but continued as long as economic conditions in the western empire as a whole permitted and ceased when they did not. In the Anglo-Saxon period the archaeological evidence for the *wics* may be interpreted to suggest that urban origins were again rooted in a desire to raise revenue, but were now also related to a desire to both control and promote economic activity. In the absence of any cataclysm comparable to the fall of the Roman empire in the west, the growth of towns and the proliferation of new ones in the late Anglo-Saxon and medieval periods continued more or less unbroken until the mid-fourteenth century. At the same time, urbanism acquired an added momentum as royalty and other leading landowners found, like the Romans before them, that towns were suitable places from which to govern their domains and develop the secular and religious ceremonial surrounding the exercise of power. Artisans and merchants, meanwhile, found towns presented rich opportunities for wealth and social advancement.

In the last twenty-five years archaeology has begun to make a substantial contribution to understanding the genesis of these developments, which lead directly to modern urban society, and there is no better place to start our examination of the evidence than Winchester (see Figure 5.3). Tracing the city's development in the ninth century from a royal and ecclesiastical centre to a place with a full range of economic functions by the early tenth century remains an important archaeological problem, but it is in the context of a growing commercial role that we should see Bishop (later Saint) Swithun's recorded construction of bridges over the Itchen outside the east gate in 859.[39] As we have already noted, the decline of Hamwic must have provided an impetus to change, and it is possible that the remarkable cemetery, with over 200 graves, probably of eighth–ninth-century date, found recently on the Staple Gardens site, just inside the west gate,[40] contains immigrants from the port. The Viking raids must have also stimulated refurbishment of the defences of Winchester and it

Figure 5.3 A late Anglo-Saxon capital city: Winchester c. 993–1066 (Winchester Research Unit)
Key: 1 Lower Brook Street; 2 Staple Gardens; 3 Site of discovery of reliquary

is possible that work was in train from the 860s. The growing economic importance of Winchester, the safety of its walls and perhaps the nascent cult of St Swithun, which gave extra authority to the church, meant that by the later part of the reign of King Alfred (870–99) there is no question that the House of Wessex had chosen Winchester as its principal seat.

One of the great achievements of archaeology in Winchester is to show how this royal favour was manifested in a spatial organisation geared to defence and commercial exploitation.[41] Its basis was the street grid which essentially survives today and can be easily understood by a brief walk around the city. Before Biddle's excavations it was thought to be of Roman origin, but, although the grid idea ultimately derives from the classical city, only the main Anglo-Saxon east–west street, the High Street, is on a Roman line predetermined by the location of the gates as ways through the Roman wall and rampart. Parallel to the High Street, on its north and south sides, was a back street probably used for servicing important town centre properties. This is a role still performed today by St George's Street on the line of the northern back street. Running north–south across the High Street was a series of side streets laid out at fixed intervals of c. 16 poles or perches (c. 5m or 16 ft 6 ins), indicating the early use of a unit of land measurement common in medieval England.[42] Running around the defences was the intra-mural street, a vital component for defence as it allowed troops to be moved rapidly to points of danger.

Although further excavation is, perhaps, needed for confirmation, there seems little doubt that the street system was largely planned and executed as a single operation.[43] The arguments supporting this assertion are: first, the regularity and predictability of the plan; second, the similarity of construction of the first surface wherever it has been seen; and, third, the use of plans of similar type in other towns at much the same time. The credit for the Winchester plan is most likely to be due to Alfred. First, because a documentary source of 904, recording lands acquired by Edward the Elder for the foundation of the New Minster, describes their bound-aries in terms of existing streets. Secondly, an early-tenth-century coin was found on the second street surface excavated at Trafalgar Street (medieval Gar Street) in 1964 and a coin of Alfred was found under the earliest surface of the same street in 1990.

Originally the spaces within the street grid would have been organised into large plots owned by the king and major landlords. Subsequently there was extensive subdivision creating a complex tenurial pattern which can be studied in some detail because of the survival of a survey carried out during the reign of Edward the Confessor in 1057 which was incor-porated into the so-called Winton Domesday, a survey of the city in 1110.[44] The freedom to create a property market, which the Edwardian survey implies, is one of the most important features of the legal arrangements in medieval towns which distinguishes them from rural areas and it is of great importance to have evidence for this before the Conquest. Another aspect of the survey, with exciting prospects for archaeological testing, is that it shows how practitioners of trades were concentrated in different parts of Winchester in a way which again foreshadows the characteristic urban scene in the medieval period.

Although excavation of late Anglo-Saxon tenements has not been extensive, except at the Lower Brook Street site, it is clear that the population of Winchester grew rapidly from the late ninth century onwards. One indication of this is the appearance of extra-mural suburbs, especially on the west side of town where the defences of the great Iron Age enclosure were retained as a boundary. Another indication of growth is the appearance of new churches. It is a well-known feature of towns emerging in the late ninth to eleventh centuries that they have an abundance of churches.[45] Winchester itself had fifty-seven by 1100 and London well over a hundred. Excavations in Winchester and elsewhere have shown that these late Anglo-Saxon urban churches were very small buildings in origin and can only have served very localised communities. Since they would have been entitled to keep the tithes, most churches were built by private landlords as something of a speculative venture, as well as a pious observance. Although it is virtually impossible to date the foundation of urban churches closely, archaeology and documents make it possible to get some impression of how the churching of towns developed. At Winchester, for example, a concentration of population in the High Street is suggested by numerous early churches, but there are others in extra-mural areas which confirm suburban expansion.

These small urban churches were, of course, but pale reflections of the great monastic churches of Winchester concentrated in what became one of the most important ecclesiastical centres of not only Anglo-Saxon England, but also contemporary western Europe. A special walled enclave which came to occupy the south-eastern quarter of the city, absorbing streets and tenements in the process, contained the extensive buildings of three great religious institutions.

At the centre was the Old Minster, most of which lay immediately north of the present cathedral.[46] The reconstruction of the Old Minster (see Figure 5.4), based principally on the excavated ground plan, and reference to likely analogues which still stand elsewhere in Europe make it easy to imagine the building as the embodiment of the artistic renaissance of late Anglo-Saxon England. It was an appropriate setting for extravagant celebration of the great ritual cycle of the Christian year and for the glorification of the West Saxon royal house, many members of which were to be buried here. The Old Minster was also a centre of pilgrimage and this explains much of its architectural history. The earliest church was, as we have seen, constructed in the mid-seventh century. The next major event in its history was the burial of St Swithun in 862, according to

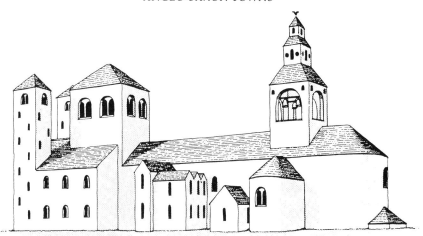

Figure 5.4 Reconstruction of Winchester's Old Minster at the time of King Cnut (1016–35) (Winchester Research Unit)

his wishes, outside the west door. In 971, however, Bishop (later saint) Aethelwold, one of the great monastic reformers of the period, had Swithun's remains moved into the church while it was extended westwards with a great double-apsed martyrium focused on the grave. Shortly afterwards this structure was remodelled with two massive towers at the west end, dedicated in 980. By 993–4 the church was extended eastwards to a new apse and the eastern part of the church was remodelled to form the principal crossing, flanked by new apses north and south, as a setting for the high altar and Swithun's relics. Over the altar there was, it is conjectured, a great tower, as shown, for example, in the Benedictional of St Aethelwold.[47] Around the site of Swithun's grave and the west end of the church (before and after extension) clustered numerous graves attracted by the 'odour of sanctity'. They were evidently of high-ranking individuals able to afford great iron-bound coffins and fine funeral vestments decorated with gold thread.

Immediately north of the Old Minster was the New Minster of 903–4. Excavations have revealed parts of the plan of this building which was probably intended for the use of the growing number of townspeople. Further east was the Nunnaminster (nun's minster), later known as St Mary's Abbey, founded by Eahlswith, Alfred's queen (died 902/3).[48]

The architectural appointments of these great buildings are likely to have matched the artistic achievements of the celebrated Winchester schools of manuscript illustration and decorative arts in ivory and metalwork. A most remarkable addition to our knowledge of the latter was made in 1978 when careful excavation of an otherwise unremarkable late-ninth/early-tenth-century rubbish pit on a site in the western suburbs produced the remains of a metal and wooden object, apparently lying in a deposit which had been cess and domestic debris. Subsequent careful cleaning in the laboratory revealed the surprisingly well-preserved remains of a burse reliquary, a purse-shaped portable container for holy relics and the first of its kind from England (see Plate 5.4).[49] It has a beechwood core in which X-radiographs revealed small hollow chambers which presumably served as containers for saints' bones, or other matter sanctified by association with holy remains. Access to the contents is not possible as the wood is completely covered with gilded copper-alloy sheets with embossed decoration; on one face, now damaged, was a figure of Christ, and on the other, three sheets with trumpet-shaped tree stems, probably representing the tree of life.

Plate 5.4 The Winchester reliquary (ninth–tenth century; height 175mm / c. 7 ins) (Photograph: Conway Library, Courtauld Institute)

The reliquary may have had pride of place in a church from where it was on special occasions carried in procession, but, as in the case of the Coppergate helmet, it is difficult to envisage the circumstances in which this precious object was discarded; perhaps it was hastily thrown away by a thief to avoid detection or in disgust at it not being gold. At all events, discoveries like this should encourage all humble excavators sent to dig out yet another rubbish pit.

Once the Winchester street plan had been discovered and dated, comparison with the layout of other towns in Wessex made it clear that they too had plans of the Winchester type, and the presumption is that they were probably laid out at much the same time and formed part of Alfred's defence of his country against the Vikings.[50] The military aspect of town foundation is apparent from a document known as the Burghal Hidage originating in the reign of Edward the Elder (899–924). It is a list of places (*burhs*) with associated hides of land; the idea was that each hide, probably c. 24ha (60 acres), supplied a man, and four men were needed for the defence of each pole or perch of *burh* wall. From the hidage figure it is therefore possible to calculate the length of a *burh*'s defences in the tenth century and this usually corresponds to the circuit known to exist on the ground.

Some of the *burhs* were quite small and may be seen solely as forts; others, however, were larger and were probably incipient towns at the time of their formal layout.[51] Good examples include Chichester, Dorchester and Exeter, which already had walls of Roman origin. Towns on new non-Roman sites include Wareham and Wallingford, where prominent ramparts of the late Anglo-Saxon period survive today, and Oxford[52] (see Figure 5.5), which is the most extensively explored burghal hidage town, apart from Winchester. Although most familiar to us as the great university city established in the thirteenth century, Oxford's origins are some 500 years earlier and appear to lie in the foundation of a monastic house in c. 727 by St Frideswide, revered, like many other Anglo-Saxon saints, for preserving her virginity against a base assault. Her site was probably that of the present cathedral, now an integral part of Christ Church College.[53] Crucial to the location of the monastery were crossings of the River Thames and its tributaries. In excavations at 79–81 St Aldate's[54] the remains were found of an eighth-century causeway built of clay, leading to a crossing of one of these tributaries, the Trill Mill stream. At this time Oxford was on the southern boundary of the kingdom of Mercia and a meeting point for east–west and north–south routes, the latter probably running as far as Hamwic. Although this combination of roads and river crossings would have favoured settlement, little trace of Mercian Oxford has yet been found.

Oxford was part of Wessex when it acquired its first defences, consisting of a gravel rampart and ditch, and making a roughly square enclosure.

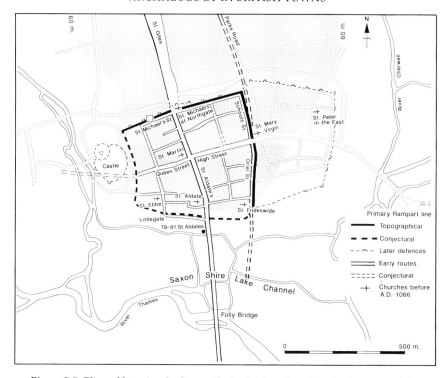

Figure 5.5 Plan of late Anglo-Saxon Oxford (also showing the location of the
Norman castle) (Oxford Archaeological Unit)

The Anglo-Saxon Chronicle implies that the defences were in place by
911, although they could be Alfredian. Recent examination of the defences
has taken place at 24a St Michael's Street and at the church of St Michael-
at-the-Northgate (see Figure 5.6).[55] It has been shown that at some stage
before the Norman Conquest the original timber-facing of the rampart
was replaced by a stone wall, an early forerunner of the sophisticated
walling of later medieval Oxford, remains of which can still be seen, well
preserved, in New College garden. At St Michael's no trace was found of
the original church, but it appears that the fine eleventh-century tower,
which can still be admired at the top of Cornmarket Street, was added
after the defensive line was moved north to allow an enlargement of the
graveyard. In addition to its ecclesiastical function, the tower would have
served as a lookout post and thus as an integral part of the defences.
Recent examination during restoration has revealed a doorway at second-
floor level facing north which would have given access to a walkway on
top of the rampart. The church itself would have served travellers wishing
to say a prayer and, equally important for the church authorities, to make
a financial offering for safety on their journeys. It is for this reason that

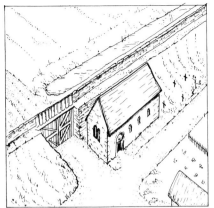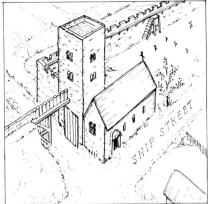

Figure 5.6 Reconstruction of St Michael-at-the-North-Gate, Oxford, in the Anglo-Saxon period. Left: the original layout with the church just inside the gate; right: the tower added and the line of defences moved northwards (Oxford Archaeological Unit)

churches at the gates are such a common feature of Anglo-Saxon and medieval towns.

Much of Oxford's Anglo-Saxon street grid survives in the present-day plan and there have been an unusual number of opportunities to examine the streets themselves. Since the earliest street surfaces, now up to 4m (13 ft) below the modern city, appear, as at Winchester, to look the same in all sightings (quartz pebbles for the main streets and limestone cobbles for the side streets), it is likely that, as at Winchester, they were laid out at the same time. Alongside the streets the discovery of numerous pits suggests a healthy growth of settlement in the tenth–eleventh centuries. Oxford was burnt by the Danes in 1009, but this had no lasting effect on the town's fortunes, except that it appears that some buildings were given cellars, perhaps to act as fire-proof stores for merchants and craftsmen.

There is no doubt that the *burh* system was a success in military terms and, although still in its early stages in 878 when Alfred was able to inflict a decisive defeat on the Vikings at Edington (Wiltshire), it served to consolidate his achievements. From then on the Vikings were confined to the Danelaw, north-east of a line roughly corresponding to Roman Watling Street (the modern A5). In the late ninth and early tenth centuries the *burh* system was extended to Mercia, which came under West Saxon influence when Alfred's daughter Aethelflaed, 'lady of the Mercians', married King Ethelred. The Mercian *burh*s also included a mixture of forts and fortified towns, the earliest of which were perhaps Hereford,[56] Worcester[57] and Gloucester,[58] followed by Chester (see Figure 5.7),[59] Tamworth, Stafford

Figure 5.7 Reconstruction of the Lower Bridge Street area, Chester, in the tenth century. As at York, the principal urban area at this time was probably outside the fortress whose south gate can be seen in the background. The buildings are shown with plank walls similar to tenth-century examples found in London and at 16–22 Coppergate, York (Grosvenor Museum, Chester)

and Warwick.[60] More followed after Wessex and Mercia were united under Edward the Elder on Aethelflaed's death in 918. Some excavation of late Anglo-Saxon levels at most of these places has occurred, but, with the exceptions of Gloucester, burial place of Aethelflaed, and Chester, little is yet known of their progress to urbanism. Other towns in Mercia and Wessex, such as Northampton[61] and Bristol (see pp. 194–6), probably emerged in the later tenth and eleventh centuries thanks as much to local economic and political factors as to royal intervention.

London – 'richer in treasure'

London does not appear in the Burghal Hidage because at the time of compilation it was still in Mercia. Only after 918 when Wessex and Mercia were united did London come permanently under what may now be called the English crown. A *burh* is named in the Burghal Hidage at Southwark on the south bank of the Thames, but little trace of it has been found; presumably it was a fort intended to guard the south side of the river crossing.

Late Anglo-Saxon London reoccupied the area bounded by the Roman walls (see Figure 5.8). It is assumed that this was largely because of the threat posed by the Viking raids, but it is only in recent years that archaeology has shown how growth of the resited settlement occurred.[62] The remains are to some extent elusive because in many areas of the City there has been severe truncation by modern cellars, leaving only rubbish pits and other deeper features cut into the underlying Roman strata. The traces of streets and timber buildings do survive in many places, however,

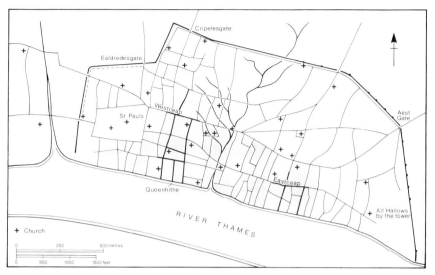

Figure 5.8 Plan of late Anglo-Saxon London. The suggested extent of the Alfredian planned town is toned (after Milne 1990, Figure 1); streets shown archaeologically to be in existence by the late tenth century are shown in bold (after Milne and Milne 1988) (drawn by Glenys Boyles; Museum of London)

and, by combining work on the structural sequences with work on pottery typology, the story of late Anglo-Saxon London is starting to emerge. An archaeological context is now apparent for the documented prosperity reached by 1018 when the city paid one-eighth of England's Danegeld.

Investigations by the DUA have been concentrated in the Billingsgate and Cheapside areas. They have shown, first of all, that London had no pan-urban street plan created at a particular time, as proposed for Winchester. There may, however, have been an initial planned grid between Cheapside – the Anglo-Saxon word *ceap* means a market – and the Thames, and in both study areas some elements in the street plan have been dated to c. 900, while others emerged later as population increased. In due course expansion would also have continued out to the line of the walls, but initially there were large, open intra-mural areas used, perhaps, for markets and even fields. The eastern and western ends of the principal late Anglo-Saxon thoroughfare (Cheapside, Lombard Street and Fenchurch Street) were predetermined by the location of the Roman gates at Newgate and Aldgate (Aest Gate), although the street itself diverged from the Roman line. To the south was another east–west market street incorporating Eastcheap. Streets at right angles to the east–west streets connected them with the riverside. Early examples include what are now known as Bow Lane and Huggin Hill, where a land grant of 889 suggests that the Roman baths (see pp. 68–9) were still a landmark. In the Billingsgate area, Fish Street Hill and Botolph Lane are also thought to have been in existence by the early tenth century. A combination of documentary research[63] and archaeology suggests that the medieval names of lanes running down to the waterfront which end in -gate or -hithe (such as Dowgate or Queenhithe) are probably of Anglo-Saxon origin and represent the southern end of the early streets. The -gate names are of interest because they probably indicate openings made in the Roman riverside wall.

Alongside the Anglo-Saxon streets the remains of some fifty late-ninth–eleventh-century buildings have been found. They are often end on to the frontages, as the strip buildings were in Roman London, and have produced vital evidence for a range of construction techniques unparalleled in the period except at York. The walls were usually built with posts set directly in the ground which either interlocked or had plank or wattle cladding. More sophisticated examples were built up from a horizontal timber ground beam. Some buildings incorporated a form of cellar, but no obvious evidence was found for upper storeys or internal partitions. Floors were usually beaten earth; other features were scarce except for hearths and ovens, but an unusual survival was a collapsed door detectable from its iron bindings, hinges, and, particularly significant, a lock. Judging by the numbers of locks and keys found in tenth–eleventh-century towns, there was an increasing concern for security among the inhabitants – another small indicator of social change in the urban environment.

There was no apparent development of building type over time in Anglo-Saxon London of the kind we shall note in York, and it has been suggested that the diverse structural techniques may reflect differing traditions of the immigrants who presumably flooded into the place. Some thought has also been given to how building form might relate to function, although this is difficult in the absence of diagnostic artefacts. Nevertheless, it seems reasonable to suggest that buildings with cellars, probably used for the storage of merchandise, were a specifically urban type, also known at Oxford, Chester and York, and indicative of London's role as a commercial centre.

In contrast to middle-Saxon London, little pottery from overseas has been found in late Anglo-Saxon deposits.[64] This is also the case in other towns of the period and may suggest that trade was almost exclusively local or regional until perhaps the early eleventh century when archaeology and written sources both suggest a revival in foreign contacts. Ships coming up the Thames in the tenth century would, as in middle Anglo-Saxon times, have been simply dragged up on the foreshore. At a number of sites excavations have revealed that purpose-built embankments of clay and rubble, consolidated with timber and wattle, were thrown up over the remains of the Roman quays to make the shore stable (see Plate 5.5).[65]

Plate 5.5 On the waterfront at Billingsgate Lorry Park, London: a small bank of the late tenth century in front of the first stave-built revetment, looking east, i.e. river is to the right. The revetment baseplate is visible on the left and protective hurdling for the bank is on the right (scale 0.50m / c. 1 ft 6 ins) (Photograph: Museum of London)

In the early eleventh century the embankment was, in places, given a vertical stave-built front, often made of re-used boat timbers, marking the first stage in the development of what became the sophisticated waterfront structures of medieval London (see pp. 189–94).

The London described by Guy, Bishop of Amiens, in 1067 as 'a great city, overflowing with froward (i.e. stubborn) inhabitants and richer in treasure than the rest of the kingdom' can, in conclusion, be described as enclosed by its Roman walls, divided up by areas of roughly rectilinear streets focused on major street markets and the waterfront. The land between the streets was densely built up in many areas, especially south of Cheapside, with single-storey timber buildings which might appear modest in our eyes, but were 'state of the art' to the Anglo-Saxons. On the waterfront ships of largely local origin were pulled up and everywhere there would be people buying and selling with, no doubt, all the cheating, thieving and gambling associated with the rapid ebb and flow of money. When they tired of serving Mammon, folk could try to serve God at the great Anglo-Saxon cathedral of St Paul's or in the numerous small churches, often built of stone from Roman buildings, as can still be seen at All Hallows by the Tower.[66]

Finally, outside the walls and upstream to the south-west lay Thorney Island which in the late Anglo-Saxon period saw the growth of a great religious and political centre to rival and eventually surpass that at Winchester. A monastic community had existed at 'west minster' since perhaps the eighth century, although the hall and farmstead remains revealed by excavation are ninth–tenth-century.[67] King Edward the Confessor (1042–66) reorganised the abbey and had a great new church built which is shown in the Bayeux Tapestry at the time of his funeral. Alongside the church was a palace which probably replaced an earlier establishment inside the walls where it was now too crowded and, on occasions, too dangerous for royal comfort.

Towns in the Danelaw

York, 'crammed with merchandise'

What is lacking from our sketches of late Anglo-Saxon Winchester and London is the intimate details of daily life. For a picture of what it was like to live in a town of this time we must go north to York (see Figure 5.9), the principal city of the Danelaw, described by a monk from Ramsey Abbey in c. 1000 as follows:

> The city of York is the capital of all the Northumbrian people. It was in old times built with magnificence and strongly defended by walls which are now decayed with age. It boasts, however, a huge population, of not less than thirty thousand of both sexes, excluding

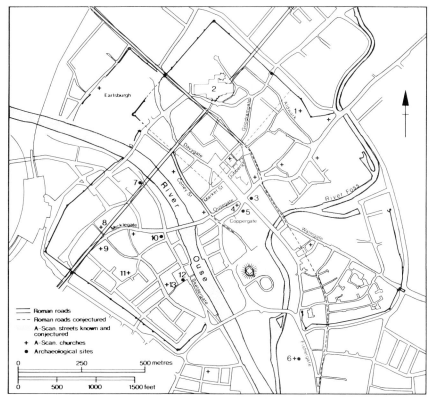

Figure 5.9 Plan of York showing excavation sites, and churches and streets thought
to be of Anglo-Scandinavian origin (drawn by Glenys Boyles)
Key: 1 St Helen-on-the-Walls; 2 Site of Anglo-Scandinavian cathedral; 3 Lloyd's Bank (6–
8 Pavement); 4 All Saint's Pavement; 5 16–22 Coppergate; 6 46–54 Fishergate and St
Andrew's, Fishergate; 7 Wellington Row; 8 St Gregory's; 9 Holy Trinity, Micklegate;
10 Queen's Hotel (1–9 Micklegate); 11 St Mary Bishophill Junior; 12 58–9 Skeldergate;
13 St Mary Bishophill Senior

children. It is crammed with the merchandise – too rich to describe –
of traders who come from all parts, but especially Danes.[68]

An important stimulus behind the abandonment of the Fishergate *wic*
and the resiting of the centre of commercial life close to the walls of the
former Roman fortress in the 'ness' (the Old Norse word for promontory,
found today in the street name Nessgate) between the rivers Foss and
Ouse was probably fear of the Viking armies in the north. According to
the Anglo-Saxon Chronicle, they first attacked York in 867. Subsequently
York, or Jorvik as it was known, was ruled by kings of Scandinavian origin
for some sixty years and, after a period of English rule, they briefly
regained control from 940 to 954. In the last two years of Scandinavian

hegemony York was ruled by one of the most famous Vikings of them all, Eric Bloodaxe.

It is likely that the re-emergence of York as an urban centre in the late ninth and tenth centuries was accompanied by an influx of settlers from Scandinavia – hence the use of the term 'Anglo-Scandinavian' by York's archaeologists for the period c. 850–1066. Clear evidence for Scandinavian influence in the city today can be found in the street names with the -gate suffix, which does not, as in London, mean a gate, but derives from the Old Norse word *gata* meaning street. A rare record of personal names of the period can be found on coins which suggest that as many as three-quarters of the moneyers were of Norse, largely Danish, origin or descent.[69]

Until recently almost as little was known of the archaeology of York which emerged after the Viking kings took control as of York in the previous 200 years. The existence of churches founded before the Norman Conquest and numerous finds of the Anglo-Scandinavian period, largely made by chance, showed, however, that the principal area of occupation lay along the line of the streets Micklegate, Coppergate and Pavement.[70] The visitor to York today often finds the street plan bewildering, but once one has some appreciation of its chronological development, it can be seen as a consequence of the Roman layout and the Anglo-Scandinavian adaptation to it. We have already seen that in the Anglian period one of the principal routes into York ran along the line of the main Roman road from the south-west, and another along a Roman road running out from the south-east gate of the fortress across the Foss to the *wic*. The main change in layout in the Anglo-Scandinavian period was the establishment of a new line for the route from the south-west creating a *mickel gata*, or great street (today Micklegate), which swung away north-east of the Roman line to a river-crossing downstream from the Roman and probable Anglian crossing at present-day Ouse bridge. This road line then continued north-east along Ousegate before meeting the line of another Roman street which ran between the south-west side of the Roman fortress and the River Ouse; this is now Coney Street (originally *kunung*'s – king's – street). The main street continued north-east along High Ousegate, and then Pavement, to meet the Roman street line coming from the south-east gate of the fortress. Another early street is probably Jubbergate/Market Street which would have taken its alignment from the south-east defences of the fortress. The original core of the Anglo-Scandinavian town on the north-east bank of the Ouse may, therefore, have lain on the south-east side of the former fortress around a rough rectangle of streets. On the south-west bank excavations have revealed tenth-century buildings at the Queen's Hotel and 58–9 Skeldergate – the street of the shield-makers.[71]

The reorganisation of Anglo-Scandinavian York was probably conducted, as in contemporary London, in several stages, with the establishment of the principal streets followed by infill with lesser streets and expansion into new areas.[72] As population rose, the spaces between the streets were laid out with characteristic long and narrow urban tenements forming a pattern which survives today in many city centre areas. At the 16–22 Coppergate site, property boundaries appear to date from c. 900 and by c. 925 four tenements were clearly recognisable running some 25m (82 ft) from the street frontage towards the River Foss, their boundaries marked by wicker fences. The street, Coppergate, was presumably laid out at much the same time.

Another major change to the topography of York in the tenth century was the demolition of Roman buildings. The stone was used for the many churches of Jorvik and its region which are testimony to the pagan Vikings' rapid conversion to Christianity. Chief among these churches was the Anglo-Scandinavian cathedral whose cemetery was found in excavation under the present Minster.[73] Alongside the cathedral, no doubt, was the royal palace, and one reason for the creation of the new south-west / north-east route was probably to prevent the urban proletariat from thronging across the old river-crossing into the royal and ecclesiastical enclave located, like its Anglian predecessor, within the former Roman fortress. In due course, however, the south-east and south-west walls of the fortress were demolished and ordinary urban tenements spread into the enclosure.

One of the greatest achievements of the York Archaeological Trust has been to discover what everyday town life in tenth–eleventh-century Jorvik was like. Unique details have come to light, first because of the damp ground conditions which allow good preservation of organic matter, from structural timbers to insect fauna. Secondly, the topographical position of Jorvik in a river valley which has since been filled in by later urban deposits has meant that those deposits of Anglo-Scandinavian date have been given some protection from erosion and the intrusion of modern structures. Thirdly, we must be grateful for the refuse disposal habits of the inhabitants who were happy to see mounds of organic waste and other debris build up in and around their dwellings.

The first excavation to demonstrate the riches of Jorvik was at the Lloyd's Bank site in 1972 where remains of a leatherworking workshop were found.[74] This was, however, only a foretaste of what was to come at 16–22 Coppergate where an area of c. 800 sq. m (960 sq. yds) was examined between 1976 and 1981.[75] Occupation clearly became intense after the layout of properties in the early tenth century, to judge by the depth of accumulated archaeological deposits and quantity of discarded artefacts.

At the Coppergate end of the site the earliest structures consisted of buildings constructed with earth-fast posts with wattles woven between them; the floors were beaten earth and the roofs presumably thatched (see Plate 5.6). A prominent feature of these buildings was large central hearths of clay, lined with stone or tile. In and around the buildings were large quantities of metalworking debris, including slag, bars and strips of

various metals, especially iron, and a number of iron tools including hammers, files and punches. Coppergate is, apart from Flaxengate, Lincoln (p. 156), the only urban site in Britain where metalworking in this crucial period of England's economic development can be studied in relation to its workshop context.

The ironworking evidence is particularly important.[76] The metal would have been smelted at the site of the ore source, probably out in the Yorkshire Moors, and then supplied to the smiths in the form of bars; at the same time redundant objects were broken up for recycling. This may be the context in which we should see two unique iron coin-stamping dies.[77] Instead of being evidence for a mint on the site they may simply have been brought in as scrap. From their bar-iron or scrap the Coppergate smiths made a wide range of tools, weapons and structural fittings, but a speciality was small tin-plated dress fittings including strap-ends and

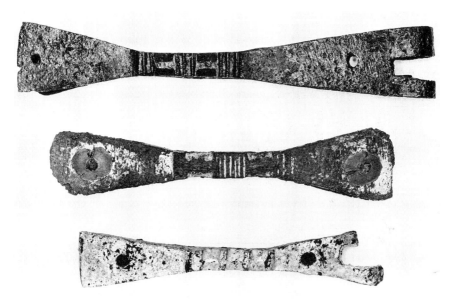

Plate 5.7 Tenth-century iron fittings from 16–22 Coppergate, York (the upper example is 81mm/c. 3 ins long) – possible products of the smiths working on the site. The central and lower examples are plated with tin (Photograph: York Archaeological Trust)

buckles (see Plate 5.7). We know this, first, because a number of part-made examples were found which had been discarded during manufacture and, second, because a number of the incomplete and complete objects are so distinctive in form and decoration that they can only have been made by the same craftsman or group of craftsmen.

Over 200 knives (see Plate 2.5) of varying sizes and forms were found and it is clear that the Anglo-Scandinavian smiths were masters of the art of making steel and of welding iron and steel together to make blades of supreme quality. Their hardness is greater than that of most machine-made knives available in the shops today and one of the problems of making sections for metallographic analysis was cutting into the metal. Compared to the Hamwic knives, we see innovations in approaches to blademaking. One of these involved welding a steel strip between two strips of ordinary iron; as the knife was sharpened and worn it would stay sharp, whereas a blade with a steel strip only a few millimetres thick on the cutting edge would eventually wear out. Another innovation was the use of pattern-welding, which involved twisting and welding together strips of different quality iron to create a decorative effect in the core of the blade. This had previously been used only on swords and larger weapons.

In c. 975 there was a major rebuilding on the Coppergate site after which metalworking ceased, and it is possible that the smiths were removed to a location where their fires and noise were less troublesome. New buildings were constructed with semi-basements whose sides were retained with planks and massive timber posts which were presumably carried through to join the above ground walls. Because the basements were used as rubbish tips after the buildings had been demolished, the timber walls were remarkably well preserved, surviving in places to a height of over 1m (3 ft).[78]

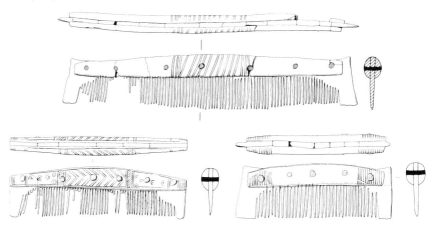

Figure 5.10 Anglo-Scandinavian antler combs from 16–22 Coppergate (scale 1:2)
(drawn by T. Pearson, York Archaeological Trust)

Prominent among the other crafts practised at the site was woodworking. The name Coppergate probably means street of the coopers or wood turners, and both incomplete and finished examples of their skill, in the form of bowls and cups, were found. The working of bone and antler[79] produced numerous handsome combs (see Figure 5.10), indicating a concern for grooming in a people whose personal freshness cannot otherwise have borne close inspection. Evidence for textile working[80] included the remains of iron combs used for preparing woollen fleece for spinning, spindle whorls to weight the spinner's distaff, and weights for securing tension on the threads of the vertical weaving loom. The numerous iron and bronze needles found on the site would have been used for sewing and embroidery. Examples of the textile itself, principally wool, survived and, together with the metal dress fittings, give us some impression of what the well-dressed townsperson of the period was wearing. Most surprising, perhaps, is that the analysis of traces of vegetable dyes shows clothing to have been brightly coloured, especially in red, blue and purple. Particularly striking individual items of dress were a woman's cap made locally of silk imported from the Near East, and a woollen sock made with a needle in a technique developed in Scandinavia, known as nålebinding. Of all the many finds from Coppergate this sock probably had the greatest world-wide press coverage (see Plate 5.8)

Plate 5.8 The most famous old sock in the world? – from 16–22 Coppergate, York (tenth century) (Photograph: York Archaeological Trust)

Much of daily life would obviously have centred on food preparation and consumption. There was no shortage of meat to judge by the vast quantity of animal bones from Coppergate.[81] In terms of weight, cattle formed c. 80 per cent of the meat eaten. The animals' age at death – youngish adults, rather than immature as today – shows, however, that they were also valued for milk, in other words tenth–eleventh-century cattle were multi-purpose in a way that their selectively-bred modern descendants are not. Mutton, rather than lamb, was also on the menu; the sheep were rather smaller than ours and again multi-purpose since they were also valued for milk and the wool provided by their hairy fleeces.

153

Most animals were brought into Jorvik on the hoof and slaughtered as required, hence the occurrence of all parts of their skeletons in the ground. It is quite likely, however, that some pigs were kept in the backyards, especially in view of the large number of their lice found. The study of butchery marks on bones suggests that, unlike later medieval towns, Jorvik had no specialist butchers and carcasses were cut up on a somewhat amateur basis.

The townspeople were also keen on fish and the bones of herrings and eels were common alongside the remains of freshwater fish, such as burbot, which can no longer live in the Ouse because of pollution. The bones of cod, probably from the Humber estuary, show that Jorvik's fishermen were rather more adventurous than their Anglian and Roman forebears who stuck to what was locally available.

Bread was the staple source of carbohydrate and large quantities of cereal bran, especially oats, were found. In amongst the bran, however, there were seeds of the corncockle, a plant with a handsome pink flower which used to be common in cornfields before selective weedkillers. If its seeds are harvested with cereal any resulting bread or porridge not only becomes unpalatable, but poisonous. While this was one source of Anglo-Scandinavian stomach-ache, another was infestation by parasitic worms,[82] evidence for which comes from the examination of the abundant faecal matter found at Coppergate in cess pits, on yard surfaces and even on building floors. The potential of the study of faeces was first realised at the Lloyds Bank site where an object described in the academic report as 'a single elongate fusiform mass of organic debris, concreted by mineral deposition',[83] and more commonly known as 'the Lloyds Bank turd', was

Plate 5.9 Tenth-century human stool from the Lloyds Bank site, 6–8 Pavement, York (length 195mm/c. 7½ins) (Photograph: York Archaeological Trust)

found (see Plate 5.9). Examination revealed the presence of the eggs of two worms which live in the human gut, the whipworm and the maw worm. Subsequent work at Coppergate has revealed untold millions of their eggs each less than one-twentieth of 1mm (one-five-hundredth of

1 in.) long. The worms themselves live primarily in the small intestine and can cause indigestion, diarrhoea and symptoms akin to ulcers.

These infestations, like many other ailments, were, of course, endemic because it is clear that the inhabitants of Jorvik had little notion of hygiene as we understand it; not only did rotting organic matter lie around in uncovered heaps, allowing flies and beetles to breed at a rapid rate, but the wells for drinking water were dug next to pits used for cess and offal. Meanwhile pigs, dogs and, no doubt, children rooted around quite happily, frequently encountering families of house mice and black rats. The latter had apparently re-introduced themselves to York after an absence in the less squalid Anglian period when suitable habitats were lacking.[84] Emanating from this teeming scene would have been the strong and putrid smell of decomposition.

In spite of this unappetising environment, where the risk of disease and worse would seem unacceptably high, the people not only survived, but grew prosperous from their crafts. Nothing in the finds from Coppergate suggests poverty; quite the opposite. Diet was good and varied, exotic luxuries such as silk were available, and we may conclude that plenty of the good-quality silver coinage was flowing through people's hands. There was probably plenty of leisure to play the board game *hnefatafl*, of which numerous pieces were found, and to sing and dance to the accompaniment of musical instruments such as boxwood pan pipes and bone whistles. Away from the squalor of the backyards, moreover, some aspects of the environment would have been pleasanter than our own; there was no pervasive pollution from motor vehicles, no noise louder than the hammering of the blacksmiths and the clang of church bells, and little poisonous effluent in the river. It would, however, be overstating the case to say that Anglo-Scandinavian York was a 'green' city; the prevailing colour was probably more a dirty brown.

Lincoln and Norwich

In contrast to tenth–eleventh-century England south-west of Watling Street, relatively few towns developed in the Danelaw, but of those few most became substantial centres able to dominate large regional hinterlands. By Domesday in 1086, for example, only three other places in Yorkshire besides York had burgesses.[85] Another Danelaw town broadly similar in its development and status to York is Lincoln, which also reappears in history in 627 when Bede reports Paulinus conducting missionary activity there.[86] Little is known of Anglian Lincoln, but in 872 the Anglo-Saxon Chronicle records that the Viking host 'took winter quarters at Torksey in Lindsey'. Although Lincoln is not mentioned, it was probably at this time that the town submitted to the control of Scandinavian rulers and became one of the five Danish boroughs – the others being Derby, Leicester, Nottingham and Stamford – referred to in the Chronicle as conquests of King Edmund of Wessex in 942.[87] As at York, much of the influx of population in the five boroughs during the late ninth and early tenth centuries may have been made up of Scandinavian settlers.

The layout of Anglo-Scandinavian Lincoln is not yet understood in any detail, although, as at York, an early origin for many streets is suggested by the -gate suffix. The course of some of them, including the main north–south street (High Street, Steep Hill and Bailgate) was determined by the location of the Roman gates, but no street follows a Roman line exactly, suggesting that all trace of the grid had vanished by the ninth century (see Figure 4.3 for Anglo-Scandinavian sites).

By the mid-tenth century the town was clearly a centre for manufacturing and trade. This was graphically demonstrated at the Flaxengate site, where a sequence of timber buildings and backyard middens was found, along with evidence for intensive metal- and glassworking.[88] At Silver Street the remains of pottery kilns are witness to production on a large scale.[89] Recent excavations on the banks of the River Witham have found evidence for the consolidation of its banks in the tenth–eleventh centuries, perhaps to enable the safe drawing up of ships engaging in local and regional trade.[90] Lincoln's economic domination of a region encompassing Lincolnshire itself and surrounding counties in the later tenth and eleventh centuries appears to be confirmed by the distribution of coins from its mint and the size of its mint output which ranks it close to York by the Norman Conquest and much superior to the other four Danish boroughs.[91]

By Domesday it is reckoned that Lincoln had a population of c. 6,000,[92] and indications of growth are, as we have seen elsewhere, an expansion into areas outside the defences and an increase in the number of churches. The principal early suburb was Wigford which took the form of ribbon development along the continuation of the High Street south of the River Witham. It has been suggested that the name Wigford incorporates the *wic* element of the middle-Saxon trading sites, but as yet no archaeological evidence for this has been found. By the twelfth century, however, Wigford was densely populated with twelve churches many of which are of pre-Norman origin, including St Mary-le-Wigford and St Peter-at-Gowt, in which substantial late Anglo-Saxon fabric can still be seen. They are complemented by the excavated church of St Mark's, latterly a Victorian building demolished in 1972,[93] but with its origins as a small timber building of the mid-tenth century.

In addition to York and Lincoln, the two other Danelaw towns of first rank were Thetford and Norwich. Although Group Captain Knocker excavated extensively in Thetford in the late 1940s and further campaigns followed in the 1960s, it is difficult to form a coherent picture of urban development at Thetford or, indeed, of urban decline, since Thetford is an unusual example of a thriving late Anglo-Saxon town which did not continue to thrive after the eleventh century.[94] The archaeology of Norwich does, however, have a vital contribution to make to the study of both Anglo-Saxon and medieval urbanism (see Figure 5.11).

By way of an introduction to Norwich we can again refer to the Anglo-Saxon Chronicle which records that in 1004 'Swein came with his fleet to Norwich and completely sacked the borough and burnt it down'. What, we may ask, did this borough consist of? The question is not a new one; it has vexed local historians and archaeologists alike for many years, giving rise to a number of fanciful theories along the way, for, as Alan Carter, director of the Norwich Survey, put it: 'Since the fifteenth century pride and covetousness have bedevilled the study of Norwich's origins – pride in its medieval splendour and size, and covetousness of the antiquity of its rivals in the English urban hierarchy.'[95]

Even after 1948 when the first systematic archaeological investigations took place on sites made available by bombing, the location of the principal Anglo-Saxon settlements was erroneously located on the River Wensum margins south of the castle, rather than, as was subsequently demonstrated, to its north. Some progress was made in the excavations of the early 1950s which, first, allowed a middle- and late Anglo-Saxon pottery typology to be identified and, second, produced that pottery on sites north of the cathedral, confirming the existence of a ninth-century or earlier settlement also suggested by the local place names at Coslany and Westwick. As elsewhere, the 1960s was a period of unrecorded destruction of archaeology and little further progress was made until 1970 when an archaeological research committee was established.

One of the principal aims of the Norwich Survey, as it became in 1971, was to examine the origins and early growth of the town,[96] and it is a measure of Carter's achievement that when the Survey concluded active fieldwork in 1980 an outline development of late Anglo-Saxon Norwich from several small middle-Anglo-Saxon settlements had become clear. Carter also believed that the principal tenth-century settlement nucleus of Northwic lay in an area now largely occupied by the cathedral close. Recent work by Brian Ayers of the Norfolk Archaeological Unit has, however, indicated that the original Northwic may lie north of the River Wensum, its name distinguishing it from Westwick. Excavations in Fishergate[97] produced substantial quantities of middle-Anglo-Saxon pottery, more than all other sites in Norwich put together, and evidence for consolidation of the river bank in the tenth century. The site lay within an area enclosed by a ditch, probably of tenth-century date, which has been found at Alms Lane and Calvert Street.[98] To the east the line probably follows Peacock Street and Blackfriars Street. The main street would have been on the line of Magdalen Street. Conclusive proof that this is Northwic must rely on further excavation, which will, it is hoped, produce evidence

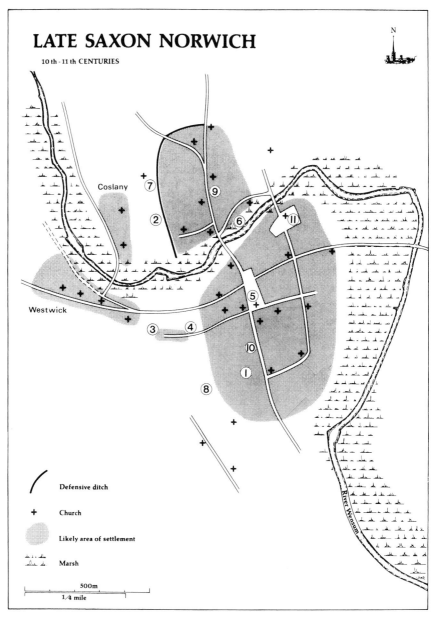

Figure 5.11 Plan of Norwich showing late Anglo-Saxon sites and streets referred to in the text (Norfolk Archaeological Unit)
Key: 1 Church in the castle bailey (Anglia TV site); 2 Alms Lane; 3 Lobster Lane; 4 Bedford Street; 5 Tombland; 6 Fishergate; 7 Calvert Street; 8 Castle Mall; 9 Magdalen Street; 10 King Street; 11 Palace Plain

of Sweyn's attack. In the meantime, Ayers has speculated that the vanished medieval church of St Margaret in Combusto – 'the burnt area' – within the enclosure derives its name from the events of 1004, as does another lost church of St Mary Unbrent in Combusto – 'unburnt in the burnt area'.

Today the area suggested as the original Northwic is something of a backwater and the centre of the modern city lies south of the Wensum. This shift is probably the result of eleventh-century developments after Sweyn's raid, deliberately encouraged perhaps by the major landowners on the south bank including the Earls and Bishops of East Anglia (the latter based in North Elmham). Recent research has identified the rudiments of a late Anglo-Saxon street grid. One of the principal north–south streets (linked to Magdalen Street on the north bank) would have been on the line of Wensum Street, Tombland and Upper King Street, but the line of the other, largely lost in the close, is now indicated only by Whitefriars north of the river. Prominent features of the plan were large open spaces at Tombland and Palace Plain which probably served as market places. By the time of the Conquest this southern settlement was the main centre of population.

In addition to trade, a variety of crafts would, as at York and Lincoln, have sustained the local economy, but the only one known archaeologically is pottery manufacture.[99] A number of sites along the line, not of Pottergate itself, but on its eastward continuation as Lobster Lane and Bedford Street, have revealed remains of kilns and dumps of waste from the manufacturing of grey wheel-made cooking pots. Recently further kilns have been found at the Castle Mall site. In the tenth–eleventh centuries these areas were on the western periphery of the town and occupied, perhaps, a distinct industrial zone where activities involving fire could be kept away from the timber dwellings.

The vessels produced in Norwich are very similar to those made at other major production centres in the Danelaw such as Thetford, Torksey (near Lincoln) and York. Potting in all these centres probably developed from the traditions of wheel-turned manufacture established at Ipswich in the middle-Anglo-Saxon period. The majority of middle-Saxon vessels, however, were hand-made, whereas later Anglo-Saxon ceramics (see Plate 2.3) were very well made on an efficient wheel. In terms of both form and fabric they were highly standardised, reflecting both improving technology and the demands of a growing urban market. The later ninth and tenth centuries also see diversification of vessel form into pitchers, lamps and bowls, and increasing vessel decoration, most notably with the production of glazed wares.

As elsewhere, the growth of Anglo-Saxon Norwich can be indicated by the number of churches; there were probably forty-six by the time of the Domesday Book in 1086 with, perhaps, a particular concentration of early foundations in the Tombland area. Only five Norwich churches have pre-

Figure 5.12 Plan of a typical late Anglo-Saxon urban church and its cemetery as excavated at the Anglia TV site, Norwich. The wall trenches and post-holes representing the church are at the bottom of the plan (Norfolk Archaeological Unit)

Conquest fabric surviving, but an opportunity to excavate a previously unknown late Anglo-Saxon timber church, unaffected by later structural alterations, came in 1979 on a site peripheral to the core of the settlement (see Figure 5.12).[100] The site had been absorbed by the north-east bailey of the Norman castle whose construction had obliterated the church as well as, perhaps, the homes of its parishioners. The remains of the earliest church consisted of just six large post-holes, graphically demonstrating the modest nature of most early urban foundations. Subsequently it was replaced by another timber building which at 9m (30 ft) by 4m (13 ft) was

160

slightly larger and also had a distinct nave and chancel. Few internal features could be identified except perhaps the site of the font. Adjacent to the church was the burial ground where skeletons of some 130 individuals were recovered, presenting a fascinating insight into the population of a late Anglo-Saxon town.[101] In this case it is suggested that we may be dealing with a relatively poor and deprived section of the community. An unusually high proportion of infant burials suggests poor health and many of the skeletons exhibited evidence for dietary deficiencies.

In the latter part of this chapter we have looked at several places in England which grew steadily from the later ninth or tenth centuries onwards until, by the mid-eleventh century, they had populations several thousand strong, making them as large or larger than the major Roman towns. Lower down the hierarchy, especially in the south of England, smaller urban centres were also flourishing. The growing body of archaeological discoveries creates an overall impression of a vigorous and enterprising approach to all aspects of town life. In every trade and craft, from construction to metalwork, there was diversification of output and innovation in techniques. At the same time there was a renaissance in the decorative and fine arts, centred on urban workshops which responded to the demands of wealthy aristocratic, ecclesiastical and commercial patrons. Thanks in no small measure to its towns, England was, by the mid-eleventh century, truly 'a precious stone set in the silver sea' and it is no surprise to see her coveted by the ambitious Duke William of Normandy, to say nothing of the last serious Viking contender for our throne, Harald Hardrada of Norway.

6

MEDIEVAL TOWNS

Analysis of the animal bones from excavations in Lincoln, has suggested that while mutton only provided about 7 per cent of the city's meat diet in the mid-eleventh century, the number of sheep which were slaughtered annually would have required a much larger percentage of the region's agricultural land for grazing. Furthermore, the usual age at death of medieval Lincoln's sheep was 4 years, that is, past the prime age for eating.[1] These data can only be explained by the value of wool. To find an example of archaeological evidence for the processing of this vital commodity we can do no better than move across the country to Winchester. At the Lower Brook Street site, one of the most striking discoveries was of an open area between two medieval houses where there was a regular pattern of small stone-packed post-holes. Found associated with them and elsewhere on the site were a number of small iron L-shaped

Figure 6.1 Iron tenterhooks from Lower Brook Street, Winchester (scale 1:2) (Winchester Research Unit)

hooks (see Figure 6.1).[2] The post-holes probably secured the base of tenting frames on which woollen cloth was stretched to dry after fulling – a process which strengthened cloth by soaking it in water and fuller's earth. The iron hooks – the tenter-hooks – held the cloth in place on the frames.

Excavated evidence of the kind I have just referred to serves to confirm the importance of the wool trade and manufacture of cloth for the medieval urban economy, but also reminds us that towns of the period remained, like their Roman and Anglo-Saxon forebears, almost completely dependent on the resources of their region. It was, however, the increasing productivity of agriculture which permitted the pace of urbanisation in the twelfth and thirteenth centuries to quicken. Although over 90 per cent of the population of medieval England remained rural, a perception of the opportunities for the acquisition of both wealth and power prompted many landowners, both ecclesiastical and secular, to lead the way in founding new towns or expanding those established in the late Anglo-Saxon period. New foundations were, moreover, made for the first time in Scotland and Wales. The resulting urban framework was to survive until the last major wave of new additions during the Industrial Revolution in the late eighteenth century.

The price landlords paid for attracting new citizens was to allow them freedom from many of the feudal restraints which stifled enterprise on the land, and, as time went on, urban communities would acquire the economic strength to seize ever greater responsibility for their own affairs and to dominate those of their region. At the same time, drawing ahead of all the others in size, wealth and status, London was to become by far the most important medieval town in Britain and the only one to compare with the great medieval centres elsewhere in Europe.

Although discoveries in Roman towns may seem more glamorous and those in Anglo-Saxon towns more intriguing, it is in illustrating the layout and character of medieval towns that urban archaeology has made many of its most significant advances.[3] Compared to those of earlier date, however, buried medieval deposits and structures are often relatively close to the surface and are therefore peculiarly vulnerable to modern disturbance. Since modern streets usually correspond to medieval streets, moreover, the destruction of archaeological deposits may be particularly severe on the frontages where modern buildings, with their cellars and basements, have replaced their medieval predecessors.

In addition to buried remains, an important part of the archaeological resource for the medieval period consists of standing buildings. The majority of those that survive from the eleventh–thirteenth centuries are the more monumental structures, such as castles and churches, but from the fourteenth–fifteenth centuries there are also many dwellings in varying states of completeness. The existence of standing structures does not, however, mean that the excavation of buried remains is any less valuable, because it can reveal details of the first stages of construction, including the foundations and earliest floors, unen-cumbered by the alterations and accretions of later periods.[4] As far as the dwellings of the lower orders are concerned, moreover, archaeology remains virtually the only source of information; houses which survive were largely erected by the rich who could afford to build soundly in either stone or good timber.

Because the survival of buried and standing remains is so uneven, medieval urban archaeology is most informative when it can be combined with the evidence from the documentary sources which become gradually more plentiful from the twelfth century onwards (see pp. 17–18). For archaeologists the documents are particularly valuable for details of the ownership, location and extent of properties, but the written record rarely approaches the status of a comprehensive guide to medieval urban topography, and gives little clue to the nature of structures within the properties or to the activities undertaken by the occupiers as opposed to the owners. Archaeology's strength lies in the evidence it reveals for the form and plan of vanished buildings, for the processes and products of craft and industry, and for the intimate picture of daily life from diet to refuse disposal. Above all, archaeology is uniquely able to illustrate the character of all parts of the urban fabric, from buildings and streets to yards, wells and middens. It is perhaps one of the few entirely positive consequences of the pervasiveness of modern development that this point has now been demonstrated in a number of the larger medieval towns of Britain by wide-ranging programmes of excavation.

Cathedrals, castles and defences

The principal effect of the Norman Conquest of England on the urban scene was the construction of new cathedrals and castles. Their function may be seen not only as, respectively, places for religious observance and military control, but also as symbols of the political power of the new regime. Norman bishops and warlords built in a grand style to legitimate the authority of the new ruling class just as the Roman emperors and Anglo-Saxon kings had done before them.

The dramatic impact of the construction of a Norman cathedral in the centre of an Anglo-Saxon town was strikingly demonstrated by excavations on the Cathedral Green in Winchester. In 1079 the first Norman bishop began his new church at its east end, but in 1093–4 work took place on the nave and the Anglo-Saxon Old Minster was systematically demolished and used as a quarry.[5] The original character of the eleventh-century building is still apparent today in the massive and simple stonework of the transepts which powerfully emphasise the Norman ascendancy in the heart of the old English kingdom. Another event of great symbolic significance in 1093 was the moving of St Swithun's bones from the original Anglo-Saxon shrine to the new high altar. Care was taken not to rupture all links with the past, however, since, as excavations showed, the old site retained its potency. It was marked by a monument and burials gathered around it as they had in the Anglo-Saxon period.[6] In York the effect of a new cathedral was even more dramatic because of a radical change of alignment. On the evidence of the burials in its graveyard,[7] the Anglo-Scandinavian cathedral, like other churches in the city founded in that period, followed the dominant north-east/south-west alignment of the Roman fortress. Archbishop Thomas of Bayeux's new cathedral, begun in the 1070s, was, however, aligned east–west and the break with tradition is still very apparent in York's townscape, as the medieval walls around the later medieval cathedral, or Minster, overlie those of the fortress, and many of the principal streets follow Roman lines.

At Norwich (see Figure 6.2), which replaced Thetford as the seat of the bishop of East Anglia in 1094, the cathedral is not on an exact east–west line and probably follows the alignment of an Anglo-Saxon street and pre-existing church,[8] but the establishment of a large monastic estate, the Prior's Fee (today's cathedral close), had a major influence on the layout of the town, serving to force the centre westwards to where it is today. Excavations at St Martin-at-Palace Plain and Whitefriar's Street[9] have shown that by the twelfth century these riverside locations, which had previously lain close to one of the main north–south routes of the Anglo-Saxon town, the market place close to the bridge and the river wharves, had become largely deserted after the route was severed by the Prior's Fee. The new commercial centre was what is known today as the Market Place. The river wharves were moved downstream to the lower end of King Street where larger ships could be accommodated.

Norman castles were, if anything, even more disruptive of the urban fabric than new cathedrals. This point also can be demonstrated at Norwich where the remodelling of the city was completed by the construction of the castle whose motte and keep still dominate the modern city, overlooking both cathedral and market. According to Domesday, construction of the castle involved the destruction of ninety-eight houses, and recent excavations south of the castle at the 2.5ha (6 acres) Castle Mall site, one of Britain's largest ever urban digs,[10] have shown how the extensive bailey works completely transformed the landscape – one consequence being the removal of the late Anglo-Saxon church described above (see pp. 159–61). In addition to the bailey ditch, a particularly impressive discovery was of a hitherto unknown ditch, 15m (50 ft) across and 8m (26 ft) deep, which had probably been dug to protect the drawbridge and gatehouse after the capture of the castle in a French raid connected with the baron's revolt against King John in 1216 (see Plate 6.1). Important as this ditch is for the history of Norwich, however, its discovery also makes it clear that even the best-known ancient monuments, whose layout is thought to be fully understood, may still have secrets which can only be revealed by archaeology.

The Normans' objective in building urban castles was to overawe the citizens and turn towns into defendable strong points in a potentially hostile country, although after the 'anarchy' of the mid-twelfth century their importance declined. The castles were either allowed to fall into decay or demolished and the land was given away for other purposes. The town defences themselves, however, remained prominent features of the medieval landscape. As a result they, like their Roman and Anglo-Saxon forerunners, became important determinants of urban topography

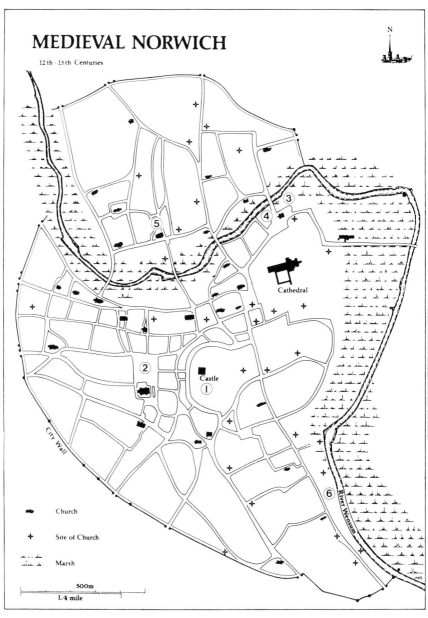

Figure 6.2 Plan of Norwich showing medieval sites referred to in the text (Norfolk Archaeological Unit)
Key: 1 Castle Mall; 2 Market Place; 3 St Martin-at-Palace Plain; 4 Whitefriars Street; 5 Alms Lane; 6 Music House

Plate 6.1 Cross-section through the 11m-deep early-thirteenth-century barbican ditch unexpectedly revealed at Castle Mall, Norwich. The excavators define the V-shaped profile of the ditch; the sides of the trench have been stepped to prevent collapse. The castle motte is beyond the picture, upper left (Photograph: Norfolk Archaeological Unit)

and are often the most prominent surviving secular monuments of the period.

Medieval towns originally founded in the Roman or Anglo-Saxon periods usually maintained and refurbished the defensive circuits they inherited, while towns founded after the Conquest often acquired defences at an early stage. In the late eleventh and twelfth centuries they were clearly thought necessary for security purposes and there are a number of towns, including Hereford and York, which extended their defences at this time to protect extra-mural settlements.[11] In general, however, strong centralised government meant that medieval England suffered little civil disorder and its island location meant that it did not suffer like most other countries in western Europe from repeated foreign invasions. After c. 1200 defences were, it seems, constructed largely to assert civic pride, to define the area covered by legal privileges particular to townsmen, and to facilitate the collection (at the gates) of taxes due on internal trade. The size of the defended enclosure is not necessarily, therefore, a good guide to urban fortunes. Norwich, for example, in spite of being one of the largest and wealthiest towns of medieval England, was undefended until the mid-thirteenth century and the wall was not completed until 1334. Even then the river side was left largely unprotected, the raid of 1216 being long forgotten.

On occasions, however, threats to security could focus minds wonderfully. At Hull, founded by Edward I in 1293, the town was surrounded by a boundary ditch from the start, but in 1317 the burgesses applied to Edward II for permission to construct a wall.[12] They were aware that the town's role as a base for the king's Scottish campaigns rendered them vulnerable to attack, especially after the victory of Robert the Bruce at Bannockburn in 1314. Initially a rampart with a palisade and wooden gates was built, but between the 1330s and 1410 this was replaced by a wall (see Figure 6.3). By this time, however, the danger had passed, which accounts for the time taken to complete the work. Even then the east side of the town was, as at Norwich, left undefended to prevent interference to its precious river commerce.

The most remarkable feature of Hull's medieval walls is that, unlike those of any other major English town, they were built of brick. This is, moreover, the earliest use of brick in a monumental structure of any kind in Britain since Roman times apart from Holy Trinity Church also in Hull, begun c. 1300. The popularity of brick in late medieval Hull and eastern England generally was probably due to the influence of trade and immigration from the Low Countries, and was immediately attractive in areas short of building stone and timber. Today Hull's medieval defences are virtually invisible except for the Beverley Gate recently rediscovered in excavation. For many years a plaque on the wall at the head of White-friargate purported to identify the site of the gate, but in 1986–7 a site c. 100m (110 yds) further west revealed the well-preserved lower part of the structure (see Plate 6.2). It had initially been built as a simple free-standing arch in c. 1350, before the town walls were completed. Subsequently the gate was enhanced with guardchambers and a tower and spire, as can be seen in Wenceslaus Hollar's view of Hull in 1640 (see Figure 6.3). The excavated remains are now on display in the new pedestrianised precinct adjacent to the Prince's Dock development. For an idea of the complete gate one should visit nearby Beverley and look for the North Bar built, in brick, in c. 1400.

A similar picture to that described at Hull emerges elsewhere; construction of anything more than a ditch and earthen bank might be a

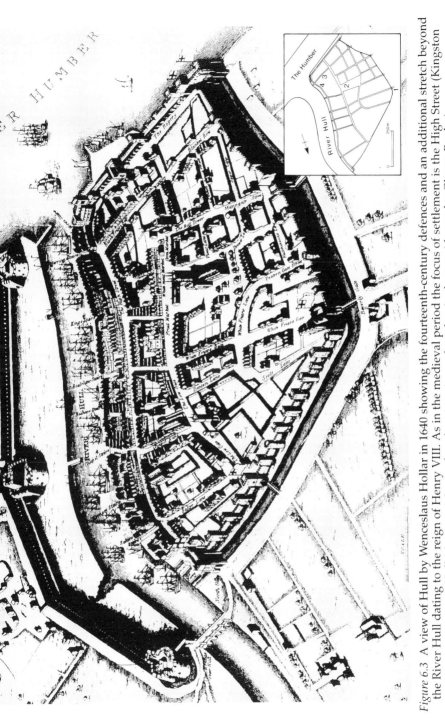

Figure 6.3 A view of Hull by Wenceslaus Hollar in 1640 showing the fourteenth-century defences and an additional stretch beyond the River Hull dating to the reign of Henry VIII. As in the medieval period the focus of settlement is the High Street (Kingston upon Hull Museums) *Inset*: plan showing sites referred to in the text (drawn by Glenys Boyles)
Key: 1 Beverley Gate; 2 Holy Trinity; 3 Wytelard property; 4 Ousefleet property

Plate 6.2 Detail of the fourteenth-century Beverley Gate at Hull showing the fine early brickwork – north buttress of the north guard house (foreground) at its junction with the town wall (vertical scale 1.50m/c. 5 ft) (Photograph: Humberside Archaeological Unit)

very protracted process in view of the expense involved and the lack of incentive resulting from long periods of peace. At Southampton a castle was constructed on the north-west side of the Anglo-Saxon town in the late eleventh century, but work on the medieval defences, which extended the enclosed area north of the original town, did not begin until 1202–3.[13] The burgesses continually resisted paying for a wall to add to the bank and ditch and for any defences at all on the west and south sides of town where access to the quays was given priority. A heavy price for obstinacy was paid, however, when a French force attacked the town in 1338 burning down many buildings whose charred remains are frequently found in excavation. After the raid the Crown insisted that a wall was built, but it was done on the cheap, as shown by excavations which have revealed poor shallow footings. On the west side of the town, as can be seen today, existing house walls were used where possible.

In Scotland poverty rather than peace probably explains the lack of substantial urban defences before the fifteenth–sixteenth centuries, even in large towns like Aberdeen. Only Berwick and Perth[14] had medieval walls which were erected during the Wars of Independence when they were in English hands. The walls of Perth, erected in c. 1306, were demolished by Robert the Bruce in 1313 and archaeological evidence for this was found for the first and only time on the High Street site (see Figure 6.4). Somewhat surprisingly, although the defensive ditch, or 'Mill Lade', which is probably twelfth-century, was found at the nearby Mill Street site, it revealed no wall, suggesting that the circuit had never been completed.

Urban colonisation – streets, tenements and rigs

Opportunities to study the development of the medieval street plan through excavation of the streets themselves are rare as they usually lie underneath their modern successors. Archaeology can, however, give some idea of the date of streets from the examination of adjacent properties. We may also note that most medieval towns of Anglo-Saxon origin inherited some kind of regular street grid, and this form of organisation of space remained in favour for urban extensions and for new towns such as Salisbury, founded c. 1220. Smaller towns had simpler plans, perhaps two streets meeting at a right angle or just a single main street. A vital component of the town plan was a market place and many examples of medieval origin can be recognised today as unusually wide streets or as rectangular or triangular open spaces. Others have become hidden due to the encroachment of surrounding properties or the conversion of temporary stalls into permanent buildings, but the study of early maps will often suggest the original layout. Most market places are relatively central and often close to a castle or monastic house, from which they drew much

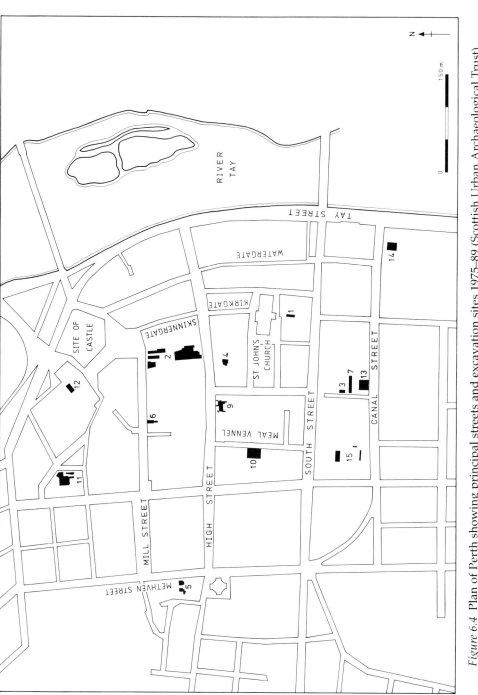

Figure 6.4 Plan of Perth showing principal streets and excavation sites 1975–89 (Scottish Urban Archaeological Trust)

Key: 1 St Anne's Lane (1975); 2 High Street excavations (1976–7); 3 Canal Street 1 (1978); 4 Kirk Close (1979); 5 Methven Street (1979); 6 Mill Street (1979–80); 7 Canal Street 2 (1981); 9 King Edward Street (1985); 10 Meal Vennel (1983–4); 11 Kinnoull Street (1982); 13 Blackfriars House (1984);

of their business and protection, but others, such as St Giles at Oxford, lay immediately outside the town gates (see Figure 5.5).

Another feature of the layout of the medieval town directly associated with its economic role is the long narrow tenement or burgage plot. We have already met elongated tenements in both Roman and late Anglo-Saxon towns, but, as a means of meeting the growing demand for space to conduct business on the street and market frontages, they are a particular characteristic of urban areas laid out after the Conquest (see Figure 2.2). Once established, the very distinctive pattern of tenement boundaries has lasted remarkably unchanged to recent times in many town centres, although modern developments have begun to create larger property units for supermarkets and the like which are more suited to today's commercial requirements.

To the casual visitor an excavation of a typical medieval urban tenement can appear extremely puzzling. The structural remains of even substantial timber buildings may be relatively ephemeral, especially when, as is common, they are disturbed both by the innumerable pits used for cess and refuse in the medieval period itself, and by intrusive modern features. It is possible, however, to identify a number of general trends in tenement development through the medieval period. The buildings, for example, were first concentrated on the street frontages and subsequently, in response to rising population, spread into the backyards, often at the same time as the properties themselves were split into smaller units. Medieval towns did not, therefore, expand solely, or even primarily, by pushing outwards from the centre, but rather by internal colonisation creating the densely occupied urban core whose character is still identifiable in Winchester, York and elsewhere. The process has been demonstrated archaeologically in a number of towns, including Canterbury where excavations[15] suggest that the principal streets were laid out in the late Anglo-Saxon period, but that the most rapid period of building-up the street frontages in the central area took place in the eleventh and twelfth centuries. In the thirteenth century the frontages of minor streets were built up and by the fourteenth century building over the backyards had become general.

New towns of the Middle Ages usually experienced several episodes of addition to the initial planned street and property layout, and they also grew through intensified occupation of core areas. To illustrate this point in more detail we may look at two Scottish towns, Perth[16] and Aberdeen.[17]

Urban archaeology in Scotland is a much more recent development than its English counterpart. The first excavation of any size took place at the Perth High Street site in 1975–6. It revealed remains of the late-sixteenth-century house in which the Scottish Parliament met in 1606, but beneath it were medieval deposits with excellent preservation of timber buildings and organic refuse. The site demonstrated the archaeological potential of Perth, and by implication that of other Scottish towns. As a result, government funding for urban archaeology became available for the first time. By 1982 the City of Aberdeen had established its own unit based in the museum, the only one funded by a local authority in Scotland. Responsibility for all other towns in the country, including Perth, lies with the Scottish Urban Archaeological Trust which has now begun the long haul of establishing an archaeological framework for well over 100 previously unexplored places.

Most medieval Scottish boroughs, including Perth and Aberdeen, were royal foundations by a crown which saw taxes on urban trade as a means to boost its hard-pressed coffers.[18] Perth received its first charter under King David I (1124–53) who, according to the Aberdonian priest, John of Fordun, 'enriched the ports of his kingdom with foreign merchandise and to the wealth of his own land added the riches and luxuries of foreign nations, changing its coarse stuffs for precious vestments, and covering its ancient nakedness with purple and fine linen'. Deriving something of its importance from proximity to the ancient royal site of Scone, Perth was the nearest Scotland came to having a capital city until the emergence of Edinburgh in the seventeenth century.

The site of Perth (see Figure 6.4) is on slightly raised ground on the banks of the River Tay, but settlement was hardly viable until trade became important. Although the river ensured good communications, flooding was also a serious hazard and in 1209 the castle was washed away. The earliest occupation known archaeologically is mid-twelfth-century and comes from the High Street site which lay on the west side of the original settlement nucleus. A combination of archaeological and documentary analysis[19] has shown that this was centred on the east end of the High Street and on two north–south streets, Watergate and Kirkgate. The latter was subsequently extended northwards, via Skinnergate, to connect kirk and castle. This development was followed – still, it is thought, in the twelfth century – by westward extensions of the High Street and by the establishment parallel to it of South Street. As witness to this medieval expansion, one can still see two slight bends in the High Street at the points where the extensions probably began. A western town boundary may have been established for a while along the line of Meal Vennel where excavations revealed a ditch running north–south. In places archaeology has suggested that colonisation lagged behind the establishment of streets. At the Canal Street II site, for example, a regular layout of rigs (i.e. tenements) fronting on to South Street was dated no earlier than the later thirteenth century. A similar dating for rigs was established at the Kirk Close site near St John's Church. Subsequent expansion westwards beyond the line of Meal Vennel took the town up to the line of the defences established in the early fourteenth century; the ditch was located at the Methven Street site.

Medieval Aberdeen was, like Perth, a dual settlement in origin with one nucleus around St Machar's Cathedral (founded c. 1150) at Old Aberdeen, and the other a few miles south at the mouth of the River Dee. Because of its fine natural harbour and good position on the local land communications network, it was the southern settlement which grew and, like Perth again, became a royal borough under David I. The insertion of Union Street in the nineteenth century has rather obscured the medieval layout of the town (see Figure 2.2), but settlement probably grew rapidly in the mid-thirteenth century from an original nucleus between the Castle and St Nicholas's Church. The principal streets, Castle Street, Broad Street and Upper Kirkgate, were laid out with long narrow rigs facing them, much as they appear on Parson Gordon's map, although excavation at the 42 St Paul Street site, north of Upper Kirkgate, suggests the pattern was not complete in some areas until c. 1300. Recent excavations on the west side of Gallowgate, north of the original centre, revealed an area originally dedicated to industrial and craft activities, such as tanning, which was not divided into rigs until the fourteenth–fifteenth centuries.[20]

Although most excavations in Aberdeen and Perth have taken place in the backs of the rigs, it is assumed that the first buildings were on the street frontages with expansion subsequently to the rear (see Figure 6.5). Colonisation is also marked by refuse tipping and because the deposits are waterlogged in both towns we can plot the intensification of settlement in a way which is rarely possible in English towns where organic preservation in medieval deposits is usually poor. In Perth the build-up of middens was particularly rapid in the thirteenth and fourteenth centuries, raising ground level by up to 3m (10 ft), creating a thoroughly squalid and unpleasant environment in the process. The High Street site was no exception, although the finds suggest that it was occupied by relatively prosperous members of the community.

The contents of the midden deposits at Aberdeen and Perth show, in the first instance, how reliant medieval towns were on local resources. The buildings used posts of oak and wattles of birch from the nearby woods for walls, and bracken and heather from the moorland for roofs, floor coverings and even bedding. Cereal remains were largely oats, used for bread, and barley, used for brewing, while wheat, difficult to grow in the climate, was a rarity, probably imported from England. Vegetable remains were not so well preserved, but indicate that turnips (the traditional accompaniment to haggis) and beans were readily available. Locally gathered moss found in the latrines served as toilet paper; the abundant eggs of intestinal worms are, as in Anglo-Scandinavian York, witness to poor hygiene. Numerous textile fragments consisted largely of undyed coarse fabrics made from the wool of hairy local sheep similar to the Orkney sheep of today.[21]

We should not get the impression, however, that these Scottish towns

Figure 6.5 Aberdeen c. 1300: a splendid evocation of life in the medieval backyards based on archaeological evidence from the 42 St Paul's Street site (drawn by G. Smith)

were no more than big villages. Apart from their distinctive layout, there are other aspects of the midden contents which indicate a characteristically urban society with a well-developed hierarchy based on wealth. This is indicated on the Perth High Street site by such finds as gold buttons, gilt spurs and three pieces of embroidered silk hair net imported from the continent to satisfy fashionable tastes (see Plate 6.3; Figure 6.6). Among the food remains there were bones of geese and swans which are witness to an unusually varied diet.[22] Foreign merchants formed another distinctive element in the population of Scottish towns and the refuse of their households may account for the small quantities of pottery imported from France and the Low Countries which occur among the mass of local wares.

In both England and Scotland medieval towns clearly had a good deal of open space within their walls which was used as gardens, allotments and even fields, but, in addition to internal colonisation, towns also grew by spawning suburbs, which we may define as settlements outside the principal circuit of defences.[23] The growth of suburbs need not, however, indicate that intra-mural areas had filled up, but may, instead, betray increasing stratification in urban society since it appears that some form

Plate 6.3 Towns as consumers of luxury goods: a piece of thirteenth-century silk textile from the Kirk Close site, Perth, with a bird pattern woven into it (see also Figure 6.6; size: 145mm × 140mm/c. $5\frac{1}{2}$ ins × $5\frac{1}{2}$ ins) (Photograph: Scottish Urban Archaeological Trust)

of social distinction constrained certain sections of the community to live outside the walls where they might be deprived of some of the rights and privileges of fully-fledged townsfolk. Documentary sources also suggest that medieval suburbanites were generally poorer than those within the walls. At the same time, extra-mural land was probably cheaper and so for those hoping to speculate in the urban property market the suburbs offered a chance of a quick profit.

The earliest suburbs clustered immediately outside the town gates or along the line of the defences. They might also grow around an extra-mural market place as at St Giles, Oxford, and it is at Oxford that some of the best archaeological evidence for the development of medieval

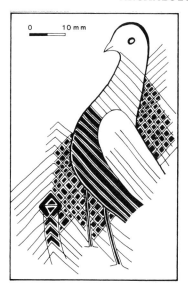

Figure 6.6 Detail of bird design on fragment of thirteenth-century silk from Perth (see Plate 6.3) (Scottish Urban Archaeological Trust)

suburbs has been found, beginning with one of the earliest rescue excavations in England, north of the walls at the New Bodleian library in 1937.[24] In 1964 a more serious threat to the medieval town arose with plans for the wholesale redevelopment of its western side, both outside and inside the defences, in advance of what was to become the Westgate Centre. Following the publication in 1966 of one of the earliest of the now familiar genre of archaeological implications surveys,[25] a full-time team of archaeologists directed by Tom Hassall, under the aegis of the Oxford Archaeological Excavation Committee, was created as the first 'urban unit' on the Winchester model. Initially the unit saw itself as having a five-year programme after which it was envisaged that the pace of redevelopment in Oxford would slow and resources could be devoted to publication.[26] In the event this was wishful thinking. In 1973 the unit extended its brief to include the county, but under the new name of the Oxford Archaeological Unit has continued to deal with the threats to the city's archaeology.

Extra-mural settlement had already taken place at Oxford in the Anglo-Saxon period and on the west side at least one building and an east–west street were covered over by the motte and bailey of the Norman castle (see Figure 5.5).[27] Urban growth both inside and outside the walls was evidently rapid in the twelfth and thirteenth centuries, not only due to the cloth industry, but also because Oxford was becoming a centre for scholarship. The survival of archaeological deposits in the suburbs is remarkably good since they often lie on lower ground near the river where rubbish dumping and artificial build-up against floods have reduced the intrusive effect of modern buildings. This has been demonstrated at 79–

178

81 St Aldates[28] (see Figure 5.5) outside the south gate, and on the western side of the medieval town at a site on a street known as The Hamel (see Figure 6.7).[29] In the twelfth century The Hamel was the property of Osney Abbey and, judging by the regular elongated shape of the tenements, settlement was probably the result of a deliberately planned, speculative venture. In the mid to late twelfth century ditches were dug to divide up and drain the site; the organic matter in them, especially the beetles,[30] show that a rural environment prevailed initially, but was soon followed by the encroachment of human occupation of an urban character, signalled by insect species living on timbers, thatch and rotting domestic refuse.

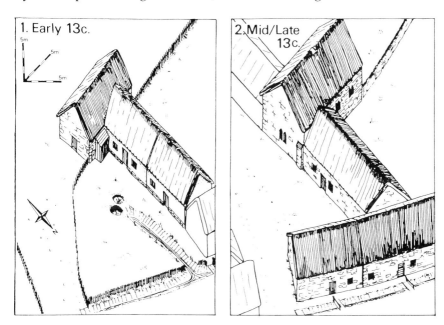

Figure. 6.7 Colonisation in the medieval suburbs: conjectural reconstruction of buildings at The Hamel, Oxford, based on archaeological evidence. The street is at the bottom of the drawings and in 2 the Hall of St Helens is at the top (Oxford Archaeological Unit)

The first buildings on the site went up in the early thirteenth century and had stone footings to support timber frames. The street-frontage buildings had their long axes parallel to the street indicating less pressure on space in a suburban location. In the later thirteenth century the southern tenement was occupied by the hall of St Helen, a stone building rather grander than its neighbours and possibly occupied by its owner, the merchant Nicholas de Weston. Thanks to subsidence, however, the hall only had a brief life and was replaced by a humbler stone structure. The burial of a new-born infant skeleton in a sub-floor layer in this building is probably testimony to some sad story of disappointed hope and to the ever-present risk of infectious diseases caused by living conditions which appear to have been squalid throughout the medieval period.

With the exception of the hall of St Helen, the character both of the buildings at The Hamel, with their simple one or two room plans, and of the artefacts, especially the pottery which was overwhelmingly local, suggests that the inhabitants were, with the exception of de Weston, humble artisans rather than prosperous merchants. This is confirmed by the documentary sources which show that men like Walter the Tanner, resident c. 1270, were typical of suburbanites in many medieval towns who travelled to work in the town centre. Their more prosperous employers required easy access to the markets or riverfront and, if for no other reason than security, preferred to live at their place of work. This situation gradually changed in the later medieval and post-medieval periods as the rich moved to landed estates or outer suburbs leaving poorer tenants in town centre properties.

Urban dwellings – a jumble of styles

As the medieval period progressed most town centre properties became a jumble of buildings of different periods and styles as a result of continual additions and alterations to satisfy the demands of both accommodation and social pretension. A factor enhancing the diversity of house types in a medieval street was that the rich and ambitious often lived cheek by jowl with the poor and humble. We have had some indication of this at The Hamel and the point has also been graphically demonstrated on such excavations as Lower Brook Street in Winchester where the remains of merchants' houses were found alongside two-roomed cottages.[31]

From both standing structures and excavations some general patterns can be detected in the development of plans and mode of construction. In both respects urban buildings, not surprisingly, adapted traditions prevailing in the countryside to the more confined spaces and complex social requirements of the town. As far as plan type is concerned, it is possible to trace a gradual move towards a greater and more formal division of interior space from the late Anglo-Saxon period onwards. Pre-Conquest dwellings, as at York (see Plate 5.6), usually consisted of a single room, albeit with space allocated to such separate functions as cooking and keeping animals. By the twelfth–thirteenth centuries dwellings were more frequently divided up by fixed partitions into several rooms to accommodate these functions. At the same time it was possible for residents to have greater privacy and to reinforce such social distinctions as those between the family of the owner and the domestic servants. In addition there was an increasing use of altogether separate buildings for dangerous or noxious activities, such as cooking or brewing.

Running parallel to changes in plan, we can trace a gradual increase in the range of materials employed for building and a greater sophistication of construction techniques. Timber, of course, remained the primary structural medium throughout the medieval period, although it rarely survives in buried buildings. In addition to what can be learned from standing structures, however, further information on medieval carpentry techniques can be gained from timber-lined pits and wells, and, as we shall see shortly, the remarkable preserved waterfronts of some medieval ports, especially London. These structures show an increasing sophistication in jointing and bracing which allowed both greater stability and the spanning of greater internal spaces. Prefabrication of the frame gave a greater efficiency and lower cost. A climax to these developments may be seen in the many-storeyed and jettied town buildings which began to emerge in the fourteenth century.

In most parts of the country the construction of dwellings entirely in stone was rare in the medieval period except in the homes of the rich. From the later twelfth and early thirteenth century onwards, however, stone was, as we have already noted at The Hamel in Oxford, increasingly used for footings and the lower parts of walls. One reason for this was presumably to prolong the life of timber which would eventually rot when in contact with the ground. From the fourteenth century onwards brick appears in footings in Hull and other east coast towns to serve the same purpose. Roofs at the time of the Conquest were usually thatch, but, with an increasing risk of fire in crowded urban areas, tiles and slates became more common and are abundant if – because of their bulk and weight – unloved archaeological finds. Between 1192–3 and 1212 Henry Fitzailwin, the first lord mayor of London, attempted to enforce the use of fire-proof materials in both walls and roofs,[32] but these and subsequent regulations were honoured more in the breach than the observance. In the Great Fire year of 1666 London was a largely timber and thatch city.

These general trends in form and fabric can be illustrated in more detail by the archaeology of a number of towns including Norwich (see Figure 6.2). One of the most remarkable discoveries here was a stone house constructed in the third quarter of the twelfth century on the banks of the Wensum at the St Martin-at-Palace-Plain site (see Plate 6.4).[33] Built of flint walls with limestone quoins and window surrounds, it originally had two floors, the lower being found almost intact with walls over 2m (6 ft 6 ins) high. This had been a store room into which commodities could easily have been off-loaded from the river. Above this had been the living quarters which, because of the slope of the bank, would have been at street level at the front. A reasonable standard of comfort was indicated by the addition, in a specially built turret, of an internal latrine chute. It would have been smelly where it emptied into the river, but at least the inhabitants were spared draughty trips outside.

The best parallel in Norwich for this building is the so-called Music House,[34] again adjacent to the river, but further downstream. It is a building with a long and complex history, but much of the surviving undercroft is also twelfth-century. At this time the Music House was owned by Jewish merchants and money-lenders who frequently built themselves stone houses at Norwich, Lincoln and elsewhere, because they were both rich and in special need of protection against anti-semitic riots. The house at St Martin-at-Palace-Plain was not a Jew's dwelling, however, but was probably the property of the cathedral priory and used by an official involved in its provisioning. The upper part of the building was reconstructed in the later fifteenth century and much of it survived until 1962 when, sadly, it was demolished at a time when the value of Norwich's rich heritage of historic buildings was less widely appreciated than it is today. There has been a more positive approach to conservation in recent years, however, and excavated remains of the undercroft can be seen in the basement of the new law courts on the site.[35]

There is little evidence from archaeology in Norwich for the twelfth–thirteenth-century buildings inhabited by the poorer classes of the urban population, but they were probably little different from those of the fourteenth century in being very simply constructed. On the Alms Lane site,[36] located on the periphery of the medieval town, two buildings of c. 1300 were only detectable from the remains of their clay floors, suggesting that they were no more than c. 5.5m (18ft) by 3.5m (11 ft 6 ins). They may have had clay walls or slight timber frames based on beams laid directly on the ground, although a third building had clay sills to reduce the problems caused by rot. The infill of the walls would have been of wattle and clay, the roofs thatch.

The smallest medieval dwellings in Norwich and elsewhere would probably have had a single room, although a more common plan had two rooms with a hall/kitchen partitioned from the parlour. To understand these humble buildings great care is required in excavation as little more than the floors may survive. Typically, surfaces were made of clay or beaten earth and were covered with rushes or straw. As a surface became worn and uneven it was patched up and replaced, so creating a build-up of thin floor layers interleaved with occupation deposits which usually contain fragmented pottery and other artefacts which can provide crucial evidence for the use of the rooms. At Alms Lane, for example, although the buildings were probably structurally similar to dwellings, one had a floor covered with a deposit including charred germinated barley, which may indicate a brew house, and the other two buildings were probably smithies because of slag on the floors.

If we now turn our attention to the dwellings of the members of the upper social echelons of the thirteenth–fourteenth centuries, we find that some of the best recently excavated examples come from in and around the High Street in Hull which runs along the west bank of the river of that name (see Figure 6.3). Preservation of the remains of this period, the first century or so of the town's existence, is good because they were buried during episodes of deliberate dumping, probably to cope with rising river level. Although it is not readily apparent today, the High Street (formerly Hull Street) was a prime residential as well as business location at this time when merchants preferred to live over the shop. Access to the quay on the river frontage was by a series of staithes, and excavation on Chapel Lane Staith revealed a very fine fourteenth-century timber waterfront comparable to those from London.[37]

The location of some of the staithes can still be identified in Hull, but there is now only one medieval timber-framed building which is to be found in Scale Lane. While enemy action was responsible for some destruction, old Hull has largely been the victim of civic redevelopment since the Second World War. The pace of this quickened in the early 1970s culminating in preparation for the South Orbital Road Scheme which, as Peter Armstrong, sometime Field Officer with the museum, put it:

> with a perversity born of innocence maximised the menace to the archaeological survival of not only thirty medieval tenements, but the fourteenth-century Gate of Myton within the circuit of the town wall together with later outlying defences, the medieval Guildhall and Gaol complex and part of the Blackfriars monastery.[38]

The imminence of this threat led, as in similar circumstances elsewhere, to the establishment in 1975 of a full-time archaeological organisation, known as the Humberside Archaeological Unit, to serve not only Hull itself, but the historic town of Beverley and the new county.

A distinctive feature of Hull's archaeology is the extra dimension provided by excellent documentary sources (see p. 18).[39] Together they have provided two splendid examples of how buildings may illustrate upward social mobility.[40] In the first instance it is known that in the late thirteenth century a property on Blackfriargate (formerly Monkgate) was owned by Simon Wytelard (see Figure 6.3, 3). At this time he occupied a relatively modest building, essentially rural in style. The principal posts rested on stone pads, which protected them from rotting, but the technique was less sophisticated than the use of sill walls which spread the roof load more effectively. In plan the building was divided into a large central hall with just one small room at each end, and it lay with its long axis parallel to the street. As a new town, Hull had yet to grow to the point where pressure on space demanded that houses be arranged gable end to the street. In the early fourteenth century, perhaps after the acquisition of the property by Nicholas de Swanland, a major rebuilding took place employing chalk and rubble footings below sill walls of brick into which limestone blocks were set to bear the main posts (see Figure 2.1). In plan a central range

184

was flanked by two wings at right angles to the street. In the east wing was the main hall with, perhaps, additional private rooms on the first floor, and in the west wing was the kitchen. This was a typical house of a merchant who may not have been in highest rank, but was benefiting from the town's growing commercial success, stimulated in part by provisioning the king for his Scottish wars.

A more marked rise in the world is probably indicated by the excavated buildings in a property on the more prestigious High Street (see Figure 6.3, 4). In the late thirteenth century this was owned by one John de Ousefleet who probably had an unremarkable timber-framed building with its long axis parallel to the street and two projecting rear wings; finds of leather scraps suggested a cobbler was among the residents. In the early fourteenth century, however, documentary evidence of a change of title appears to coincide with a major redevelopment of the property featuring the earliest use of brick in a private house in Hull (see Figure 6.8). As we have noted (see p. 168), brick was used in Holy Trinity and in the town walls at this time and its use in a house may be as much an assertion of status as a recognition of any merit in the material. In plan the building probably had two wings, separated by a central passage, each of which had its long axis at 90 degrees to the street. It is likely that there was an imposing gabled façade comparable, perhaps, to that of the brick-built fifteenth-century St Mary's Guildhall in Boston. Excavation suggests that the south wing was residential, since hearths were found, and new standards of comfort are again indicated by a generous internal garderobe pit. In the pit were eighteen date stones which are the first recorded examples from an English medieval site. Fig seeds and grape pips also suggest a taste for the imported luxuries which passed through the port of Hull. The north wing, without hearths, was probably a warehouse where commodities from the owner's activities on the adjacent, and graphically named, Rottenherring Staith were stored.

While Hull is an example of a late medieval port which was booming, Chester is an example of one which, due to silting of the River Dee, was doomed to decline. This decline was, however, to ensure the survival of a unique form of urban development currently being researched by survey and excavation.

One of the great glories of Chester today is the city walls. On the north and east sides of the circuit they are on the line of the Roman fortress and incorporate a good deal of Roman masonry, while on the west and south sides the surviving parts are medieval extensions of the Roman circuit to the banks of the Dee. Within the walls there are, as the twelfth-century monk Lucan put it in *De Laude Cestrie* ('In Praise of Chester'): 'two excellent straight streets in the form of the blessed Cross, which through meeting and crossing themselves, then make four out of two, their heads ending in four gates'.[41] On the east, south and west streets (today Eastgate Street,

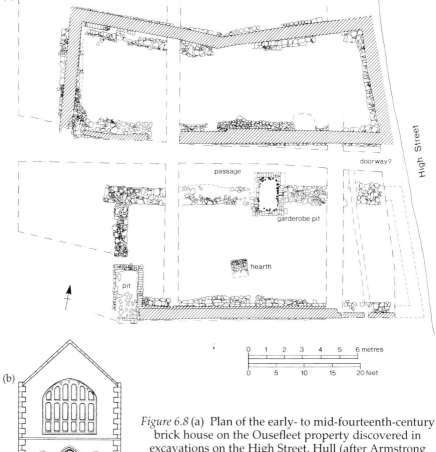

(a)

High Street

doorway?

passage

garderobe pit

hearth

pit

0 1 2 3 4 5 6 metres

0   5   10   15   20 feet

(b)

Figure 6.8 (a) Plan of the early- to mid-fourteenth-century brick house on the Ousefleet property discovered in excavations on the High Street, Hull (after Armstrong and Ayers 1987, Figure 20). (b) Sketch to show conjectured appearance of the façade (drawn by Glenys Boyles)

Westgate Street and Bridge Street) are The Rows, buildings, typically of several storeys, which incorporate stretches of continuous covered galleries at first-floor level (see Figure 6.9).[42] These galleries are public rights of way connecting shops which are situated above other shops at street level. The buildings themselves are now of various dates and architectural styles, but the origin of The Rows appears to lie in the late thirteenth century, judging by the earliest timberwork identified using the techniques of dendrochronology. The development of this unique streetscape may be connected with the stimulus to building – and the local economy generally – when Edward I used Chester as a base for his campaigns of conquest in Wales.

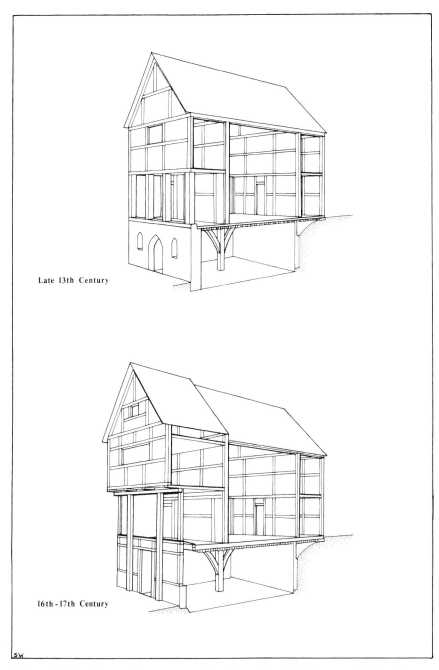

Late 13th Century

16th-17th Century

SW

Figure 6.9 The Chester Rows: a reconstruction of the building recorded in advance of demolition at 12 Watergate Street (drawn by Simon Ward, Grosvenor Museum, Chester)

Since medieval times the ownership of the ground floor and upper storeys appears to have been in separate hands and this has been an important reason for the complex structural history of the Row buildings. A common feature, however, is a stone-built and vaulted undercroft which is not dug down into the hard underlying rock, but runs with a level floor back into the ground whose surface slopes up from the streets. Above the undercroft the buildings are timber-framed, but many alterations, involving the addition of extra storeys, and a variety of plans are known. The crucial factor in understanding The Rows, however, appears to be the slope at ground level. Excavations at 12 Westgate Street[43] showed that in the medieval period the ground surface at the back of the property was at first-floor level not street level. This was due to the survival of remains of the Roman fortress headquarters building which had formed a mound on the north side of the east–west street. The street itself had presumably remained in use since Roman times at more or less its original level. If, as is likely, the Westgate Street site is typical, then it may be suggested that at a time of medieval growth the two-tier landscape lent itself to a new method of maximising the number of shops on the street frontage. Rather than being planned at one time, however, it is currently believed that The Rows gradually evolved in the late thirteenth and fourteenth centuries and became fossilised in the fifteenth century when the loss of port facilities caused Chester's economic decline.

The urban economy – of sheep and ships

In late twelfth-century London William FitzStephen observed that: 'those engaged in business of various kinds, sellers of merchandise, hirers of labour are distributed every morning into their several localities according to their trade'. Other documentary sources also indicate that the medieval period saw a gradual move towards a division of towns into zones occupied principally, but not exclusively, by the practitioners of a particular craft, or group of related crafts, who would sell their products in adjacent street markets. It is not easy to detect this specialisation process from purely archaeological evidence, however, as most medieval crafts were what we might call 'low tech'. They used little fixed equipment and recycled waste materials if at all possible which means that their archaeological traces are minimal. Important exceptions, however, are crafts which used water and heat which usually required substantial structural facilities. As far as water-using crafts are concerned, ready availability determined the location of the workshops and dwellings of practitioners. This has been very strikingly illustrated by the Lower Brook Street site in the low-lying centre of Winchester which in medieval times was criss-crossed by numerous streams.[44] The site was excavated over a ten-year period in one of the most extensive investigations ever of urban medieval tenements. A long sequence of building was examined, dating from the tenth to the fifteenth centuries, during which time the frontage of Lower Brook Street – medieval Tanner Street – became more and more crowded and extensions into the backyards took place in the usual manner.

The earliest evidence for craft activity consisted of two eleventh-century timber-lined pits perhaps used in tanning, hence the original street name. From the twelfth century onwards both archaeology and documentary sources suggest that the properties excavated were occupied by people engaged in cloth finishing. Three houses had dyeing workshops on the street frontage with heated vats whose locations were indicated by numerous hearths and other emplacements. Fulling is, as we have already noted (p. 162), attested by the site of the tenting frames. Timber-lined water channels brought water from the adjacent brook, but in the early to mid-thirteenth century when the building footings were, as elsewhere, converted to stone, substantial water channels built of chalk were constructed (see Plate 6.5).

While cloth manufacturing was responsible for many medieval fortunes, an equally important source of wealth for the super-rich in medieval urban society, which also served to establish the dominance of certain towns in the urban hierarchy, was inter-regional and international trade. We have noted that the evidence for overseas trade in the late Anglo-Saxon town appears small relative to that in the middle Anglo-Saxon *wic* sites, but during the eleventh century a revival took place, based largely, perhaps, on wool and cloth exports, which in turn allowed increasing imports of raw materials and manufactured goods. In archaeological terms the network of trading contacts of both England and Scotland is primarily indicated by the growing number and range of foreign pottery which until the fifteenth century came largely from northern France and the Low Countries. Although waterfront sites have been examined in Bristol (see pp. 196–7), Hull and elsewhere, the most spectacular evidence for the facilities serving sea-borne and river-borne trade comes from London. The medieval timber waterfronts, like their Roman and Anglo-Saxon predecessors, have been found in good condition at a number of sites in the City.[45]

The Anglo-Saxon waterfront had been characterised principally by reinforced beaching positions, but between the mid-twelfth and early thirteenth century a new form of waterfront structure emerged employing vertical timber revetments (see Plate 6.6). These were not quays as such, to which ships would be drawn up, but were intended to keep the banks sound. Large ships were moored in the centre of the river channel and served by small boats carrying goods to and from the shore where the quays were furnished with stairs and occasionally cranes. As in the Roman

Plate 6.5 Lower Brook Street, Winchester – remains of a thirteenth-century fuller's house with a chalk-lined water channel in the foreground (Photograph: Winchester Research Unit)

period the line of the waterfront was regularly moved out into the channel, in part to allow replacement of rotted timbers and in part to overcome the problem of silting. The second element in this consolidation and

190

reclamation process was the dumping of material, consisting largely of domestic refuse, behind the revetments in order to support them. These waterfront dumps have produced substantial quantities of artefacts whose date of disposal, if not manufacture, can be closely and independently determined by dendrochronology of the revetment timbers. The dumps are therefore a unique and invaluable source of information on such everyday objects as pottery, shoes, clothing and knives, as used in the capital over some 200 years (see Figure 6.10).[46]

The waterfront structures reveal a gradually increasing sophistication of carpentry techniques developing from the use of supporting braces both in front of and behind the uprights to a system in which only back bracing was required. As in dwellings and other buildings of the day, prefabrication for rapid erection on site was an advance mastered by the late fourteenth century. Equally important is the evidence that the process of innovation on the waterfront seems to have lain in the hands of individuals, and there is no suggestion of concerted rebuilding episodes on the waterfront organised by municipal authorities. Each property owner was responsible for his own stretch of waterfront and maintained it as he thought fit.

The commercial riverfront of medieval London extended from Baynard's Castle in the west to the Tower in the east and running behind it was Thames Street, on the line of the Roman riverside wall which had probably been demolished by the end of the twelfth century. As in Anglo-Saxon times the riverfront complemented the market streets which ran east–west along the line of Cheapside and Eastcheap. Connecting them, and no doubt continually busy with the movement of goods, were north–south streets. By the twelfth century they had probably reached their full complement and many of them survive today. South of Thames Street there was a maze of small lanes. While some of them are of Anglo-Saxon origin, many others were created in medieval times frequently taking their names from those of adjacent property owners or occupants.[47] Trig Lane, for example, was adjacent to the property of the Trig family, fishmongers in the late fourteenth century.

As the commerce on the waterfront grew, so did the need for regulation by the municipal authorities and the desire for a cut of the profits on the part of the Crown (see Plate 6.7). Documentary sources suggest that the first permanent and systematic exaction of customs dues, as we would understand them, on wool, woolfells and hides, took place in 1275. The location of the first Custom House is unknown, but in 1382 a new one was built on the waterfront near the Tower. Although it was substantially destroyed in the nineteenth century, the Old Custom House excavations in 1973 did locate some stone footings of the fourteenth-century building.[48] Of particular interest, however, was an enclosed timber drain which led from the building to the river. This is clearly referred to in a royal patent

Plate 6.6 London's medieval waterfront at the Thames Exchange site: a front-braced timber revetment of the twelfth century looking north (i.e. from the contemporary river bank). The free-standing timbers in the foreground were probably part of a scissor-braced jetty which served warehouses in the waterfront area (scale 0.50m / c.1 ft 6ins) (Photograph, Museum of London)

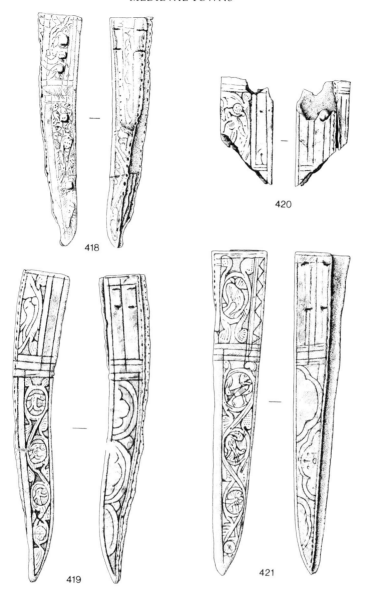

Figure 6.10 Early- to mid-fourteenth-century leather knife scabbards from the Thames waterfront, London (drawn by Nick Griffith, Museum of London)

document of 1383 in which an extra sum was given to John Churchman, builder of the Custom House:

> because he has added a small chamber for a latrine and a sollar over the counting house 38 feet long and $21\frac{1}{2}$ feet broad containing two

Plate 6.7 The taxman is always with us: twelfth-century ivory seal matrix of Snarrus the toll collector – note the coins and the bag (diameter 38mm/c. 1½ ins). Ebor Brewery site, York (Photograph: York Archaeological Trust)

chambers and a garret as a further easement for the customs controllers and clerks.

Chief controller at this time was Geoffrey Chaucer, much better known, of course, as the author of the *Canterbury Tales*, but archaeology somehow brings the life of the great man closer to us when we realise that some of his daily stooling probably passed along this humble drain to medieval London's main sewer, the River Thames.

Competition between the ports of the south and east coasts, including London, Hull and Southampton, had been fierce in the thirteenth and early fourteenth centuries, but by Chaucer's time London had started to pull ahead of the others in importance. Less involved in rivalry with the capital, however, was the western port of Bristol near the mouth of the River Avon (see Figure 6.11). In showing how water-borne commerce might be a motor of medieval urban growth, the recent archaeological programme organised by the City Museum is of the greatest interest.[49]

The seeds of Bristol's medieval prosperity were probably sown in the

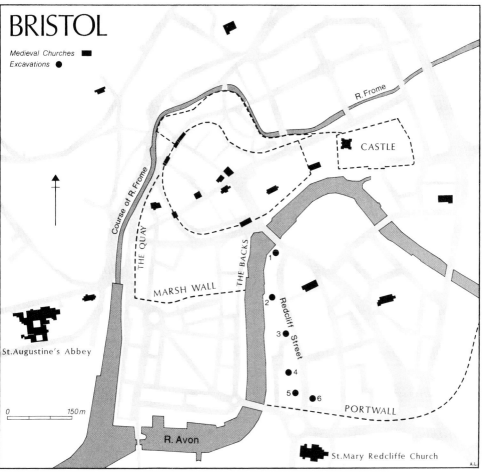

Figure 6.11 Plan of medieval Bristol showing principal topographical features and excavation sites on the Redcliffe waterfront (City of Bristol Museum and Art Gallery)

Key: 1 Bristol Bridge (1981); 2 127–9 Redcliffe Street, Dundas Wharf (1982–3); 3 110–12 Redcliffe Street (1985–6); 4 95–7 Redcliffe Street (1983–5); 5 80–7 Redcliffe Street (1980); 6 Port Wall Lane (1982)

late Anglo-Saxon period.[50] There was certainly an important mint with six moneyers from the time of King Cnut (1016–35), and at the time of the Domesday Book Bristol yielded tax revenue as high as London or York. Bristol's importance was confirmed by the siting of a Norman castle at the east end of a spur of raised ground between the rivers Frome and Avon on which the late Anglo-Saxon town had grown up. There were two main thoroughfares, which can still be identified on the ground, one running north–south (Broad Street and High Street) and the other east–west (Corn Street and Wine Street). No Anglo-Saxon defences are known, but in the twelfth century the so-called 'Inner Wall' was built[51] as the first of a series of defensive circuits which reflect the prosperity and civic pride of Bristol. The site of the original bridge after which Bristol, originally Brigstowe, was named is unknown, but it may have been on the north-west side of the town, across the Frome, forming a link with another early settlement nucleus around what became the Augustinian priory (now the cathedral). Excavations on the south-east side of the modern Bristol Bridge which crosses the Avon have produced no evidence for Anglo-Saxon occupation.

The Anglo-Saxon quays were probably on the north bank of the Avon, but in the twelfth century the focus of commercial activity moved across the river to Redcliffe.[52] This was not part of Bristol at this time and the riverfront along Redcliffe Street was developed as a speculative venture by the lords of the manor, the Berkeley family. Another source of wealth in Redcliffe was the presence of the Temple Fee (the name still preserved in that of the railway station at Temple Meads), an area on its east side acquired for a residence by the crusading Knights Templar in 1145.

In 1247 the River Frome was diverted to join the Avon to the south-west of the original confluence and this allowed ships to use deep-water quays on the north-west side of Bristol. In the thirteenth century also the defended area was extended out to the new line of the Frome and re-claimed areas to the south-west were enclosed with the 'Marsh Wall'. Redcliffe continued to flourish after the river diversion and in the mid-thirteenth century was also dignified with defences known as the 'Port Wall'. On sites on Redcliffe Street archaeology has, as in London, found evidence for the outward movement of the river banks, which in this case was probably intended to gain new land in a crowded urban environment as well as to combat silting. An important item of medieval Bristol's trade was, of course, cloth, and clothworking in the form of fulling and dyeing evidently took place close to the riverside in the thirteenth–fifteenth centuries, judging by discoveries at 87 Redcliffe Street.[53] A number of well-preserved vat bases were found (see Plate 6.8) and, as at Lower Brook Street, Winchester, the presence of an adjacent water supply was crucial, as shown by an extensive drain system. At the Dundas Wharf site deposits behind the riverfront produced well-preserved remains of a number of plants used by medieval dyers including dyer's greenweed, madder (red) and weld (yellow).[54]

Another site of great interest was 95–7 Redcliffe Street[55] where, after reclamation in the late twelfth and early thirteenth centuries, a stone river wall was constructed in the mid-thirteenth century with a fine slipway running through it which was used for drawing up small boats (see Plate 6.9). Subsequently in the fourteenth century the wall line was moved out

Plate 6.8 Fourteenth-century dyer's stone vat-base and drain from 80–7 Redcliffe Street, Bristol (longer scale 2m/c. 6 ft 6 ins) (Photograph: City of Bristol Museum and Art Gallery)

15m (50 ft) into the channel, while a complex of stone buildings was erected between river and street. The property may have been owned in this and the following century by the Canynge family, great merchant aristocrats of Bristol, who grew rich on the cloth and wine trade. Still surviving on the site is a stretch of rather battered stone wall reputedly part of a tower built by the younger William Canynge (1402–74) to glorify his property.

The lives of the prosperous urban merchant class have also been revealed by archaeology in medieval Southampton.[56] Excavations have

Plate 6.9 Bristol's medieval waterfront at 95–7 Redcliffe Street: thirteenth-century river wall and slipway from the west – i.e. from the contemporary river bank (foreground scale 2m/c. 6 ft 6 ins) (Photograph: City of Bristol Museum and Art Gallery)

shown that there was rapid growth in the later twelfth century and a building boom which produced some fine stone houses such as 'Canute's Palace' and 'King John's House' whose remains can still be seen. The principal thoroughfare which joined the quays to the south with the north gate, known today as the Bargate, was English Street, now the High Street. Many of the merchants had properties fronting on to it, often with stone vaults below their houses for the storage of goods including the wine from Gascony on which much of their wealth depended. Examples of these vaults still survive, including Quilter's Vault of c. 1270[57] which can be seen at the south end of High Street. There is also a vault at **58 French Street**,[58] a fine early-fourteenth-century timber-framed house recently restored and opened to the public by English Heritage. With its central hall open to the roof and smaller rooms at either end, it gives the visitor a very good impression of what a medieval merchant's dwelling was like to live in.

An insight into the private tastes of the merchant class came from the remains of a house in nearby Cuckoo Lane[59] which could be associated with a burgess of the town named Richard of Southwick (died c. 1290) because of the lucky find of his seal in a stone-lined rubbish pit. This pit had not been cleaned out for re-use, as was customary, because a fire had

Plate 6.10 Luxury table ware from Southampton: late-thirteenth-century Saintonge ware jugs from excavations (height c. 37cm/c. 1 ft 2 ins) (Photograph: Southampton City Museums)

caused it to be clogged with rubble leaving the contents intact. They included a range of household artefacts including imported glass from Italy, pewter tableware, imported ceramics, notably gaily painted Saintonge Ware from Gascony (see Plate 6.10), fashionable shoes, and luxury foods such as grapes, figs and walnuts. Most remarkable of all the finds, perhaps, was the skull of a monkey presumably brought back to England as a pet.

The estate of the holy church

Another significant find in Richard of Southwick's pit was a pair of ampullae or pilgrim badges showing that he had been to Canterbury to what was then England's holiest shrine of St Thomas à Becket (martyred in 1170). The ampullae of St Thomas and other saints' shrines are common archaeological finds (see Plate 6.11) and but one indication of the dominant role played by the ceremony and ritual of the Christian church in the lives of medieval townsfolk. This is also reflected in the amount of land occupied and owned by religious institutions in towns which included not only cathedrals and parish churches, but also monastic houses, friaries and hospitals. While archaeology can contribute to our knowledge of all these establishments, for the smaller and less well-endowed which are usually poorly documented, it may be virtually the only source.

Plate 6.11 Small lead ampulla (length 50mm/c. 2 ins). It would have contained holy water and depicts the murder of Thomas à Becket. Thames Exchange Site, London (Photograph: Museum of London)

The archaeology of the urban parish church has received considerable attention in recent years and is no longer merely a branch of art and architectural history. Excavation and survey in standing buildings have occurred in a number of towns, but particular interest attaches to the discovery of churches which went out of use during the medieval period as they offer a chance to study early developments in building form unencumbered by the late and post-medieval additions in surviving churches.

In the twelfth century the practice of church foundation by private landlords, which had created so many small churches in late Anglo-Saxon towns, came to an end. It is a characteristic, therefore, of towns founded or expanding rapidly in the twelfth and thirteenth centuries that they have relatively few churches, which are, at the same time, of relatively large size. Medieval Hull, for example, had only two churches and one of them, Holy Trinity, is the largest parish church in England. The end of private ownership and changing patterns of population, including the effects of the Black Death of the mid-fourteenth century, often led to the closure of parish churches in towns with large numbers inherited from earlier times, a process which culminated in a major programme of parish amalgamation and church closure in the sixteenth century.

A good example of a medieval redundant church is St Helen-on-the-Walls in Aldwark, York. It was made redundant in 1549–50, and after demolition its exact location was lost, only to be unexpectedly rediscovered in excavation in 1972.[60] The earliest documentary sources to refer to the church are twelfth-century, but excavation established that its origin lay in the tenth century when it was a rectangular stone building only 7.8m (25 ft 6 ins) by 5.8m (19 ft). Like other churches founded on the northeast bank of the Ouse at this time, it was built north-east/south-west, rather than true east–west, to correspond to the alignment of the Roman fortress which still dominated the urban plan.

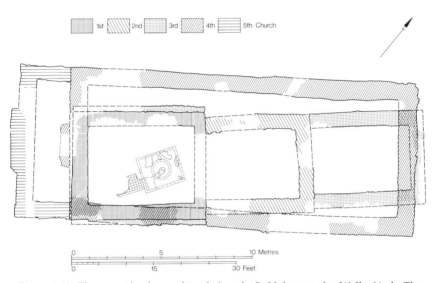

Figure 6.12 The growth of a medieval church: St Helen-on-the-Walls, York. The location of the Roman mosaic (p. 104) is shown in the centre (York Archaeological Trust)

St Helen's is amongst the smallest of pre-Conquest churches and throughout its history its relatively small size and simple plan reflect its position in one of York's poorer parishes. Nevertheless, the gradual expansion of the church (see Figure 6.12) as population rose is part of a pattern detectable in urban churches all over England. In the twelfth century a chancel was added and subsequently the earliest of many burials in the church was made. They were all of adult males who presumably belonged to the leading families in the parish. In the early fourteenth century there was a substantial rebuilding of the church with the chancel extended north-eastwards. A complete rebuilding, on a slightly different alignment, took place in the later fifteenth century, although the nave remained only 6m (19 ft 6 ins) wide and, unlike most other York churches, it had no aisles. The final archaeologically determined alteration was a short extension of the nave in the late fifteenth or early sixteenth century shortly before abandonment.

An incursion of major monastic houses into towns began in the late eleventh century forming part of the great revival of monasticism in Norman England. This was based both on the cathedrals and on Benedictine houses such as St Mary's Abbey in York (founded 1088–9) with its great walled precinct on the west side of the city. Particularly attracted to the urban environment, however, were the Augustinian Canons who often acquired redundant churches and their lands. The first Augustinian house, dated to the late eleventh century, was at St Botolph's, Colchester where much of the church survives, but the Augustinian priory which is best known archaeologically is the recently excavated St Gregory's, Canterbury where the complete plan of the buildings and most of the cemetery were uncovered (see Plate 6.12).[61]

In 1070 Lanfranc was installed by William the Conqueror as Archbishop of Canterbury and began rebuilding the cathedral, but this was only the beginning of his construction programme. In c. 1085, outside the north gate of the town, Lanfranc built a new church dedicated to St Gregory, with a house of secular canons to care for the sick, destitute and aged in the Hospital of St John on the opposite side of Northgate Street. The excavated plan of the earliest church revealed two chapels – one on each side of the chancel – which had probably accommodated the remains of St Eadburg and St Mildred. The trouble taken to remove them from churches elsewhere is, as at Winchester Cathedral, evidence for the potency of relics in medieval Christianity, which would in turn encourage the financial contributions of pilgrims. In the 1120s St Gregory's became a house of Augustinian canons and a new church was built. Among the interesting features found in excavation were stone-lined channels in the chancel which were intended to make the priors' singing more resonant. On the north side of the church, excavations revealed the complete plan of the cloister surrounded by the usual monastic buildings. On the south side was the cemetery containing some 1,250 burials.

St John's Hospital, with its fine sixteenth-century gatehouse, still survives today as an alms house. More remarkable is the survival of the north end of the Norman dormitory and contemporary *necessarium* (lavatory) – in use until 1948 – which, although in urgent need of repairs, still boasts some original fittings including drains and seating.

Urban monasteries were usually located on the periphery of the settled area, partly because they were latecomers to the scene and partly because they wished to avoid the distractions of the secular world. The former is

Plate 6.12 'Big is beautiful' in urban archaeology: St Gregory's Priory, Canterbury, during excavation, looking east; the church is on the right of the site, peppered with grave pits. Northgate Street runs left to right in the foreground with St John's Hospital at the bottom of the picture opposite the excavation (Photograph: Canterbury Archaeological Trust)

also true of the friaries which were to make such an impact on the medieval town from the 1220s and 1230s onwards, and their sites were often on marginal land, such as riverside marshes. The friars were not, however, concerned to avoid the distractions of town life, rather they sought to carry their ministry into the streets and relied on the generosity of the townspeople for their livelihood. Because of this the date at which the friaries were founded and the number which a town acquired are good guides to late medieval urban fortunes; large towns like London, York and Bristol each had at least four by 1300.[62]

In their early years the friars may have rejoiced in their sites on poor land, as they deliberately sought an austere and self-denying regime, but, paradoxically, because of their spiritual purity they soon attracted large endowments as townsmen turned to them and away from what was considered a corrupt and venal parish clergy. Royal favour was bestowed on certain houses; Edwards I, II and III all stayed and held Parliaments at the house of the Franciscans (Greyfriars) at York. In the circumstances the friars found it increasingly difficult to maintain high standards and fourteenth-century literature, including Chaucer's *Canterbury Tales*, is full of references to their vices. The grandeur of their buildings was criticised by Matthew Paris, a thirteenth-century monk, who noted that 'they rivalled royal palaces in height'. There was also considerable tension between the friars and parish priests, especially over burial rights, an important source of income for both parties.

Very few friary buildings, of course, survive in Britain today as most were destroyed following Henry VIII's dissolution of the monasteries, but there have been numerous excavations on friary sites in recent years, and by studying building form and plan, along with rubbish dumps and burials, it is possible to get a new perspective on what is already known from historical sources.

As an example of one of the most extensively explored friaries we may look at the house of the Dominicans (Blackfriars) at Oxford[63] discovered, along with the Franciscan friary, in the important series of excavations in the south-western suburbs of the medieval town (see Figure 6.13). The Dominicans' first site had been accommodated within the walls, but, with expansion, the move to a new site was made in c. 1245. Although spacious, it was also very damp being close to the Thames, and to ensure the building stood up in the marshy ground the land was artificially built up and the footings made unusually deep. The plan included a church with a large nave suitable for preaching to a sizeable congregation, and a long narrow chancel to accommodate the friars themselves. In common with most other friaries, a particularly distinctive feature would probably have been a tower at the junction of nave and chancel above an open passage. This gave townsfolk easy access to the Great Cloister around which were the friars' quarters. Beyond, there was another cloister surrounded by

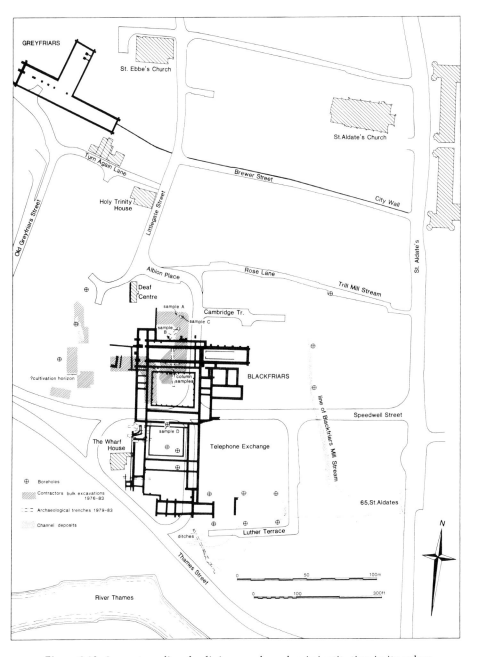

Figure 6.13 A great medieval religious and academic institution in its urban context; plan of the Blackfriars, Oxford, based on excavations in advance of new development. The site of the Greyfriars and City Wall is also shown (Oxford Archaeological Unit)

workshops and other buildings. The great size of the Oxford Dominican house reflects its role as the training centre of the English province, where large numbers of visiting friars had to be accommodated, and this in turn reflects the growing status of medieval Oxford as England's first university town.

Burials were excavated in four distinct areas, which presumably indicate differences in the status of the deceased. Male skeletons found in the west cloister alley were probably friars, but there were also, to judge by the presence of women, examples of lay burials in the cemetery to the north of the church and at the west end of the nave. The ratio of males to females was 5:1, as at the Franciscan friary, which may reflect the large number of single men in holy orders who were associated with the university. At the west end of the chapter house were children, probably of high social rank.

Medieval townsfolk – a skeleton crew

Organic remains suggest that the Oxford Blackfriars had a cleaner environment and better diet than the inhabitants of the tenements at The Hamel and elsewhere in the town. Similar advantages may have been enjoyed by those able to afford burial here and in other urban friaries. This may account for the evidence of a greater physical robustness and life expectancy in the skeletons of both friars and layfolk than is perhaps usual in medieval populations, which was revealed at the Franciscan friary in Hartlepool.[64] By way of a conclusion to the scientific analysis of some 150 skeletons it was remarked that: 'One can imagine these inhabitants of medieval Hartlepool enjoying life and not spending their time imagining where the next day's food and energy would come from.'

For a more balanced view of the human physiology of the period, however, we must turn to skeletal material from church cemeteries, a number of which have been excavated in recent years including those at St Nicholas Shambles (on the GPO Newgate site), London[65] with 234 individuals, and at St Helen-on-the-Walls, York,[66] with 1,041 individuals. The London burials were largely of the eleventh and twelfth centuries; the earliest burials at York may be eleventh-century or earlier and the latest fifteenth-century. Dating individual burials at both sites was, however, difficult unless they could be related to church building phases, as continual grave-digging tends to destroy distinct stratigraphy. It remains difficult, therefore, to plot changes in the physiology of medieval populations.

At both sites the graves themselves were simple shallow pits with little evidence for coffins. Markers were presumably rare as there was considerable intercutting of graves; the job of a sexton in the cramped graveyards of medieval towns must have been rather unpleasant as one was always likely to dig up the partly decomposed remains of previous interments (see Plate 6.13). There was little evidence for the segregation of burials on the basis of sex or age, although at St Helen's the majority of the burials in the church were of older males, probably the more senior and prosperous members of the community. The extra expense of burying wives in the church probably made many families think twice.

Life expectancy was clearly low in our terms; neither London nor York produced many individuals over c. 45 and at York it is suggested that 27 per cent of the population died as children, that is under 14–15 years, with the greatest risk being between 6 and 10 years. No doubt infant mortality was also high, but the skeletons rarely survive in the disturbed ground of medieval churchyards. As we saw in the Roman period there was some difference in life expectancy between males and females, which again favoured the former; at York 56 per cent of adult women and 36 per cent of men were probably dead by their mid-thirties. In terms of physical appearance some interest attaches to skull shape. York and other sites suggest the medieval population was largely brachycephalic, that is heads were relatively short (from forehead to back) and broad whereas in Anglo-Saxon or Anglo-Scandinavian cemeteries, including that found at York Minster, skulls were largely doliocephalic, that is heads were relatively long and narrow. The reason for this distinction is unknown but a gradual change in skull shape in the medieval period has also been observed elsewhere in Europe.[67]

The cause of death of most medieval townsfolk was probably infectious diseases, such as cholera, typhoid and tuberculosis, which swept through the crowded tenements in great epidemics – the plague known as the Black Death of 1348–50 is only the most well known. These diseases, however, leave little trace on the skeleton. For women there was, as in earlier times, the added hazard of childbirth, and there are several examples from London and York of female skeletons accompanied by new or still-born infants. Given the popular image of the medieval period as one of frequent wars and general lawlessness, one might expect good evidence for violent deaths in males. Many wounds would not, of course, leave a trace on the skeleton, but nevertheless it is perhaps surprising that few examples of heavy blows were found in either the York or London cemeteries; the fractures which were detected were mostly on the arms and were probably the result of accidents in the home or at work. Some inferences regarding physical well-being were made on the basis of tooth loss; on average adults had lost 3–4, but probably due more to gum disease than caries which is particularly associated with consumption of refined sugar in more recent times. Osteoarthritis was common in both London and York bodies, especially on the spine, and must indicate that there were numerous disabled people with a limited capacity for work. In the London cemetery, however, there was evidence of self-inflicted injury in

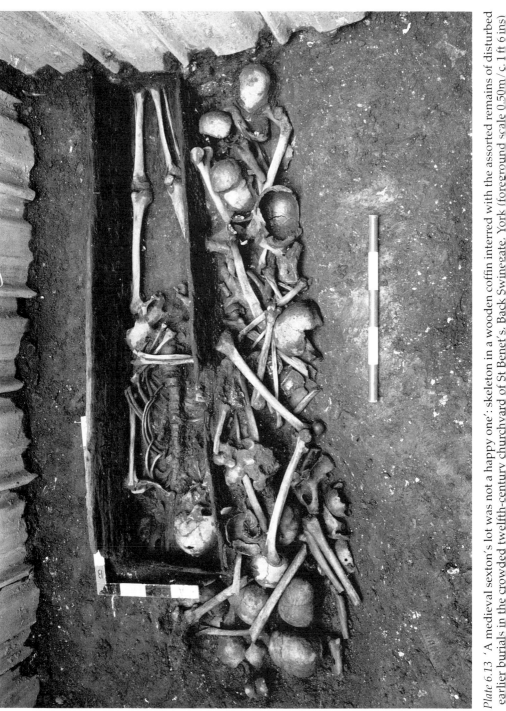

Plate 6.13 'A medieval sexton's lot was not a happy one': skeleton in a wooden coffin interred with the assorted remains of disturbed earlier burials in the crowded twelfth-century churchyard of St Benet's, Back Swinegate, York (foreground scale 0.50 m / c. 1 ft 6 ins)

examples of toe deformities, probably due to wearing tight, but fashion-able, shoes.

Medieval towns – dirty, diseased and dynamic?

The Black Death brings us to a watershed in the history of British towns and to the end of the principal period covered by this book. It is difficult to estimate the proportion of townsfolk who died between 1348 and 1350, but it may have been as much as a third or more in places. Archaeology does not usually, however, find mortal remains which can be securely associated with the plague, but at the Royal Mint site in East Smithfield, London, one of two special cemeteries created to relieve pressure on churchyards during the Black Death was excavated.[68] As well as ordinary graves with a single individual, two mass burial trenches were found, one 67m (73 yds) long and the other 125m (136 yds) metres long, both densely packed with skeletons.

In addition to its immediate effects, the Black Death, and subsequent recurrences of plague, caused major social and economic disruption in Britain, and the population may not have recovered its pre-plague level until about 1500.[69] Towns were less affected than the countryside because of continuing immigration, but most of them did decline in prosperity and fifteenth-century historical sources contain many appeals to the king for a reduction in tax burden. Archaeology usually confirms that there was relatively little new urban building in the period except in a few centres like Norwich and York which bucked the trend. While population may have been thinner on the ground in places like Lincoln and Winchester, however, it is difficult to detect this from archaeological evidence alone. The extent of pit-digging and refuse-tipping, for example, cannot be treated as a reliable indicator since it appears that from the late fourteenth century onwards refuse disposal customs were changing with increasing use of both re-usable stone-lined pits and communal tips outside town centres. The evidence for a markedly reduced number of pits in the late medieval period need not, therefore, indicate reduced occupation.

Our brief archaeological journey down the medieval town streets of Britain is now at an end. While we have seen some fine buildings, it is, perhaps, the all-embracing squalor that would have struck the visitor from our own time most forcibly. As confirmation of the latter, if confirmation were needed, we have the words of Edward III on his visit to York in 1332 when he ordered the streets to be cleaned on account of 'the abominable smell abounding in the said city more than in any other city in the realm from dung and manure and other filth and dirt wherewith the streets and lanes are filled and obstructed'.

Plague affected rich and poor alike because all classes continued to live side by side in the mid-fourteenth century in a way which would largely disappear in Tudor times. Archaeology makes us aware, however, of very marked differences in life style between rich and poor. Medieval town life may have been communal, with its shared pits, wells and party walls, but it was not egalitarian; there was no question of the sort of big happy family conjured up by 'medieval banquets' of our own day. At the top of the heap there were some of the most dynamic and ambitious entrepreneurs in the country, winners in a very uncertain economic climate who had benefited from what little opportunity there was for social mobility. From the eleventh century onwards these urban aristocrats began to use their wealth to build houses of considerably greater size and sophistication than those of their fellows and to assert their rank and status ever more markedly in other ways, from the consumption of imported foodstuffs to burial in prominent reserved plots inside churches and religious houses.

Much more numerous in our town street would be the lowly artisans and labourers, of both sexes, who were always in danger of slipping into the ranks of the destitute with hopes of privilege and wealth unrealised. The near complete reliance of medieval townsfolk on local trade meant that they were peculiarly vulnerable to fluctuations in the fortunes of agriculture in their region whose failures would not only depress business but bring the constant danger of famine. At the same time, periods of poverty would create an increased susceptibility to the diseases for which there was no cure or solace but a grave whose site was quickly forgotten. We should not, however, allow the filth or the oppressive shadows of death and poverty to confirm our prejudices surrounding the word 'medieval' as indicating backwardness, ignorance and barbarity. What ultimately strikes one most about townsfolk of the period is, on the one hand, the intense vitality, which allowed them to overcome the disadvantages of circumstance, and, on the other, the intellectual curiosity which lay behind even the simplest developments in building technique, sanitation, town planning or fortification. It is a curiosity only matched by that of the archaeologist who painstakingly brings this hidden world to our attention.

7

POSTSCRIPT – PRESENTING THE PAST TO THE PUBLIC

A glance at many of the plans in this book, those of Perth (see Figure 6.4) or York (see Figure 4.1) for example, will immediately show what a small proportion of Britain's towns have been examined archaeologically. While urban archaeology has come a long way in a relatively short period of time, a vast array of problems remains for future investigation. Some of these are of a general nature covering all periods of the past, others are more specific to particular periods or localities. It is crucial therefore to continue to monitor and record the deposits and structures which are disturbed or threatened daily in historic towns. At the same time, however, the necessary access and funding cannot be taken for granted in an environment where there is continual pressure for new development. This may be subject to cyclical highs and lows, but in the long term it seems that our destination is an all-engulfing urban hive which will probably mean the end of the town itself as we know it.

While local and national governments appear, at present, to have accepted the claims of archaeology as a legitimate consideration in the planning process, there can be no guarantee, in the absence of further legislation, that developers will remain the main funding agency of urban archaeology or that planning authorities will retain the will to make them face their responsibilities. As these words are written an article in the *Museums Journal*[1] on the provision of archaeological services by the Museum of London notes the 'controversial plans to integrate its three archaeology departments into a largely self-financing trading organisation, selling its expertise to planning authorities and building developers'. This expertise will be 'charged at cost and with cash up front, a bill which could run into millions of pounds a year for developers'. The museum's director is quoted as warning: 'There are sites of archaeological importance where costs will be more than the developer can absorb.'

In the absence of a public subsidy, it would appear that the long-term future for archaeology in London is, to say the least, uncertain. To secure such a subsidy, however, archaeology, like most other cultural activities in this country, will have to continue to justify its existence to government and to the public at large. In a sense archaeology has an advantage over many other activities because it can offer the layman a chance to participate with a minimum of knowledge and training. Most archaeological units encourage new volunteers and it is quite possible for them to make a crucial find which, while not necessarily altering the course of history, can fundamentally affect the interpretation of a site. There can be few other professions where the inexperienced newcomer can make a comparable contribution. The number of people who have the time and energy to get actively involved in archaeology in a non-professional capacity is, however, restricted and the majority of the public will consume the subject in a more passive way. It is vital, therefore, that people are encouraged to do this in a way which is stimulating both to the intellect and the imagination. The belief that there is no more effective way of understanding urban archaeology than seeing a building or monument set in its surrounding townscape has led me to make a point of referring to examples which have been the subject of recent archaeological investigation. I do this in the hope that the reader will be encouraged to seek them out. Equally rewarding, I believe, is a visit to an excavation in progress, and most archaeological units make the effort to open their sites to visitors where possible (see Plate 7.1). Public relations have come a long way from an unfortunate episode at Wroxeter c. 1860 described as follows:

> When hypocaust K was first uncovered one hundred and twenty pillars were counted standing in it, but these were shortly afterwards ruthlessly overthrown by a party who came to inspect the ruins of the Roman city. The visitors expecting to see more than met their view, declared the whole affair a 'a sell'; when, arrived at this hypocaust, Bill and Jack, to make up for their disappointent, amused themselves Englishmen-like, by shying at its interesting group of pillars, until everyone of these were laid low.[2]

Archaeology in towns does, of course, present a rather particular and intense sort of public relations challenge. The very fact that they are working in densely populated surroundings means that field archaeologists are continually on show, not only to fellow scholars, but also to all sorts and conditions of men and women whose shared history is under examination. Archaeologists therefore have a very varied responsibility to their fellow citizens, at one extreme seeking to present serious academic information and at the other providing a form of street theatre. I have found, however, that far from being onerous, the exercise of this responsibility is enormously stimulating and there can be no more rewarding task than presenting the rudiments of a very rigorous intellectual discipline to a mass audience.

Experience tells us that it is only the power of public interest which will create a climate of opinion at all levels of society favourable to

Plate 7.1 Visitors welcome and a message from our sponsors: Leadenhall Court Site, London, 1985

archaeological endeavour. While the pursuit of knowledge for its own sake is a fine thing, it is, if I may mix my metaphors, 'bums on seats' which focus minds, especially those of people with money to spend. It is this sort of thinking which led the York Archaeological Trust to take advantage of the great interest shown by over 1 million visitors to the excavation at 16–22 Coppergate between 1976 and 1981, and create the Jorvik Viking Centre, an attempt to present the results of the dig in the heart of the Anglo-Scandinavian town in a serious, yet entertaining, manner.

A visit to the Centre essentially involves travelling in a small electric car, with a built-in commentary tape, through a reconstructed street in tenth-century York where houses, people, animals and objects are based as far as possible on the archaeological evidence studied by specialists. The tape also allows you to hear people speaking in some approximation of the Norse language of the day. The visitor is shown how the reconstruction was arrived at when the car travels through a re-creation of a frozen moment in the life of the original excavation. Models of staff are seen at work on digging and recording the actual timbers surrounded by reconstituted archaeological layers. Mock-up laboratories show how finds are conserved and organic material is studied and are followed by a conventional museum display of finds from the site. Finally there is a shop selling replica objects and other souvenirs.

The primary objective of the Jorvik Viking Centre is to communicate an archaeological message to as many people as possible, and the results speak for themselves with close to 900,000 visitors per year since 1984. By the success of the Centre it is hoped that a more educated climate of understanding about the past can be created which can only be good for the care and preservation of its remains in York and elsewhere. Equally important, the Centre is extremely profitable; the Trust raises in excess of £1 million per annum which goes to fund further archaeological projects in the city. This is vital now that there is relatively little public funding and the Trust must otherwise rely on funds from site developers to pay for excavations.

Another consciousness-raising venture by York Archaeological Trust is the Archaeological Resource Centre (ARC) which aims to introduce the visitor to archaeological techniques by a hands-on approach. In the pleasant ambience of a restored church one can learn about such things as sorting pottery, ancient crafts, and computer techniques, guided by trained staff. Recently voted Archaeological Museum of the Year, the ARC, and a comparable venture in Lincoln, seem certain to win more converts.

York is, perhaps, in a unique position to create facilities like the Jorvik Viking Centre because of its huge tourist numbers. It is unlikely that anything quite comparable will be attempted again, either in York itself or elsewhere, but it is to be hoped that archaeologists will continue to look for new opportunities to present their work to the public. If there is one lesson we can learn from the study of urban archaeology and history down the ages it is that, whether you were a Roman *negotiator*, an Anglo-Scandinavian blacksmith or medieval wool exporter, success depended on taking your chances when they came along.

NOTES

For unpublished excavations readers are referred to the annual excavation reports in *Britannia* and *Medieval Archaeology,* the journals of, respectively, the Society for the Promotion of Roman Studies and the Society for Medieval Archaeology.

Reports on excavations also appear in:

Current Archaeology, available bi-monthly on subscription from 9 Nassington Road, London NW3 2TX

Archaeology in Britain, available annually from the Council for British Archaeology (CBA), 112 Kennington Road, London SE11 6RE. The CBA also publishes *British Archaeological News* which reports monthly on current issues in archaeology.

Rescue News, available three times a year to members of Rescue – The British Archaeological Trust, from 15A Bull Plain, Hertford, SG14 1DX.

In addition, most of the major urban archaeological units publish an annual report on their excavations and research.

Abbreviations for primary sources in translation

Agricola	Tacitus, *The Agricola and the Germania,* translated by Mattingly (1970).
Ammianus Marcellinus	*The Later Roman Empire,* translated by Hamilton (1986).
Annals	Tacitus, *The Annals of Imperial Rome,* translated by Grant (1977).
Bede	*A History of the English Church and People,* translated by Sherley Price (1968).
Histories	Tacitus, *The Histories,* translated by Wellesley (1975).

Preface

1. English Heritage 1990, p. 16.

1 Archaeology in towns

1 Marsden 1980, pp. 198–205; B. Jones 1984, p. 122.
2 S. Reynolds 1977, p. 62.
3 See Wacher 1974, pp. 1–35 for a sound introductory discussion of the status of Roman towns in a British context.
4 Beresford 1967, p. 273. A burgage, or burgage plot, was an urban property held

in return for a yearly rent which did not require the rendering of feudal labour dues. The tenant was known as a burgess.

5 Braudel 1988, p. 181.
6 For further discussions of how a town may be defined, see Biddle 1976, pp. 98–100 for an archaeologist's approach, and see the preface to S. Reynolds 1977, for a historian's approach.
7 For the Roman period see Burnham and Wacher 1990, especially chapter 1 for the problems of definition. For settlement classification in medieval and later periods see Braudel 1988.
8 R.A. Hall 1984a, p. 53.
9 Wright 1872.
10 For the history of archaeology at Silchester see Boon 1974.
11 Hassall 1986, p. 115; 1987, pp. 2–3.
12 Wheeler 1920; 1921.
13 Wheeler and Wheeler 1936.
14 Frere 1983, p. 1.
15 C.F.C. Hawkes and Hull 1947, p. 23.
16 Grimes 1968.
17 Frere and Stow 1983; Frere 1984a.
18 Maitland Muller 1949; 1950; Morton forthcoming.
19 Frere 1972; 1983; 1984b.
20 Rogerson and Dallas 1984.
21 Jope 1952–3; 1958; Pantin 1958.
22 Platt and Coleman-Smith 1975.
23 Biddle 1964, p. 188.
24 Hammond 1978.
25 Biddle 1983, p. 94.
26 B. Jones 1984, 57–61; Horsman and Davison 1989.
27 For the foundation of Rescue see B. Jones 1984, pp. 50–4; Barker 1987.
28 Heighway 1972; Biddle 1974.
29 Biddle and Hudson 1973.
30 Department of the Environment 1990, *Planning Policy Guidelines*, no. 16, clause 25.
31 *British Archaeological News*, June 1986; Hobley 1987.

2 Urban archaeologists at work

1 Biddle 1984, p. 26; Vince 1984, p. 311.
2 Pilbrow 1871.
3 For a good summary of documentary sources for towns see Palliser 1975.
4 For a collection of papers discussing the *Notitia Dignitatum* see Goodburn and Bartholomew (eds) 1976.
5 D. H. Hill 1969.
6 Stenton 1934; Brooke and Keir 1975, pp. 112–21.
7 Horrox 1978.
8 Urry 1967.
9 Norwich Survey 1980; Atkin, Carter and Evans 1985.
10 Keene 1984.
11 Bailey 1988; King 1990; *Medieval Archaeology* 1988, p. 257.
12 *Medieval Archaeology* 1989, p. 202.
13 Biddle and Hudson 1973.
14 Carver 1980; 1987.
15 Garrod and Heighway 1984, p. 1.

16 Wheeler describes his approach to excavation in *Archaeology from the Earth* (1954).

17 Frere 1972, p. 6.

18 Biddle 1965, p. 245.

19 For a history of excavation and recording techniques see Harris 1989, especially chapters 3 and 4.

20 Wheeler 1954, p. 67.

21 Atkinson 1942, p. 126.

22 For a sound description and discussion of archaeological recording techniques see Barker 1982. The best how-to-do-it-on-site manual is produced by the Museum of London, Department of Urban Archaeology, edited by Spence 1990.

23 Barker 1982, pp. 197–203, and for a full discussion see Harris 1989.

24 Hillam and Morgan 1981; Morgan 1982; Hillam 1985.

25 The essential field guide to archaeological conservation is Rescue's publication *First Aid for Finds* edited by Watkinson (1987).

26 Tylecote 1986, chapters 6–8.

27 For a useful group of general papers on the subject of environmental archaeology see A.R. Hall and Kenward (eds) 1982.

28 A.R. Hall, Kenward, Williams and Greig 1983.

29 For a recent study of animal bones from urban contexts see O'Connor 1989a.

30 Noddle 1975, pp. 332–4.

31 Watts and Rahtz 1985, p. 128.

32 See Brothwell 1981 for a sound introduction to the study of human bones from archaeological sites.

33 W. White 1988, p. 29.

34 Stirland 1985, p. 54.

35 Wheeler 1956, p. 100.

36 Ayers 1988.

37 P. Crummy 1984, pp. 42–4.

38 Wheeler 1954, p. 2.

3 Early Roman towns

1 Wacher 1974, pp. 39–40.

2 *The Agricola* XXI.

3 *Britannia* 1981, pp. 364–5.

4 For a brief introduction to the late Iron Age in the Colchester area see Dunnett 1975, pp. 15–27.

5 Piggott 1985, p. 147; P. Crummy 1979a, pp. 3–4.

6 For excavations at Sheepen see C.F.C. Hawkes and Hull 1947; Niblett 1985.

7 For the temples of Roman Colchester see P. Crummy 1980.

8 For a stimulating brief account of Colchester's archaeological history see P. Crummy 1979a.

9 Morant 1748.

10 *Annals* XIV.

11 Morant 1748, p. 20.

12 Wheeler 1921.

13 *Annals* XIV.

14 Wheeler and Laver 1919; Wheeler 1920.

15 Dunnett 1967.

16 For reports on recent archaeological discoveries at Lion Walk and other sites in Colchester see N. Crummy 1983; N. Crummy (ed.) 1987; P. Crummy 1977;

1982a; 1984; 1985; 1988. For Culver Street see Crummy forthcoming; *Britannia* 1982, p. 371; 1985, pp. 245–6; 1986, pp. 405–6.

17 Hurst 1988.
18 In the introduction to P. Crummy 1975.
19 Bidwell 1979; 1980; Henderson 1988.
20 M.J. Jones and Gilmour 1980; M.J. Jones 1985. For an overview of recent archaeology of all periods in Lincoln see Vince and Jones 1990.
21 Drury 1984.
22 P. Crummy 1982b.
23 *The Agricola*, XVI.
24 *Annals*, XIV.
25 Wheeler 1956, p. 59.
26 P. Crummy forthcoming.
27 P. Crummy 1987; 1988–9.
28 For recent general surveys of Roman London covering most of the points discussed here see Marsden 1980; Merrifield 1983; J. Hall and Merrifield 1986; Hobley 1986; Perring 1991. See also The Ordnance Survey's *Londinium: A Descriptive Map and Guide to Roman London* (1983). Annual summaries of work in London are published in *The London Archaeologist*.
29 *Annals* XIV. For the social composition of early Roman London see T. Williams 1990.
30 For the river regime in Roman London see Milne 1985 (especially chapter 7); Milne, Battarbee, Straker and Yule 1983.
31 For Roman roads in Southwark see Graham and Hinton 1988; for other recent work in Roman Southwark see P. Hinton (ed.) 1988; Heard, Sheldon and Thompson 1990; Mills and Whittaker 1991. For irregular Claudian coins see Hammerson 1978a; 1988; Kenyon 1987.
32 For a good history of the Roman archaeology of London see Marsden 1980, chapter 9.
33 Reproduced in J. Hall and Merrifield 1986, inside front cover, and on the cover of the Ordnance Survey's *Londinium: A Descriptive Map and Guide to Roman London* (1983).
34 Roach Smith 1859.
35 Wheeler 1930, p. 4.
36 Grimes 1968.
37 *News Chronicle*, 23 September, 1954.
38 Museum of London 1989, p. 8.
39 Biddle and Hudson 1973, p. 51.
40 Sites at Aldgate, Chapman and Johnson 1973; 94–7 Fenchurch Street and 9 Northumberland Alley, Rivière and Thomas 1987; *Britannia* 1987, p. 334.
41 Including sites at 5–12 Fenchurch Street, Hammer 1985; Watling Court and GPO Newgate, Perring 1985; 36–7 King Street, *Britannia* 1986, p. 407; Rowsome 1987.
42 Marsh and West 1981.
43 I am grateful to Gustav Milne for this suggestion.
44 Milne and Wootton 1990.
45 C. Maloney 1991.
46 Perring 1987; Perring and Roskans 1991.
47 Tatton-Brown 1974; 1975.
48 The most recent studies of the Roman waterfront are by Milne 1985 and Brigham 1990a.
49 Dillon 1988; 1989; Mills and Whittaker 1991, pp. 159–61.
50 Marsden 1974.

51 Described as 'the sauce of the Thames' by N. Bateman in Milne 1985, p. 87.
52 Marsden 1987.
53 Brigham 1990b.
54 Marsden 1975.
55 J. Maloney 1988; *Britannia* 1988, p. 461; Museum of London 1989, pp. 11–12.
56 For discussion of the Huggin Hill discoveries and controversy see Orton 1989; Rowsome and Wooldridge 1989.
57 Marsden 1976.
58 *Independent*, 6 May, 1989.
59 *Independent*, 15 April, 1989.
60 Rowsome and Wooldridge 1989.
61 For the most recent discussion of dark earth in London see McPhail 1981; 1983; Yule 1990.
62 For discussion of the sequence and circumstances of *civitas* capital foundation see Wacher 1974; Todd 1989; Wacher 1989.
63 Wheeler and Wheeler 1936; Frere 1972; 1983; 1984b.
64 Frere 1983, p. 19.
65 For archaeological discoveries in Roman Canterbury see Frere 1962; Wacher 1974, p. 178–95; Blagg 1982; Frere and Stow 1983; Bennett 1984; 1989. See also the Canterbury Archaeological Trust Annual Reports, annual summaries in *Archaeologia Cantiana*, and the Ordnance Survey's *Historical Map and Guide to Roman and Medieval Canterbury* (1990).
66 Frere and Stow 1983; Frere 1984a.
67 Frere 1970.
68 Tatton-Brown 1977.
69 77–9 Castle Street: *Britannia* 1978, p. 468.
70 3 Beer Cart Lane: *Britannia* 1980, p. 400.
71 69a Stour Street: *Britannia* 1981, p. 366.
72 Millett 1990, pp. 69–72
73 Walthew 1983.
74 Frere 1962, p. 12.
75 Linden Grove site: *Britannia* p. 323.
76 For excavations in Roman Winchester, see Biddle 1964–70; 1972; 1975a; 1983; Wacher 1974, pp. 277–88; Collis 1978; for burials see Clarke 1979.
77 The Hyde Street site will be published as a monograph of the Winchester City Museum.
78 Ross 1967, pp. 321–33.
79 Ross 1967, pp. 312–13.
80 Down and Rule 1971.
81 In archaeology the term 'cremation burial' is usually used to refer to a burial in which the body has been interred after burning, while the term 'inhumation burial' is usually used to refer to a burial in which the body has been buried unburnt (often surviving as a skeleton), although strictly speaking 'inhumation' should refer to all methods of placing human remains in the ground.
82 Whimster 1981.

4 Late Roman towns

1 For general surveys of archaeological discoveries in Roman York see RCHM 1962; Wacher 1974, pp. 156–77; Brinklow 1984; Ottaway 1984. See also *Interim*, the quarterly bulletin of the York Archaeological Trust.
2 *The Agricola*, XVII; *Histories*, III, 45.

3 Hope-Taylor 1971; Phillips 1975; Phillips and Heywood forthcoming.
4 Brinklow, Hall, Magilton and Donaghey 1986.
5 Radley 1972.
6 Wellbeloved 1842, p. 66.
7 Addyman and Rumsby 1971.
8 For an account of the early aims and discoveries of the York Archaeological Trust see Addyman 1974; 1975.
9 Carver, Donaghey and Sumpter 1978.
10 Ramm 1976.
11 Tomlin 1986.
12 Ottaway 1988; *Britannia* 1990, pp. 325–6.
13 Ottaway 1989.
14 *Independent*, 17 October, 1989; *Daily Telegraph*, 11 December, 1989.
15 Ottaway forthcoming; *Britannia* 1982, p. 349.
16 Pearson forthcoming; *Britannia* 1984, p. 282–3; *Britannia* 1985, p. 279.
17 *Britannia* 1987, pp. 373–4.
18 A.R. Hall and Kenward 1990.
19 For a review of the discoveries at the Queen's Hotel see Ottaway 1989; *Britannia* 1990, pp. 325–6.
20 For the controversy at the Queen's Hotel see R.A. Hall 1988a; Sheldon 1989.
21 See, for example, a letter from Albert Cowen, Chairman of York City Council Planning Committee under the heading 'Don't blame the Council' in *Yorkshire Evening Press*, 1 February, 1989.
22 Department of the Environment 1990, *Planning Policy Guidelines* no.16.
23 For a description of Septimius Severus' campaigns in Britain see Birley 1988, chapter 16.
24 RCHM 1962, p. 120 (inscription 57).
25 Crickmore 1984; Frere 1984c; M.J. Jones and Bond 1987.
26 Frere 1984b, pp. 33–54.
27 For Gloucester see Hurst 1986; for Lincoln see M.J. Jones 1980; for Exeter see Bidwell 1980.
28 For Chichester see Down 1988; for Cirencester see Brown and McWhirr 1966; 1967; McWhirr 1988, p. 83.
29 *Britannia* 1984, p. 318; *Britannia* 1985, p. 303.
30 Fulford 1984.
31 J. Maloney 1983.
32 Millett 1990, p. 140.
33 Thompson and Whitwell 1973; M.J. Jones 1980.
34 Colyer 1975; M.J. Jones 1990; forthcoming.
35 N. Reynolds 1979, pp. 85–6; Wacher 1979, p. 81.
36 Frere, Stow and Bennett 1982; Bennett 1989, pp. 126–8.
37 C. Hill, Millett and Blagg 1980.
38 Sheldon and Tyers 1983; Hillam and Morgan 1986.
39 Miller, Schofield and Rhodes 1986.
40 Brigham 1990a.
41 Brigham 1990b.
42 223–5 St Peter's Hill site: T. Williams 1989; forthcoming; *Britannia* 1982, p. 374.
43 For Southwark see Heard, Sheldon and Thompson 1990, pp. 611–15.
44 Hammerson 1978b.
45 At Paul Street, *Britannia* 1984, p. 318; *Britannia* 1985, p. 303; and Lower Coombe Street, *Britannia* 1990, p. 350.
46 Esmonde-Cleary 1989, pp. 72–4. See Reece 1980 for a stimulating, if extreme, view of the decline of towns in late Roman Britain.

47 Wacher 1974, pp. 408–10; Burnham and Wacher 1990, pp. 81–91.
48 For Roman archaeology in Cirencester see Wacher 1974, pp. 289–315; McWhirr 1981, pp. 28–37; Wacher and McWhirr 1982; McWhirr, Viner and Wells 1982; McWhirr 1986, pp. 21–58; 1988.
49 R.M. Butler 1971.
50 St Mary Bishophill Senior site, Ramm 1976; sites at Bishophill Junior and St Mary Bishophill Junior, Ottaway and Wenham forthcoming.
51 Brinklow and Donaghey 1986.
52 Magilton 1986.
53 For a review of the evidence for public buildings in the later Roman period see Mackreth 1987, pp. 138–40.
54 Fulford 1985.
55 Thomas 1981; Esmonde-Cleary 1989, pp. 120–8.
56 Boon 1974, pp. 173–84.
57 Gilmour 1979; Lincoln Archaeological Trust 1984, p. 30.
58 *Britannia* 1980, pp. 376–8.
59 P. Crummy 1987, p. 22; 1989; 1989–90.
60 Clarke 1979; MacDonald 1979.
61 McWhirr, Viner and Wells 1982.
62 Warwick 1968, p. 147.
63 Wells 1982, p. 135.
64 Wells 1982, p. 171.
65 *Ammianus Marcellinus*, XXVII.
66 J. Maloney 1980; 1983.
67 Parnell 1985.
68 Bartholomew 1982; Thompson 1983; Esmonde-Cleary 1989, p. 138.
69 Frere 1983, pp. 21–5.
70 Frere and Stow 1983, pp. 31–40; D.A. Brooks 1988; Bennett 1989, pp. 128–9.
71 Blockley 1986, pp. 206–7.
72 69a Stour Street site, *Britannia* 1981, p. 366.
73 Johns and Potter 1985.
74 Marlowe III/Rose Lane site see *Britannia* 1980, p. 400.
75 *Current Archaeology*, no. 80, pp. 272–3.
76 S.C. Hawkes 1982.
77 N.P. Brooks 1984, p. 25 and see chapter 2 for historical background to Anglo-Saxon Canterbury.
78 Bede I, 26.
79 Taylor and Taylor 1980, p. 143.
80 Biddle 1983, pp. 111–12.
81 Biddle 1975a, pp. 109–19.
82 Biddle 1983, pp. 115–19.
83 R.A. Hall forthcoming; Phillips and Heywood forthcoming.
84 Phillips and Heywood forthcoming.
85 Bede II, 14.
86 For summaries of recent work at Wroxeter see: Barker 1975; Wacher 1974, pp. 358–74; Webster 1975, pp. 56–73; Webster 1988; R. White 1990.
87 R. White 1990, p. 5.
88 For a review of the evidence for towns in the fifth century see D.A. Brooks 1986.
89 Wright 1872, p. 68.
90 Webster 1975, pp. 120–1.

5 Anglo-Saxon towns

1 Stenton 1971, p. 71.
2 For a discussion of the place name see Rumble 1980.
3 S. Reynolds 1977, pp. 24–7. For an introduction to the revival of towns in the seventh–eighth centuries see Hodges 1982; 1988.
4 For the history of archaeology in Hamwic see Morton forthcoming, and see also Crawford 1942; Maitland Muller 1949; 1950.
5 Addyman and Hill 1968; 1969.
6 Addyman and Hill 1969, p. 90.
7 *Current Archaeology*, no.79.
8 Addyman and Hill 1969, p. 89.
9 Holdsworth 1980, p. 1.
10 Holdsworth 1984, p. 335.
11 Brisbane 1988, p. 102.
12 Morton forthcoming, and for a brief popular account of archaeology in Hamwic see Pay 1987.
13 Andrews in preparation; *Medieval Archaeology* 1980, p. 222; 1981, p. 168; 1982, p. 184; 1983, pp. 178–9.
14 McDonnell 1989.
15 For a recent discussion of northern European trade AD 600–900 see Hodges 1982. For the correspondence between Offa and Charlemagne see Stenton 1971, pp. 220–1.
16 For the Hamwic pottery see Hodges 1981; Timby 1988.
17 Andrews and Metcalf 1984; Metcalf 1988.
18 Yorke 1982.
19 For the date of the Old Minster see *Bede*, III, 7 and the Anglo-Saxon Chronicle for 648. For reports on the excavations see Biddle and Quirk 1962; Biddle 1964–70, 1972; Kjølbye-Biddle 1986.
20 Biddle 1983, pp. 115–19.
21 J.H. Williams, Shaw and Denham 1985.
22 Barclay and Biddle 1990; S.C. Hawkes 1990.
23 Biddle 1976, pp. 112–14.
24 Wade 1988.
25 For the archaeology of middle Anglo-Saxon London see Biddle 1984; Vince 1984; 1988; 1990; Hobley 1986; Cowie and Whytehead 1989; Milne and Goodburn 1990.
26 *Bede* II, 3.
27 Biddle 1984; Vince 1984.
28 Milne and Goodburn 1990, p. 630.
29 For recent excavations in Anglian York see Kemp 1987; 1991, R.A. Hall 1988b; Tweddle forthcoming.
30 Whitelock 1955, p. 725.
31 Reproduced in Palliser and Palliser 1979.
32 Addyman, Pearson and Tweddle 1982; Tweddle 1984.
33 Binns, Norton and Palliser 1990.
34 Morris 1986; Briden and Stocker 1987, pp. 85–9.
35 RCHM 1972, xli; Moulden and Tweddle 1986, 10–11; Tweddle 1987; forthcoming.
36 *Yorkshire Gazette*, 8 December 1821.
37 O'Connor 1991.
38 'Happy town of Winchester' as described in the poem *Unum beati Swithuni miracolum*, BM Royal MS 15 c.vii, fol.125v; quoted in Biddle 1975b.

39 Referred to in *Unum beati Swithuni miracolum* (see above). Biddle and Keene 1977a, pp. 271–2.
40 *Medieval Archaeology* 1986, p. 149; 1990, p. 188.
41 Biddle 1983, pp. 121–2. For the topography of Anglo-Saxon Winchester see Biddle and Keene 1977b, pp. 449–69.
42 P. Crummy 1979b.
43 Biddle 1983, pp. 125–6.
44 Barlow, Biddle, von Feilitzen and Keene 1977.
45 Brooke and Keir 1975, pp. 120–43; Morris 1989, pp. 168–226.
46 For the documentary background see Quirk 1957; 1961. For the excavations see Biddle and Quirk 1962; Biddle 1964–70; 1972; 1986.
47 British Library additional manuscript 49598.
48 For recent excavations of the *Nunnaminster* see *Current Archaeology*, no. 102, pp. 204–7. Some remains are on view near the Guildhall.
49 D. Hinton, Keene and Qualmann 1981.
50 D.H. Hill 1969; Biddle and Hill 1971; Biddle 1976.
51 For a recent review of archaeology in towns in southern England including most of the burghal hidage towns see Haslam (ed.) 1984.
52 For the latest reviews of work in Oxford see Hassall 1986; 1987; Durham 1990.
53 Blair 1990.
54 Durham 1977.
55 Durham, Halpin and Palmer 1983.
56 Shoesmith 1982.
57 Carver 1980, pp. 3–7.
58 For recent summaries of the development of Anglo-Saxon Gloucester see Heighway 1984; 1987, pp. 154–6.
59 Mason 1985; Thacker 1988; Ward forthcoming.
60 Rahtz 1977.
61 J.H. Williams 1984.
62 For the historical background to Anglo-Saxon London see Brooke and Keir 1975; for excavations in late Anglo-Saxon London see Hobley 1986; 1988; Horsman, Milne and Milne 1988; Milne 1990; Milne and Goodburn 1990.
63 Dyson 1989.
64 Vince 1988; 1990.
65 Sites include Billingsgate Lorry Park, New Fresh Wharf, Thames Exchange and Vintry House, see Hobley 1988; Museum of London 1989; Milne and Goodburn 1990; *Medieval Archaeology* 1990, pp. 179–80.
66 Schofield 1984, pp. 21–2; Taylor and Taylor 1980, pp. 399–400.
67 Schofield 1984, pp. 40–2; Gem 1986.
68 Reproduced in Palliser and Palliser 1979.
69 Dolley 1986.
70 For early discussions of Anglo-Scandinavian York see Waterman 1959; Cramp 1967; Radley 1971.
71 Donaghey 1986; R.A. Hall 1986.
72 For the topography of Anglo-Scandinavian York see R.A. Hall 1978; 1984a, pp. 49–51; 1988b; 1988c; 1991.
73 Phillips 1985, pp. 44–6; Phillips and Heywood forthcoming.
74 A.R. Hall, Kenward, Williams and Greig 1983; Addyman and Hall 1991.
75 For a summary of the 16–22 Coppergate excavation see R.A. Hall 1984a. For the craft evidence see MacGregor 1978; Tweddle 1990.
76 Ottaway 1992.
77 Pirie 1986, pp. 33–7.
78 R.A. Hall 1984b. These timbers can now be seen in the Jorvik Viking Centre.

79 For bone combs from Anglo-Scandinavian sites in York see MacGregor 1978; 1982.
80 Walton 1989.
81 O'Connor 1989b.
82 A.K.G. Jones 1982; 1983.
83 A.R. Hall, Kenward, Williams and Greig 1983, p. 206.
84 O'Connor 1991, pp. 257–8.
85 Hey 1986, p. 39.
86 *Bede* II, 16. For Anglian Lincoln see R.A. Hall 1989, pp. 174–6.
87 For a summary of the late Anglo-Saxon archaeology of the five boroughs including Lincoln see R.A. Hall 1989.
88 Perring 1981.
89 Miles, Young and Wacher 1989.
90 Waterside North site, Chitwood 1989; *Medieval Archaeology* 1989, p. 202.
91 Blackburn, Colyer and Dolley 1983.
92 F. Hill 1990, p. 54.
93 Gilmour and Stocker 1986.
94 For recent work on the archaeology of Thetford see Davison 1967; Dunmore and Carr 1976; Rogerson and Dallas 1984.
95 Carter 1978, p. 175.
96 Atkin and Carter 1985.
97 *Medieval Archaeology* 1986, p. 159.
98 For Alms Lane see Atkin 1985; for Calvert Street see *Medieval Archaeology* 1990, p. 203.
99 Atkin, Ayers and Jennings 1983.
100 Ayers 1985.
101 Stirland 1985.

6 Medieval towns

1 O'Connor 1982, especially pp. 47–8.
2 Goodall 1990; Keene 1990.
3 For a good introduction to the subject of medieval towns see Platt 1976.
4 Addyman 1979.
5 Biddle 1966, p. 325.
6 Biddle 1967, pp. 267–8; 1968, pp. 275–80; 1986.
7 Phillips 1985, pp. 44–53; Phillips and Heywood forthcoming.
8 Whittingham 1980.
9 Ayers and Murphy 1983; Ayers 1988.
10 *Medieval Archaeology* 1989, p. 202; 1990, pp. 202–3.
11 Keene 1975, p. 77; for Hereford see Shoesmith 1982.
12 For Hull defences see Bartlett 1971; Hull City Council 1987; 1990.
13 For Southampton castle see Platt and Coleman-Smith 1975, pp. 176–86 and Oxley (ed.) 1986; for the town defences see Platt 1973, pp. 36–9, 113–16, 122–30; Platt and Coleman-Smith 1975, pp. 36–8, 142–9.
14 Stell 1988, p. 62. For Perth see Bogdan and Wordsworth 1978; Holdsworth (ed.) 1987, p. 17; Brann 1991 unpublished.
15 Frere and Stow 1983.
16 For recent work in Perth see Bogdan 1977; Bogdan and Wordsworth 1978; Scottish Urban Archaeological Trust 1984; Holdsworth (ed.) 1987.
17 For recent work in Aberdeen see Murray (ed.) 1982; Evans, Murray and Stones 1987.

18 For an introduction to Scottish medieval towns, largely from documentary sources, see Lynch, Spearman and Stell 1988.
19 For a detailed analysis of the plan of Perth see Spearman 1988.
20 *Medieval Archaeology* 1986, p. 191; 1987, p. 185; 1988, p. 303.
21 Ryder 1983.
22 Hodgson 1983.
23 For a good discussion of medieval suburbs see Keene 1975.
24 Bruce-Mitford 1939. For a review of the history of Oxford's archaeology see Hassall 1986.
25 Benson and Cook 1966.
26 Hassall 1969.
27 Hassall 1976.
28 Durham 1977.
29 Palmer 1980.
30 Robinson 1980.
31 Biddle 1967, pp. 264–5.
32 Schofield 1984, p. 75.
33 Ayers 1988.
34 Carter 1980.
35 By prior arrangement with the Norfolk Archaeological Unit.
36 Atkin, Carter and Evans 1985; Atkin and Margeson 1985.
37 Ayers 1979.
38 Armstrong 1980, p. 1.
39 Horrox 1978.
40 Armstrong and Ayers 1987.
41 Reproduced in Palliser 1980, pp. 6–7.
42 Brown, Grenville and Turner 1988; Ward 1988; Willshaw forthcoming.
43 Ward 1988.
44 Biddle 1964–70; 1972; 1975a.
45 Sites include Old Custom House, Seal House and Thames Exchange and Trig Lane. For a review of medieval waterfront sites in London see Milne 1981; Schofield 1981; Milne and Goodburn 1990. For Trig Lane see Milne and Milne 1982; for Thames Exchange see Museum of London 1990, pp. 26–7, *Medieval Archaeology* 1990, pp. 179–80.
46 Cowgill, de Neergaard and Griffith 1987; Grew and de Neergaard 1988.
47 Dyson 1989.
48 Tatton-Brown 1974.
49 For a good introduction to the archaeology of Bristol see Ponsford 1986. For a guide to sources for the archaeology of Bristol see Dixon 1987. Work on current sites is reported on in *Bristol and Avon Archaeology* and *Transactions of the Bristol and Gloucestershire Archaeological Society.*
50 For late Anglo-Saxon Bristol see Ponsford 1980, pp. 28–9; Watts and Rahtz 1985, pp. 15–16; Heighway 1987, pp. 149–52.
51 For the archaeology of Bristol's defences see Price 1979.
52 For recent work on the waterfront at Bristol see Ponsford 1981; 1985; B. Williams 1981; R.H. Jones 1986. For dendrochronology dating at Dundas Wharf see Nicholson and Hillam 1987.
53 B. Williams 1981.
54 J. Jones and Watson 1987, p. 154.
55 R.H. Jones 1986.
56 Platt 1973; Platt and Coleman-Smith 1975.
57 Walker 1977.

58 Platt and Coleman-Smith 1975, pp. 104–7.
59 Platt 1973, pp. 103–5; Platt and Coleman-Smith 1975, pp. 285–317.
60 Magilton 1980.
61 Hicks 1990; Hicks and Hicks 1991; Tatton-Brown 1990; *Current Archaeology,* no. 123, pp. 100–6.
62 For an introduction to the archaeology of friaries see L.A.S. Butler 1984.
63 Lambrick and Woods 1976; Lambrick 1985.
64 Birkett 1986.
65 W. White 1988.
66 Dawes and Magilton 1980.
67 I am grateful to Gill Stroud for this information.
68 Hawkins 1990.
69 Dobson 1977; Keen 1990, pp. 84–90.

7 Postscript – presenting the past to the public

1 Greene 1991. In December 1991 the Museum of London amalgamated its two archaeological units into the Museum of London Archaeological Services (MOLAS), which will be run on a self-financing basis.
2 Corbet Anderson 1867, p. 25.

BIBLIOGRAPHY

Primary sources in translation

Garmonsway, G.N. (1972), *The Anglo-Saxon Chronicle*, London, Everyman edition, Dent.

Grant, M. (1977), Tacitus, *The Annals of Imperial Rome*, London, Penguin (revised edition).

Hamilton, W. and Wallace-Hadrill, A. (1986), Ammianus Marcellinus, *The Later Roman Empire*, London, Penguin edition.

Mattingly, H. (1970), Tacitus, *The Agricola and the Germania*, London, Penguin edition (revised by S.A. Handford).

Sherley-Price, L. (1968), Bede, *A History of the English Church and People*, London, Penguin edition (revised by R.E. Latham).

Wellesley, K. (1975), Tacitus, *The Histories*, London, Penguin (revised edition).

Secondary sources

Addyman, P.V. (1974), 'York, the anatomy of a crisis in urban archaeology', in P. Rahtz (ed.) (1975), *Rescue Archaeology*, London, Penguin, pp. 153–62.

——(1975), 'Excavations in York', 1972–73: first interim report, *Antiquaries Journal*, vol. 54, pp. 200–31.

——(1979), 'Vernacular buildings below the ground', *Archaeological Journal*, vol. 136, pp. 69–75.

Addyman, P.V. and Black, V.E. (eds) (1984), *Archaeological Papers from York Presented to M.W. Barley*, York, York Archaeological Trust.

Addyman, P.V. and Hall, R.A. (1991), 'Urban structures and defences', *The Archaeology of York*, vol. 8, no. 3, London, CBA.

Addyman, P.V. and Hill, D.H. (1968), 'Saxon Southampton: a review of the evidence, part 1', *Proceedings of the Hampshire Field Club and Archaeological Society*, vol. 25, pp. 61–93.

——(1969), 'Saxon Southampton: a review of the evidence, part 2', *Proceedings of the Hampshire Field Club and Archaeological Society*, vol. 26, pp. 61–96.

Addyman, P.V., Pearson, N.F. and Tweddle, D. (1982), 'The Coppergate Helmet', *Antiquity*, vol. 56, pp. 189–94.

Addyman, P.V. and Rumsby, J. (1971), *The Archaeological Implications of Proposed Development in York*, London, CBA.

Andrews, P. (in preparation), 'Excavations at Six Dials', *Excavations in Hamwic*, vol. 2, CBA Research Report, London, CBA.

Andrews, P. (ed.) (1988), 'The coins and pottery from Hamwic', *Southampton Finds*, vol. 1, Southampton, Southampton City Museums.

Andrews, P. and Metcalf, D.M. (1984), 'A coinage for King Cynewulf of Wessex', in D.H. Hill and D.M. Metcalf (eds), 'Sceattas in England and on the Continent: the seventh Oxford symposium on coinage and monetary history', *British Archaeological Reports, British Series*, no. 128, Oxford.

Armstrong, P. (1980), 'Excavations in Scale Lane/Lowgate 1974', Hull Old Town Report Series, no. 4, *East Riding Archaeologist*, vol. 6.

Armstrong, P. and Ayers, B. (1987), 'Excavations in High Street and Blackfriargate', Hull Old Town Report Series, no. 5, *East Riding Archaeologist*, vol. 8.

Atkin, M. (1985), 'Excavations on Alms Lane', in M. Atkin, A. Carter and D.H. Evans, 'Excavations in Norwich, 1971–8, part 2', *East Anglian Archaeology*, vol. 26, Gressenhall, Norwich Survey, pp. 144–260.

Atkin, M., Ayers, B. and Jennings, S. (1983), 'Thetford-type ware production in Norwich', in P. Wade-Martins (ed.), 'Waterfront excavation and Thetford ware production, Norwich', *East Anglian Archaeology*, no. 17, Gressenhall, Norfolk Archaeological Unit, pp. 61–97.

Atkin, M. and Carter, A. (1985), 'General Introduction', in M. Atkin, A. Carter and D.H. Evans, 'Excavations in Norwich, 1971–8, part 2', *East Anglian Archaeology*, vol. 26, Gressenhall, Norwich Survey, pp. 1–9.

Atkin, M., Carter, A. and Evans, D.H. (1985), 'Excavations in Norwich, 1971–8, part 2', *East Anglian Archaeology*, vol. 26, Gressenhall, Norwich Survey.

Atkin, M. and Margeson, S. (1985), *Life on a Medieval Street*, Norwich, Norwich Survey.

Atkinson, D. (1942), *Excavations at Wroxeter, 1923–27*, Oxford, Birmingham Archaeological Society.

Ayers, B. (1979), 'Excavations at Chapel Lane Staith, Hull Old Town Report Series, no. 3', *East Riding Archaeologist*, vol. 5.

——(1985), 'Excavations within the north-east bailey of Norwich Castle, 1979', *East Anglian Archaeology*, vol. 28, Gressenhall, Norfolk Archaeological Unit.

——(1988), 'Excavations at St Martin-at-Palace-Plain, Norwich, 1981', *East Anglian Archaeology*, vol. 37, Gressenhall, Norfolk Archaeological Unit.

Ayers, B. and Murphy, P. (1983), 'A waterfront excavation at Whitefriars Street car park, Norwich, 1979', in P. Wade-Martins (ed.), 'Waterfront excavation and Thetford ware production, Norwich', *East Anglian Archaeology*, no. 17, Gressenhall, Norfolk Archaeological Unit, pp. 1–60.

Bailey, J. (1988), *The Brooks, Winchester: The First Year of Excavation*, Winchester, Winchester City Council and Cultural Resource Management.

Barclay, K. and Biddle, M. (1990), 'Gold working: archaeological evidence', in M. Biddle (ed.), 'Object and Economy in Medieval Winchester', *Winchester Studies*, vol. 7.2, Oxford, Oxford University Press, pp. 75–6.

Barker, P. (1975), 'Excavations at the baths basilica at Wroxeter 1966–74: interim report', *Britannia*, vol. 6, pp. 106–17.

——(1982), *Techniques of Archaeological Excavation*, London, Batsford.

——(1987), 'Rescue: Ante natal, birth and early years', in H. Mytum and K. Waugh (eds), 'Rescue archaeology – what's next?', *Department of Archaeology, University of York, Monograph*, no. 6, pp. 7–10.

Barlow, F., Biddle, M., von Feilitzen, O. and Keene, D.J. (1977), 'Winchester in the early middle ages: an edition and discussion of the Winton Domesday', *Winchester Studies*, vol. 1, Oxford, Oxford University Press.

Bartholomew, P. (1982), 'Fifth-century facts', *Britannia*, vol. 13, pp. 261–70.

Bartlett, J. (1971), 'The medieval walls of Hull', *Hull Museums Bulletin*, vols 3 and 4.

Bennett, P. (1984), 'The topography of Roman Canterbury: a brief reassessment', *Archaeologia Cantiana*, vol. 100, pp. 47–56.

——(1989), 'Canterbury', in V. Maxfield (ed.), 'The Saxon Shore', *Exeter Studies in History*, vol. 25, pp. 118–29.

Benson, D. and Cook, J. (1966), *City of Oxford Redevelopment: Archaeological Implications*, Oxford, City of Oxford.

Beresford, M.W. (1967), *New Towns of the Middle Ages*, London, Lutterworth.

Biddle, M. (1964), 'Excavations at Winchester 1962–3, second interim report', *Antiquaries Journal*, vol. 44, pp. 188–219.

——(1965), 'Excavations at Winchester 1964, third interim report', *Antiquaries Journal*, vol. 45, pp. 230–64.

——(1966), 'Excavations at Winchester 1965, fourth interim report', *Antiquaries Journal*, vol. 46, pp. 308–32.

——(1967), 'Excavations at Winchester 1966, fifth interim report', *Antiquaries Journal*, vol. 47, pp. 251–79.

——(1968), 'Excavations at Winchester 1967, sixth interim report', *Antiquaries Journal*, vol. 48, pp. 250–84.

——(1969), 'Excavations at Winchester 1968, seventh interim report', *Antiquaries Journal*, vol. 49, pp. 295–328.

——(1970), 'Excavations at Winchester 1969, eighth interim report', *Antiquaries Journal*, vol. 50, pp. 277–326.

——(1972), 'Excavations at Winchester 1970, ninth interim report', *Antiquaries Journal*, vol. 51, pp. 93–131.

——(1974), 'The future of the urban past', in P. Rahtz (ed.) (1975), *Rescue Archaeology*, London, Penguin, pp. 95–112.

——(1975a), 'Excavations at Winchester 1971, tenth interim report', *Antiquaries Journal*, vol. 55, pp. 96–126, 295–337.

——(1975b), 'Felix Urbs Winthonia: Winchester in the age of monastic reform', in D. Parsons (ed.), *Tenth Century Studies*, Chichester, Phillimore, pp. 123–40.

——(1976), 'Towns', in D.M. Wilson (ed.), *Anglo-Saxon England*, London, Methuen, pp. 99–150.

——(1983), 'The study of Winchester, archaeology and history in a British town', *Proceedings of the British Academy, London*, vol. 69, pp. 93–135.

——(1984), 'London on the Strand', *Popular Archaeology*, vol. 6, no. 1 (July), pp. 23–7.

——(1986), 'Archaeology, architecture and the cult of saints in Anglo-Saxon England', in L.A.S. Butler and R.K. Morris (eds), 'The Anglo-Saxon Church', *CBA Research Report*, no. 60, London, CBA, pp. 1–31.

Biddle, M. and Hill, D. (1971), 'Late Saxon planned towns', *Antiquaries Journal*, vol. 51, pp. 70–85.

Biddle, M. and Hudson, D. (1973), *The Future of London's Past*, Worcester, Rescue.

Biddle, M. and Keene, D.J. (1977a), 'Winchester in the eleventh and twelfth centuries', in F. Barlow, M. Biddle, O. von Feilitzen and D.J. Keene, 'Winchester in the early middle ages: an edition and discussion of the Winton Domesday', *Winchester Studies*, vol. 1, Oxford, University Press, pp. 241–448.

——(1977b), 'General survey and conclusions', in F. Barlow, M. Biddle, O. von Feilitzen and D.J. Keene, 'Winchester in the early middle ages: an edition and discussion of the Winton Domesday', *Winchester Studies*, vol. 1, Oxford, Oxford University Press, pp. 449–508.

Biddle, M. and Kjølbye-Biddle, B. (1969), 'Metres, areas and robbing', *World Archaeology*, vol. 1, pp. 208–19.

Biddle, M. and Quirk, R.N. (1962), 'Excavations near Winchester Cathedral, 1961', *Archaeological Journal*, vol. 119, pp. 150–94.

Biddle, M. (ed.) (1990), 'Object and economy in medieval Winchester', *Winchester Studies*, vol. 7.2, Oxford, Oxford University Press.

Bidwell, P.T. (1979), 'The legionary bath-house and basilica and forum at Exeter', *Exeter Archaeological Reports*, vol. 1, Exeter, Exeter City Council and Exeter University.

——(1980), *Roman Exeter: Fortress and Town*, Exeter, Exeter Museums.

Binns, J.W., Norton, E.C. and Palliser, D.M. (1990), 'The Latin inscription on the Coppergate Helmet', *Antiquity*, vol. 64, pp. 134–9.

Birkett, D.A. (1986), 'The human burials', in R. Daniels, 'The excavation of the church of the Franciscans, Hartlepool, Cleveland', *Archaeological Journal*, vol. 143, pp. 291–8.

Birley, A.R. (1988), *The African Emperor, Septimius Severus*, London, Batsford.

Blackburn, M, Colyer, C. and Dolley, M. (1983), 'Early medieval coins from Lincoln and its shire, c. 770–1000', *The Archaeology of Lincoln*, vol. 6, no. 1, London, CBA.

Blagg, T.F.C. (1982), 'Roman Kent', in P.E. Leach (ed.), 'Archaeology in Kent to AD 1500', *CBA Research Report*, no. 48, London, CBA, pp. 51–60.

Blair, J. (1990), 'St Frideswide's monastery: problems and possibilities', in J. Blair (ed.), *St Frideswide's Monastery at Oxford*, Gloucester, Alan Sutton pp. 221–58.

Blockley, P. (1986), 'Excavations at Ridingate', *Archaeologia Cantiana*, vol. 103, pp. 205–9.

Bogdan, N.Q. (1977), 'Progress at Perth', *Rescue News*, no. 13, pp. 8–9.

Bogdan, N.Q. and Wordsworth, J.W. (1978), *The Medieval Excavations at the High Street, Perth, 1975–76: An Interim Report*, Perth, High Street Archaeological Committee.

Boon, G.C., (1974), *Silchester: The Roman Town of Calleva*, Newton Abbot, David & Charles.

Brann, M. (1991 unpublished), 'Excavations at Mill Lane, Perth', Perth, Scottish Urban Archaeological Trust.

Braudel, F. (1988), *The Identity of France*, vol. 1: *History and Environment*, London, Fontana (English translation by S. Reynolds).

Briden, C.M. and Stocker, D.A. (1987), 'The tower of the church of St Mary Bishophill Junior', in L.P. Wenham, R.A. Hall, C.M. Briden and D.A. Stocker, 'St Mary Bishophill Junior and St Mary Castlegate', *The Archaeology of York*, vol. 8, no. 2, London, CBA, pp. 84–141.

Brigham, T. (1990a), 'The late Roman waterfront in London', *Britannia*, vol. 21, pp. 99–184.

——(1990b), 'A reassessment of the second basilica in London, AD 100–400: excavations at Leadenhall Court, 1984–86', *Britannia*, vol. 21, pp. 53–98.

Brinklow, D.A. (1984), 'Roman settlement around the legionary fortress at York', in P.V. Addyman and V.E. Black (eds), *Archaeological Papers from York Presented to M.W. Barley*, York, York Archaeological Trust, pp. 22–7.

Brinklow, D.A. and Donaghey, S. (1986), 'A Roman building at Clementhorpe', in D.A. Brinklow, R.A. Hall, J.R. Magilton and S. Donaghey, 'Coney Street, Aldwark and Clementhorpe, minor sites and Roman roads', *The Archaeology of York*, vol. 6, no. 1, London, CBA, pp. 54–73.

Brinklow, D.A., Hall, R.A., Magilton, J.R. and Donaghey, S. (1986), 'Coney Street, Aldwark and Clementhorpe, minor sites and Roman roads', *The Archaeology of York*, vol. 6, no. 1, London, CBA.

Brisbane, M. (1988), 'Hamwic (Saxon Southampton): an eighth-century port and production centre', in R. Hodges and B. Hobley (eds), 'The rebirth of towns in the west', *CBA Research Report*, no. 68, London, CBA, pp. 101–8.

Brooke, C.N.L. and Keir, G. (1975), *London 800–1216, The Shaping of a City*, London, Secker & Warburg.

Brooks, D.A. (1986), 'A review of the evidence for continuity in British towns in the fifth–sixth centuries', *Oxford Journal of Archaeology*, vol. 5 (1), pp. 77–102.

——(1988), 'The case for continuity in fifth-century Canterbury re-examined', *Oxford Journal of Archaeology*, vol. 7 (1), pp. 99–114.

Brooks, N.P. (1984), *The Early History of the Church in Canterbury: Christchurch from 597–1066*, Leicester, Leicester University Press.

Brothwell, D. (1981), *Digging up Bones*, London, British Museum (Natural History) and Oxford University Press (third edition).

Brown, A.N., Grenville, J.C. and Turner, R.C. (1988), 'Watergate Street. The Rows Research Project,' *Journal of the Chester Archaeological Society*, vol. 69, pp. 3–35.

Brown, P.D.C. and McWhirr, A.D. (1966), 'Cirencester 1965', *Antiquaries Journal*, vol. 46, pp. 240–55.

——(1967), 'Cirencester 1966', *Antiquaries Journal*, vol. 47, pp. 185–97.

Bruce-Mitford, R.L.S. (1939), 'The archaeology of the site of the Bodleian extension in Broad Street, Oxford', *Oxoniensia*, vol. 4, pp. 89–146.

Burnham, B.C. and Wacher, J. (1990), *The Small Towns of Roman Britain*, London, Batsford.

Butler, L.A.S. (1984), 'The houses of the mendicant orders in Britain: recent archaeological work', in P.V. Addyman and V.E. Black (eds), *Archaeological Papers from York Presented to M.W. Barley*, York, York Archaeological Trust, pp. 123–36.

Butler, L.A.S. and Morris, R.K. (eds) (1986), 'The Anglo-Saxon Church', *CBA Research Report*, no. 60, London, CBA.

Butler, R.M. (1971), 'The defences of the fourth century fortress at York', in R.M. Butler (ed.), *Soldier and Civilian in Roman Yorkshire*, Leicester, Leicester University Press, pp. 97–105.

Carter, A. (1978), 'The Anglo-Saxon origins of Norwich: the problems and approaches', *Anglo-Saxon England*, vol. 7, Cambridge, Cambridge University Press, pp. 175–204.

——(1980), 'The Music House and Wensum Lodge, King Street, Norwich', *Archaeological Journal*, vol. 137, pp. 310–12.

Carver, M.O.H. (1980), 'The site and settlements at Worcester', in M.O.H. Carver (ed.), 'Medieval Worcester, an archaeological framework', *Transactions of the Worcestershire Archaeological Society*, third series, vol. 7, pp. 15–30.

——(1987), *Underneath English Towns*, London, Batsford.

Carver, M.O.H., Donaghey, S. and Sumpter, A.B. (1978), 'Riverside structures and a well in Skeldergate and buildings in Bishophill', *The Archaeology of York*, vol. 4, no. 2, London, CBA.

Chapman, H. and Johnson, T. (1973), 'Excavations at Aldgate and Bush Lane House in the City of London', *Transactions of the London and Middlesex Archaeological Society*, vol. 24, pp. 1–73.

Chitwood, P. (1989), 'Waterside North', in M. Jones (ed.), *Lincoln's Archaeology 1988–89*, first Annual Report of the City of Lincoln Archaeological Unit, pp. 4–7.

Clarke, G. (1979), 'The Roman cemetery at Lankhills', *Winchester Studies*, vol. 3.2, Oxford, Oxford University Press.

Collis, J. (1978), *Winchester Excavations*, vol. 2: *1949–60*, Winchester, City of Winchester.

Colyer, C. (1975), 'The Roman and medieval defences of the lower city', *Antiquaries Journal*, vol. 55, pp. 227–66.

Colyer, C. and Jones, M.J. (eds) (1979), 'Excavations at Lincoln, second interim report: excavations in the lower walled town 1972–8', *Antiquaries Journal*, vol. 59, pp. 50–91.

Corbet Anderson, J. (1867), *The Roman City of Uriconium*, London, J. Russell Smith.

Cowgill, J., de Neergaard, M. and Griffith, N. (1987), 'Knives and Scabbards', *Medieval Finds from Excavations in London*, vol. 1, London, HMSO.

Cowie, R. and Whytehead, R. (1989), 'Lundenwic: the archaeological evidence for middle Saxon London', *Antiquity*, vol. 63, pp. 706–18.

Cramp, R. (1967), 'Anglian and Viking York', *Borthwick Papers*, no. 33.

Crawford, O.G.S. (1942), 'Southampton', *Antiquity*, vol. 16, pp. 36–50.

Crickmore, J. (1984), 'Romano-British urban defences', *British Archaeological Reports, British Series*, no. 126, Oxford.

Crummy, N. (1983), 'The Roman small finds from excavations in Colchester', *Colchester Archaeological Report*, no. 2, Colchester, Colchester Archaeological Trust.

Crummy, N. (ed.) (1987), 'The coins from excavations in Colchester 1971–9', *Colchester Archaeological Report*, no. 4, Colchester, Colchester Archaeological Trust.

Crummy, P. (1975), *Not Only a Matter of Time*, Colchester Excavation Committee.

——(1977), 'Colchester, the Roman fortress and the development of the *colonia*', *Britannia*, vol. 8, pp. 65–105.

——(1979a), *In Search of Colchester's Past*, Colchester, Colchester Archaeological Trust.

——(1979b), 'The system of measurement used in town planning from the ninth to the thirteenth centuries', in S.C. Hawkes, D. Brown and J. Campbell (eds), 'Anglo-Saxon Studies in Archaeology and History', *British Archaeological Reports, British Series*, no. 72, Oxford, pp. 149–63.

——(1980), 'The temples of Roman Colchester', in W. Rodwell (ed.), 'Temples, churches and religion, recent research in Roman Britain', *British Archaeological Reports, British Series*, no. 77, Oxford.

——(1982a), 'The origins of some major Romano-British towns', *Britannia*, vol. 13, pp. 125–34.

——(1982b), 'The Roman theatre at Colchester', *Britannia*, vol. 13, pp. 299–302.

——(1984), 'Excavations at Lion Walk, Balkerne Lane and Middleborough, Colchester, Essex', *Colchester Archaeological Report*, no. 3, Colchester, Colchester Archaeological Trust.

——(1985), 'Colchester, the mechanics of laying out a town', in F. Grew and B. Hobley (eds), 'Roman urban topography in Britain and the western Empire', *CBA Research Report*, no. 59, London, CBA, pp. 78–85.

——(1987), 'Laying sites out for the public', *Colchester Archaeologist*, no. 1, pp. 21–2.

——(1988), 'Colchester', in G. Webster (ed.), *Fortress into City*, London, Batsford, pp. 24–47.

——(1988–9), 'Colchester's town wall', *Colchester Archaeologist*, no. 2, pp. 6–11.

——(1989), *Secrets of the Grave*, Colchester, Colchester Archaeological Trust and Essex County Council.

——(1989–90), 'Unique ancient monument', *Colchester Archaeologist*, no. 3, pp. 20–2.

——(forthcoming), 'Excavations at Culver Street and miscellaneous sites in Colchester, 1971–85, *Colchester Archaeological Report*, no. 6, Colchester, Colchester Archaeological Trust.

Davison, B.K. (1967), 'The late Saxon town of Thetford', *Medieval Archaeology*, vol. 11, pp. 189–208.

Dawes, J.D. and Magilton, J.R. (1980), 'The cemetery of St Helen-on-the-Walls, Aldwark', *The Archaeology of York*, vol. 12, no. 1, London, CBA.

Department of the Environment (1990), *Planning Policy Guidelines (PPG)*, no. 16, London, HMSO.

Dillon, J. (1988), 'Excavations at Courage's, Park Street, Southwark', *Rescue News*, no. 46, p. 3.

——(1989), 'A Roman timber building from Southwark', *Britannia*, vol. 20, pp. 229–31.

Dixon, N. (1987), *An Archaeological Bibliography of Bristol*, Bristol, Bristol City Museum and Art Gallery.

Dobson, R.B. (1977), 'Urban decline in late medieval England', *Transactions of the Royal Historical Society*, vol. 27, pp. 1–22; also reprinted in R. Holt and G. Rosser, (1990), *The Medieval Town – a Reader in English Urban History*, London, Longman, pp. 265–86.

Dolley, M. (1986), 'The Aethelraed penny from the York mint', in E.J.E. Pirie, 'Post-Roman coins from York excavations', *The Archaeology of York*, vol. 18, no. 1, pp. 30–3.

Donaghey, S. (1986), 'Anglo-Scandinavian structures and features at Skeldergate and Bishophill: 58–9 Skeldergate', in J. Moulden and D. Tweddle, 'Anglo-Scandinavian settlement south-west of the Ouse', *The Archaeology of York*, vol. 8, no. 1, London, CBA, pp. 37–48.

Down, A. (1988), *Roman Chichester*, Chichester, Phillimore.

Down, A. and Rule, M. (1971), *Chichester Excavations*, vol. 1, Chichester, Phillimore.

Drury, P.J., (1984), 'The temple of Claudius at Colchester reconsidered', *Britannia*, vol. 15, pp. 7–51.

Dunmore, S. and Carr, R. (1976), 'The late Saxon town of Thetford', *East Anglian Archaeology*, vol. 4, Gressenhall, Norfolk Archaeological Unit.

Dunnett, B.R.K. (1967), 'Excavations on North Hill, Colchester 1965', *Archaeological Journal*, vol. 73, pp. 27–61.

——(1975), *The Trinovantes*, London, Duckworth.

Durham, B. (1977), 'Archaeological investigations in St Aldate's', *Oxoniensia*, vol. 42, pp. 83–203.

——(1990), 'The city of Oxford', *Current Archaeology*, no. 121, pp. 28–33.

Durham, B., Halpin, C. and Palmer, N. (1983), 'Oxford's north defences: archaeological studies 1971–82', *Oxoniensia*, vol. 48, pp. 13–40.

Dyson, T. (1989), 'Documents and archaeology, the medieval London waterfront', *Museum of London Annual Archaeology Lecture 1987*, London, Museum of London.

English Heritage (1990), *Developing Frameworks: Policies for our Archaeological Past*, London.

Esmonde-Cleary, A.S. (1989), *The Ending of Roman Britain*, London, Batsford.

Evans, D.H., Murray, J.C. and Stones, J.A. (1987), *A Tale of Two Burghs: The Archaeology of Old and New Aberdeen*, Aberdeen, Art Gallery and Museums.

Frere, S.S. (1962), *Roman Canterbury*, third edn, Canterbury, Canterbury Archaeological Committee.

——(1970), 'The Roman theatre at Canterbury', *Britannia*, vol. 1, pp. 83–113.

——(1972), 'Verulamium Excavations, vol. 1', *Report of the Research Committee of the Society of Antiquaries*, London, no. 28.

——(1983), 'Verulamium Excavations, vol. 2', *Report of the Research Committee of the Society of Antiquaries*, London, no. 41.

——(1984a), 'Canterbury: the post-war excavations', *Archaeologia Cantiana*, vol. 100, pp. 29–46.

——(1984b), 'Verulamium Excavations, vol. 3', *Oxford University Committee for Archaeology Monograph*, no. 1.

——(1984c), 'British urban defences in earthwork', *Britannia*, vol. 15, pp. 63–74.

Frere, S.S. and Stow, S. (1983), 'Excavations in the St George's Street and Burgate Street areas', *The Archaeology of Canterbury*, vol. 7, Maidstone, Canterbury Archaeological Trust.

Frere, S.S., Stow, S. and Bennett, P. (1982), 'Excavations on the Roman and medieval defences of Canterbury', *The Archaeology of Canterbury*, vol. 2, Maidstone, Canterbury Archaeological Trust.

Fulford, M. (1984), *Silchester Defences 1974–80*, Gloucester, Alan Sutton.

——(1985), 'Excavations on the sites of the Amphitheatre and Forum-Basilica at Silchester, Hampshire: an interim report', *Antiquaries Journal*, vol. 65, pp. 39–81.

Garrod, A.P. and Heighway, C. (1984), *Garrod's Gloucester*, Gloucester, Western Archaeological Trust.

Gem, R. (1986), 'The origins of the abbey', in C. Wilson, *Westminster Abbey*, London, Bell & Hyman.

Gilmour, B.J.J. (1979), 'The Anglo-Saxon church at St Paul in the Bail, Lincoln', *Medieval Archaeology*, vol. 23, pp. 214–17.

Gilmour, B.J.J. and Stocker, D. (1986), 'St Mark's church and cemetery', *The Archaeology of Lincoln*, vol. 3, no. 1, London, CBA.

Goodall, I.H. (1990), 'Tenterhooks', in M. Biddle (ed.), 'Object and Economy in Medieval Winchester', *Winchester Studies*, vol. 7.2, Oxford, Oxford University Press, pp. 234–9.

Goodburn, R. and Bartholomew, P. (eds) (1976), 'Aspects of the *Notitia Dignitatum*', *British Archaeological Reports, International Series*, no. 15, Oxford.

Graham, A.H. and Hinton, P. (1988), 'The Roman roads in Southwark', in P. Hinton (ed.), 'Excavations in Southwark 1973–6, Lambeth 1973–9', *London and Middlesex Archaeological Society, Surrey Archaeological Society Joint Publication*, no. 3, pp. 19–26.

Greene, M., (1991), 'Admission charge for Museum of London', *Museums Journal*, vol. 91, no. 6 (June).

Grew, F. and de Neergaard, M. (1988), 'Shoes and Pattens', *Medieval Finds from Excavations in London*, vol. 2, London, HMSO.

Grew, F. and Hobley, B. (eds) (1985), 'Roman urban topography in Britain and the western Empire', *CBA Research Report*, no. 59, London, CBA.

Grimes, W. (1968), *The Archaeology of Roman and Medieval London*, London, Routledge & Kegan Paul.

Hall, A.R. and Kenward, H.K. (1990), 'Environmental evidence from the colonia: General Accident and Rougier Street', *The Archaeology of York*, vol. 14, no. 6, London, CBA.

Hall, A.R. and Kenward, H.K. (eds) (1982), 'Environmental archaeology in the urban context', *CBA Research Report*, no. 43, London, CBA.

Hall, A.R., Kenward, H.K., Williams, D. and Greig, J.R.A. (1983), 'Environment and living conditions at two Anglo-Scandinavian sites', *The Archaeology of York*, vol. 14, no. 4, London, CBA.

Hall, J. and Merrifield, R. (1986), *Roman London*, London, HMSO.

Hall, R.A. (1978), 'The topography of Anglo-Scandinavian York', in R.A. Hall (ed.), 'Viking Age York and the North', *CBA Research Report*, no. 27, London, CBA, pp. 31–6.

——(1984a), *The Viking Dig*, London, Bodley Head.

——(1984b), 'A late pre-Conquest urban building tradition', in P.V. Addyman and V.E. Black (eds), *Archaeological Papers from York Presented to M.W. Barley*, York, York Archaeological Trust, pp. 71–7.

——(1986), 'Anglo-Scandinavian structures and features at Skeldergate and Bishophill: discussion', in J. Moulden and D. Tweddle, 'Anglo-Scandinavian settlement south-west of the Ouse', *The Archaeology of York*, vol. 8, no. 1, London, CBA, pp. 48–52.

——(1988a), 'Queen's Hotel: introduction', *Interim* (Bulletin of the York Archaeological Trust), vol. 13, no. 4, pp. 2–4.

——(1988b), 'York 700–1050', in R. Hodges and B. Hobley (eds), 'The rebirth of towns in the west', *CBA Research Report*, no. 68, London, CBA, pp. 125–32.

——(1988c), 'The making of Domesday York', in D. Hooke (ed.), *Anglo-Saxon Settlements*, Oxford, Oxford University Press, pp. 233–47.

——(1989), 'The five boroughs of the Danelaw: a review of present knowledge', *Anglo-Saxon England*, no. 18, Cambridge, Cambridge University Press, pp. 149–206.

——(1991), 'Sources for pre-conquest, York', in *People and Places in Northern Europe 500–1600*, Woodbridge, The Boydell Press.

——(forthcoming), 'Excavations at City Garage, Blake Street', *The Archaeology of York*, vol. 3, no. 4.

Hammer, F. (1985), 'Early Roman buildings in Fenchurch Street', *Popular Archaeology*, vol. 6, no. 12 (October), pp. 7–14.

Hammerson, M. (1978a), 'The coins', in Southwark and Lambeth Archaeological Excavation Committee (SLAEC) (ed.), 'Southwark Excavations 1972–74', *London and Middlesex Archaeological Society, Surrey Archaeological Society, Joint Publication*, no. 1, pp. 587–600.

——(1978b), 'Excavations under Southwark Cathedral', *London Archaeologist*, vol. 3, no. 8, pp. 206–12.

——(1988), 'Roman coins from Southwark', in P. Hinton (ed.), 'Excavations in Southwark 1973–6, Lambeth 1973–9', *London and Middlesex Archaeological Society, Surrey Archaeological Society Joint Publication*, no. 3, pp. 417–26.

Hammond, N. (1977), 'Archaeologists of the seventies: Martin Biddle', *Rescue News*, no. 15, p. 8.

Harris, E.C. (1989), *Principles of Archaeological Stratigraphy*, London, Academic Press (second edn).

Haslam, J. (ed.) (1984), *Anglo-Saxon Towns in Southern England*, Chichester, Phillimore.

Hassall, T.G. (1969), 'Excavations at Oxford, 1968, first interim report', *Oxoniensia*, vol. 34, pp. 5–20.

——(1972), 'Excavations at Oxford, 1971, fourth interim report', *Oxoniensia*, vol. 37, pp. 137–49.

——(1976), 'Excavations at Oxford Castle, 1965–73', *Oxoniensia*, vol. 41, pp. 232–308.

——(1986), 'Archaeology of Oxford city', in G. Briggs, J. Cook and T. Rowley (eds), *The Archaeology of the Oxford Region*, Oxford, Oxford University Department of External Studies.

——(1987), *Oxford: The Buried City*, Oxford, Oxford Archaeological Unit.

Hawkes, C.F.C and Hull, M.R. (1947), *Camulodunum*, Oxford, Oxford University Press.

Hawkes, S.C. (1982), 'Anglo-Saxon Kent', in P.E. Leach (ed.), 'Archaeology in Kent to AD 1500', *CBA Research Report*, no. 48, London, CBA, pp. 64–78.

——(1990), 'The Anglo-Saxon necklace from Lower Brook Street', in M. Biddle (ed.), 'Object and Economy in Medieval Winchester', *Winchester Studies*, vol. 7.2, Oxford, Oxford University Press, pp. 621–7.

Hawkins, D., (1990), 'Black Death cemeteries of 1348', *Antiquity*, vol. 64, pp. 637–42.

Heard, K., Sheldon, H. and Thompson, P. (1990), 'Mapping Roman Southwark', *Antiquity*, vol. 64, pp. 608–19.

Heighway, C.M. (1984), 'Saxon Gloucester', in J. Haslam (ed.), *Anglo-Saxon Towns in Southern England*, Chichester, Phillimore, pp. 359–84.

——(1987), *Anglo-Saxon Gloucestershire*, Gloucester, Alan Sutton.

Heighway, C.M. (ed.) (1972), *The Erosion of History, Archaeology and Planning in Towns*, London, CBA.

Henderson, C. (1988), 'Exeter', in G. Webster (ed.) (1988), *Fortress into City*, London, Batsford, pp. 91–119.

Hey, D. (1986), *Yorkshire from AD 1000*, London, Longman.

Hicks, A. and Hicks, M. (1991), 'St Gregory's Priory', in *Canterbury's Archaeology 1989–90*, Canterbury, Canterbury Archaeological Trust, pp. 1–5.

Hicks, M. (1990), 'St Gregory's Priory: the church and conventual buildings', in *Canterbury's Archaeology 1988–9*, Canterbury, Canterbury Archaeological Trust, pp. 16–20.

Hill, C., Millett, M. and Blagg, T. (1980), 'The Roman riverside wall and monumental arch in London', *London and Middlesex Archaeological Society, Special Paper, no. 3.*

Hill, D.H. (1969), 'The Burghal Hidage: the establishment of a text', *Medieval Archaeology*, vol. 13, pp. 84–92.

Hill, Sir F. (1990), *Medieval Lincoln* (originally published 1948, reprinted with an introduction by D. Owen in 1990), Stamford, Paul Watkins.

Hillam, J.A. (1985), 'Theoretical and applied dendrochronology: how to make a date with a tree', in P. Phillips (ed.), 'The Archaeologist and the Lab.', *CBA Research Report*, no. 58, London, CBA, pp. 17–23.

Hillam, J. and Morgan, R.A. (1981), 'What value is dendrochronology to waterfront archaeology?' in G. Milne and B. Hobley (eds), 'Waterfront archaeology in Britain and northern Europe', *CBA Research Report*, no. 41, London, CBA, pp. 39–46.

——(1986), 'Tree ring analysis of the Roman timbers', in L. Miller, J. Schofield and M. Rhodes, 'The Roman quay at St Magnus House, London', *London and Middlesex Archaeological Society, Special Paper*, no. 8, pp. 75–86.

Hinton, D., Keene, S. and Qualmann, K. (1981), 'The Winchester reliquary', *Medieval Archaeology*, vol. 25, pp. 45–77.

Hinton, P. (ed.), (1988), 'Excavations in Southwark 1973–6, Lambeth 1973–9', *London and Middlesex Archaeological Society, Surrey Archaeological Society Joint Publication*, no. 3.

Hobley, B. (1979), 'Rescue archaeology in the City of London', *Popular Archaeology*, vol. 1, no. 3 (September), pp. 32–8.

——(1986), 'Roman and Saxon London – a reappraisal', *Museum of London Annual Archaeology Lecture*, London, Museum of London.

——(1987), 'The Archaeologists' and Developers' Code of Practice – a great leap forward', in H. Mytum and K. Waugh (eds), 'Rescue archaeology – what's next?', *Department of Archaeology, University of York, Monograph*, no. 6, pp. 35–40.

——(1988), 'Saxon London: *Lundenwic* and *Lundenburh*: two cities rediscovered', in R. Hodges and B. Hobley (eds), 'The rebirth of towns in the west', *CBA Research Report*, no. 68, London, CBA, pp. 69–82.

Hodges, R. (1981), 'The Hamwic pottery: the local and imported wares from 30 years' excavations at Middle Saxon Southampton, and their European context', *CBA Research Report*, no. 37, London, CBA.

——(1982), *Dark Age Economics*, London, Duckworth.

——(1988), 'The rebirth of towns in the west', in R. Hodges and B. Hobley (eds), 'The rebirth of towns in the west', *CBA Research Report*, no. 68, London, CBA, pp. 1–7.

Hodges, R. and Hobley, B. (eds) (1988), 'The rebirth of towns in the west', *CBA Research Report*, no. 68, London, CBA

Hodgson, G.W.I. (1983), 'The animal remains from medieval sites within three royal burghs on the eastern Scottish seaboard', in B. Proudfoot (ed.), 'Site, environment and economy', *British Archaeological Reports, International Series*, no. 173, Oxford, pp. 3–32.

Holdsworth, P. (1980), 'Excavations at Melbourne Street, Southampton, 1971–6', *CBA Research Report*, no. 33, London, CBA.

——(1984), 'Saxon Southampton', in J. Haslam (ed.) (1984), *Anglo-Saxon Towns in Southern England*, Chichester, Phillimore, pp. 331–44.

Holdsworth, P. (ed.) (1987), 'Excavations in the medieval burgh of Perth', *Society of Antiquaries of Scotland Monograph*, no. 5.

Hope-Taylor, B. (1971), *Under York Minster – Archaeological Discoveries 1966–71*, York.

Horrox, R. (1978), *The Changing Plan of Hull, 1290–1650*, Hull, Kingston-upon-Hull City Council.

Horsman, V. and Davison, B.K. (1989), 'The New Palace Yard and its fountain: excavations in the palace of Westminster, 1972–74', *Antiquaries Journal*, vol. 69, pp. 279–97.

Horsman, V., Milne, C. and Milne, G. (1988), 'Aspects of Saxo-Norman London: 1, building and street development', *London and Middlesex Archaeological Society Special Paper*, no. 11.

Hull City Council (1987), *The Archaeology of the Beverley Gate, Hull, Interim Report*, Hull, Hull City Council.

——(1990), *Beverley Gate: The Birthplace of the English Civil War*, Hull, Hutton Press.

Hurst, H. (1986), 'Gloucester, the Roman and later defences', *Gloucester Archaeological Reports*, no. 2, Gloucester, Alan Sutton.

——(1988), 'Gloucester', in G. Webster (ed.), *Fortress into City*, London, Batsford, pp. 48–73.

Johns, C.M. and Potter, T.W. (1985), 'The Canterbury late Roman treasure', *Antiquaries Journal*, vol. 65, pp. 312–52.

Jones, A.K.G. (1982), 'Human parasite remains: prospects for a quantitative approach', in A.R. Hall and H.K. Kenward (eds), 'Environmental archaeology in the urban context', *CBA Research Report*, no. 43, London, CBA, pp. 66–70.

——(1983), 'A coprolite from 6–8 Pavement', in A.R. Hall, H.K. Kenward, D. Williams and J.R.A. Greig, 'Environment and living conditions at two Anglo-Scandinavian sites', *The Archaeology of York*, vol. 14, no. 4, London, CBA, pp. 225–9.

Jones, B. (1984), *Past Imperfect – the Story of Rescue Archaeology*, London, Heinemann.

Jones, J. and Watson, N. (1987), 'The early medieval waterfront at Redcliffe, Bristol: a study of environment and economy', in N.D. Balaam, B. Levitan and V. Straker, 'Studies in palaeoeconomy and environment in south west England', *British Archaeological Reports, British Series*, no. 181, Oxford, pp. 135–62.

Jones, M.J. (1980), 'The defences of the upper Roman enclosure', *The Archaeology of Lincoln*, vol. 7, no. 1, London, CBA.

——(1985), 'New streets for old: the topography of Roman Lincoln', in F. Grew and B. Hobley (eds), 'Roman urban topography in Britain and the western Empire', *CBA Research Report*, no. 59, London, CBA, pp. 86–93.

——(1990), 'Lincoln's Roman defences: the Lower City', in M.J. Jones (ed.), *Lincoln Archaeology 1989–90: second annual report of the City of Lincoln Archaeology Unit*, Lincoln, City of Lincoln Archaeological Unit, pp. 23–4.

——(forthcoming), 'The defences of the Lower City', *The Archaeology of Lincoln*, vol. 7, no. 2, London, CBA.

Jones, M.J. and Bond, C.J. (1987), 'Urban defences', in J. Schofield and R. Leech (eds), 'Urban archaeology in Britain', *CBA Research Report*, no. 61, London, CBA, pp. 81–116.

Jones, M.J. and Gilmour, B. (1980), 'Lincoln, *principia* and forum: a preliminary report', *Britannia*, vol. 11, pp. 61–72.

Jones, R.H. (1986), *Excavations in Redcliffe 1983–5*, Bristol, City of Bristol Museum and Art Gallery.

Jope, E.M. (1952–3), 'Excavations in the city of Norwich 1948', *Norfolk Archaeology*, vol. 30, pp. 287–323.

——(1958), 'The Clarendon Hotel, Oxford Part 1: The site', *Oxoniensia*, vol. 23, pp. 1–83.

Keen, M. (1990), *English Society in the Late Middle Ages: 1348–1500*, London, Penguin.

Keene, D.J. (1975), 'Suburban growth', in M.W. Barley (ed.), 'The plans and top-ography of medieval towns in England and Wales', *CBA Research Report*, no. 14, London, CBA, pp. 71–82; also reprinted in R. Holt and G. Rosser (1990), *The Medieval Town – a Reader in English Urban History*, London, Longman, pp. 97–116.

——(1984), 'Survey of medieval Winchester', *Winchester Studies*, vol. 2, Oxford, Oxford University Press.

——(1990), 'The textile industry', in M. Biddle (ed.) (1990), 'Object and Economy in Medieval Winchester', *Winchester Studies*, vol. 7.2, Oxford, Oxford University Press, pp. 200–14.

Kemp, R. (1987), 'Anglian York – the missing link', *Current Archaeology*, no. 104, pp. 259–63.

——(1991), 'The archaeology of 46–54 Fishergate', in T.P. O'Connor, 'Bones from 46–54 Fishergate', *The Archaeology of York*, vol. 15, no. 4, London, CBA, pp. 211–20.

Kenyon, R. (1987), 'The Claudian coinage', in N. Crummy (ed.), 'The coins from excavations in Colchester 1971–9', *Colchester Archaeological Report*, no. 4, Colchester, Colchester Archaeological Trust, pp. 24–41.

King, A. (1990), *The Story of The Brooks, Winchester: Archaeological Excavations 1987–88*, Winchester, Winchester Museums Service.

Kjølbye-Biddle, B. (1986), 'The seventh century minster at Winchester interpreted', in L.A.S. Butler and R.K. Morris (eds), 'The Anglo-Saxon Church', *CBA Research Report*, no. 60, London, CBA, pp. 196–209.

Lambrick, G. (1985), 'Further excavations on the second site of the Dominican Priory, Oxford', *Oxoniensia*, vol. 50, pp. 131–208.

Lambrick, G. and Woods, H. (1976), 'Excavations on the second site of the Dominican Priory, Oxford', *Oxoniensia*, vol. 41, pp. 168–231.

Leach, P.E. (ed.) (1982), 'Archaeology in Kent to AD 1500', *CBA Research Report*, no. 48, London, CBA.

Lincoln Archaeological Trust (1984), *Lincoln: 21 Centuries of Living History*, Lincoln.

Lynch, M., Spearman, M. and Stell, G. (1988), *The Scottish Medieval Town*, Edinburgh, John Donald.

MacDonald, J.L. (1979), 'Religion', in G. Clarke, 'The Roman Cemetery at Lankhills', *Winchester Studies*, vol. 3, no. 2, Oxford, Oxford University Press, pp. 404–33.

McDonnell, J.G. (1989), 'Iron and its alloys in the fifth to eleventh centuries in England', *World Archaeology*, vol. 20, no. 3, pp. 373–82.

MacGregor, A. (1978), 'Industry and commerce in Anglo-Scandinavian York', in R.A. Hall (ed.), 'Viking Age York and the North', *CBA Research Report*, no. 27, London, CBA, pp. 37–57.

——(1982), 'Anglo-Scandinavian finds from Lloyds Bank, Pavement, and other sites', *The Archaeology of York*, vol. 17, no. 3, London, CBA.

Mackreth, D.F. (1987), 'Roman public buildings', in J. Schofield and R. Leech (eds), 'Urban archaeology in Britain', *CBA Research Report* no. 61, London, CBA, pp. 133–46.

McPhail, R. (1981), 'Soil and botanical structures of the dark earth', in M. Jones and G. Dimbleby (eds), 'The environment of man: the late Iron Age to the Anglo-Saxon period', *British Archaeological Reports, British Series*, no. 87, Oxford, pp. 309–31.

——(1983), 'The micromorphology of dark earth from Gloucester, London and Norwich: an analysis of urban anthropogenic deposits from the late Roman to early medieval periods in England', in P. Bullock and C.P. Murphy (eds), *Soil Micromorphology*, Berkhamsted, A.B. Academic Publishers, pp. 245–52.

McWhirr, A. (1981), *Roman Gloucestershire*, Gloucester, Alan Sutton.

——(1986), 'Houses in Roman Cirencester', *Cirencester Excavations*, vol. 3, Cirencester, Cirencester Excavations Committee.

——(1988), 'Cirencester,' in G. Webster (ed.) (1988), *Fortress into City*, London, Batsford, pp. 74–90.

McWhirr, A., Viner, L. and Wells, C. (1982), 'Romano-British cemeteries at Cirencester', *Cirencester Excavations*, vol. 2, Cirencester, Cirencester Excavations Committee.

Magilton, J. (1980), 'The church of St Helen-on-the-Walls, Aldwark', *The Archaeology of York*, vol. 10, no. 1, London, CBA.

——(1986), 'A Roman building and Roman roads in Aldwark', in D.A. Brinklow, R.A. Hall, J.R. Magilton and S. Donaghey, 'Coney Street, Aldwark and Clementhorpe, minor sites and Roman roads', *The Archaeology of York*, vol. 6, no. 1, London, CBA, pp. 32–47.

Maitland Muller, M.R. (1949), 'Southampton excavations: first interim report', *Proceedings of the Hampshire Field Club and Archaeological Society*, vol. 17, pp. 65–71.

——(1950), 'The Southampton excavations: second interim report, 1947', *Proceedings of the Hampshire Field Club and Archaeological Society*, vol. 17, pp. 125–9.

Maloney, C. (1991), 'The upper Walbrook in the Roman period: The archaeology of Roman London: 1', *CBA Research Report*, no. 69, London, CBA.

Maloney, J. (1980), 'The discovery of bastion 4A and its implications', *Transactions of the London and Middlesex Archaeological Society*, vol. 31, pp. 68–76.

——(1983), 'Recent work on London's defences', in J. Maloney and B. Hobley (eds), 'Roman urban defences in the west', *CBA Research Report*, no. 51, London, CBA, pp. 96–117.

——(1988), 'The Guildhall amphitheatre', *Illustrated London News*, May.

Marsden, P. (1974), 'The County Hall ship, London', *International Journal of Nautical Archaeology*, vol. 3, pp. 55–65.

——(1975), 'The excavation of a Roman palace site in London 1961–72', *Transactions of the London and Middlesex Archaeological Society*, vol. 26, pp. 1–102.

——(1976), 'Two Roman public baths in London', *Transactions of the London and Middlesex Archaeological Society*, vol. 27, pp. 1–70.

——(1980), *Roman London*, London, Thames & Hudson.

——(1987), *The Roman Forum Site in London*, London, HMSO.

Marsh, G. and West, B. (1981), 'Skullduggery in Roman London?', *Transactions of the London and Middlesex Archaeological Society*, vol. 32, pp. 86–102.

Mason, D.J.P. (1985), 'Excavations at Chester: 26–42 Lower Bridge Street 1974–6. The Dark Age and Saxon periods', *Grosvenor Museum Archaeological Excavation and Survey Report*, no. 3, Chester, Grosvenor Museum.

Merrifield, R. (1983), *London, City of the Romans*, London, Batsford.

Metcalf, D.M. (1988), 'The coins', in P. Andrews (ed.), 'The coins and pottery from Hamwic', *Southampton Finds*, vol. 1, Southampton, Southampton City Museums, pp. 17–59.

Miles, P., Young, J. and Wacher, J. (1989), 'A late Saxon kiln site at Silver Street, Lincoln', *The Archaeology of Lincoln*, vol. 17, no. 3, London, CBA.

Miller, L., Schofield, J. and Rhodes, M. (1986), 'The Roman quay at St Magnus House, London', *London and Middlesex Archaeological Society, Special Paper*, no. 8.

Millett, M. (1990), *The Romanisation of Britain*, Cambridge, Cambridge University Press.

Mills, J. and Whittaker, K. (1991), 'Southwark', *Current Archaeology*, no. 124, pp. 155–62.

Milne, G. (1981), 'Medieval riverfront reclamation in London', in G. Milne and B. Hobley (eds), 'Waterfront archaeology in Britain and northern Europe', *CBA Research Report*, no. 41, London, CBA, pp. 32–6.

——(1985), *The Port of Roman London*, London, Batsford.

——(1990), 'King Alfred's plan for London', *London Archaeologist*, vol. 6, no. 8, pp. 206–7.

Milne, G., Battarbee, R., Straker, V. and Yule, B. (1983), 'The London Thames in the mid-first century', *Transactions of the London and Middlesex Archaeological Society*, no. 34, pp. 19–30.

Milne, G. and Goodburn, D. (1990), 'The early medieval port of London, 700–1200', *Antiquity*, vol. 64, pp. 629–36.

Milne, G. and Milne, C. (1982), 'Medieval waterfront development at Trig Lane, London', *London and Middlesex Archaeological Society, Special Paper*, no. 5.

Milne, G. and Wootton, P. (1990), 'Urban development in Londinium, AD 50–120: Leadenhall Hall Court excavations, 1984–86', *London Archaeologist*, vol. 6, no. 7, pp. 179–87.

Milne, G. and Hobley, B. (eds) (1981), 'Waterfront archaeology in Britain and northern Europe', *CBA Research Report*, no. 41, London, CBA.

Morant, P. (1748), *The History and Antiquities of the Most Ancient Town of Colchester*, London.

Morgan, R. (1982), 'Tree ring studies on urban waterlogged wood: problems and possibilities', in A.R. Hall and H.K. Kenward (eds), 'Environmental archaeology in the urban context', *CBA Research Report*, no. 43, London, CBA, pp. 31–9.

Morris, R.K. (1986), 'Alcuin, York and the *Alma Sophia*', in L.A.S. Butler and R.K. Morris (eds), 'The Anglo-Saxon Church', *CBA Research Report*, no. 60, London, CBA, pp. 80–9.

——(1989), *Churches in the Landscape*, London, Dent.

Morton, A.D. (forthcoming), 'Excavations at Hamwic: 1', *CBA Research Report*, London, CBA.

Moulden, J. and Tweddle, D. (1986), 'Anglo-Scandinavian settlement south-west of the Ouse', *The Archaeology of York*, vol. 8, no. 1, London, CBA.

Murray, J.C. (ed.) (1982), 'Excavations in the medieval burgh of Aberdeen 1973–81', *Society of Antiquaries of Scotland Monograph*, no. 2.

Museum of London (1989), *Digging in the City: The Annual Review, 1988*, London, Museum of London.

——(1990), *Digging in the City: The Annual Review, 1989*, London, Museum of London.

Mytum, H. and Waugh, K. (eds) (1987), 'Rescue archaeology – what's next?', *Department of Archaeology, University of York, Monograph*, no. 6.

Niblett, B.R.K. (1985), 'Sheepen: an early Roman industrial site at Camulodunum', *CBA Research Report*, no. 57, London, CBA.

Nicholson, R.A. and Hillam, J. (1987), 'A dendrochronological analysis of oak timbers from the early medieval site at Dundas Wharf, Bristol', *Transactions of the Bristol and Gloucestershire Archaeological Society*, no. 105, pp. 133–45.

Noddle, B. (1975), 'The animal bones', in C. Platt and R. Coleman-Smith, *Excavations in Medieval Southampton 1953–69*, 2 vols, Leicester, Leicester University Press, pp. 332–9.

Norwich Survey (1980), *Norwich Survey 1971–80*, Norwich, Centre of East Anglian Studies, University of East Anglia.

O'Connor, T.P. (1982), 'Animal bones from Flaxengate', *The Archaeology of Lincoln*, vol. 18, no. 1, London, CBA.

——(1989a), 'What shall we have for dinner?: food remains from urban sites', in D. Sergeantson and T. Waldron (eds), 'Diet and Crafts in Towns', *British Archaeological Reports, British Series*, no. 199, Oxford, pp. 13–24.

——(1989b), 'Bones from Anglo-Scandinavian levels at 16–22 Coppergate', *The Archaeology of York*, vol. 15, no. 3, London, CBA.

——(1991), 'Bones from 46–54 Fishergate', *The Archaeology of York*, vol. 15, no. 4, London, CBA.

Ordnance Survey (1983), *Londinium: A Descriptive Map and Guide to Roman London* (second edn), Southampton.

——(1990), *Roman and Medieval Canterbury: Historical Map and Guide*, Southampton.

Orton, C. (1989), 'A tale of two sites', *London Archaeologist*, vol. 6. no. 3, pp. 59–65.

Ottaway, P. (1984), '*Colonia Eburacensis*: a review of recent work', in P.V. Addyman and V.E. Black (eds), *Archaeological Papers from York Presented to M.W. Barley*, York, York Archaeological Trust, pp. 28–33.

——(1988), 'Road in the hole – first course at the Stakis Hotel site, York', *Rescue News*, no. 46, p. 8.

——(1989), 'The empire strikes back – new discoveries in the Roman town at York', *Rescue News*, no. 49, p. 3.

——(1992), 'Anglo-Scandinavian ironwork from 16–22 Coppergate', *The Archaeology of York*, vol. 17, no. 6, London, CBA.

——(forthcoming), 'Excavations at 5 Rougier Street', *The Archaeology of York*, vol. 4, no. 2, London, CBA.

Ottaway, P. and Wenham, L.P. (forthcoming), 'Excavations at St Mary Bishophill Junior and Bishophill Junior', *The Archaeology of York*, vol. 4, no. 2, London, CBA.

Oxley, J. (ed.) (1986), 'Excavations at Southampton Castle', *Southampton City Museums Archaeology Monograph*, no. 3, Southampton.

Palliser, D.M. (1975), 'Sources for urban topography: documents, buildings and archaeology', in M.W. Barley (ed.), 'The plans and topography of medieval towns in England and Wales', *CBA Research Report* no. 14, London, CBA, pp. 1–6; also reprinted in R. Holt and G. Rosser (1990) *The Medieval Town – a Reader in English Urban History*, London, Longman.

——(1980), *Chester: Contemporary Descriptions by Residents and Visitors*, Chester, Council of the City of Chester.

Palliser, D. and Palliser, M. (1979), *York As They Saw It*, York, Sessions.

Palmer, N. (1980), 'A beaker burial and medieval tenements in The Hamel, Oxford', *Oxoniensia*, vol. 45, pp. 124–225.

Pantin, W.A. (1958), 'The Clarendon Hotel, Oxford, Part 2: the buildings', *Oxoniensia*, vol. 23, pp. 84–129.

Parnell, G. (1985), 'The Roman and medieval defences and later development of the inmost ward, Tower of London: excavations 1955–77', *Transactions of the London and Middlesex Archaeological Society*, vol. 26, pp. 1–79.

Pay, S. (1987), *Hamwic: Southampton's Saxon Town*, Southampton, Southampton City Museum, Archaeology Service.

Pearson, N.F. (forthcoming), 'The General Accident site, Tanner Row', *The Archaeology of York*, vol. 4, no. 2, London, CBA.

Perring, D. (1981), 'Early medieval occupation at Flaxengate, Lincoln', *The Archaeology of Lincoln*, vol. 9, no. 1, London, CBA.

——(1985), 'London in the first and early second centuries', in F. Grew and B. Hobley (eds), 'Roman urban topography in Britain and the western Empire', *CBA Research Report*, no. 59, London, CBA, pp. 94–8.

——(1987), 'Domestic buildings in Romano-British towns', in J. Schofield and R. Leech (eds), 'Urban archaeology in Britain', *CBA Research Report*, no. 61, London, CBA, pp. 147–155.

——(1991), *Roman London*, London, Seaby.

Perring, D. and Roskams, S. (with Allen, P.) (1991), 'Early development of Roman London west of the Walbrook. The archaeology of Roman London: 2', *CBA Research Report*, no. 70, London, CBA.

Phillips, A.D. (1975), 'Excavations at York Minster 1967–73', *Friends of York Minster, 46th Annual Report*, pp. 19–27.

——(1985), 'The cathedral of Archbishop Thomas of Bayeux', *Excavations at York Minster*, vol. 2, London, HMSO.

Phillips, A.D. and Heywood, B. (forthcoming), *Excavations at York Minster*, vol. 1, London, HMSO.

Piggott, S. (1985), *William Stukeley*, New York, Thames & Hudson (revised and enlarged edition).

Pilbrow, J. (1871), 'Discoveries made during excavations at Canterbury in 1868', in a letter from J. Pilbrow Esq., FSA to Earl Stanhope, PSA, *Archaeologia*, vol. 43, pp. 151–64.

Pirie, E.J.E. (1986), 'Post-Roman coins from York excavations 1971–81', *The Archaeology of York*, vol. 18, no. 1.

Platt, C. (1973), *Medieval Southampton: the Port and Trading Community*, London, Routledge & Kegan Paul.

——(1976), *The English Medieval Town*, London, Martin Secker & Warburg.

Platt, C. and Coleman-Smith, R. (1975), *Excavations in Medieval Southampton 1953–69*, 2 vols, Leicester, Leicester University Press.

Ponsford, M. (1980), 'Towns', in E. Fowler, 'Earlier medieval sites (410–1066) in and around Bristol and Bath, the south Cotswold and Mendip', *Bristol Archaeological Research Group, Field Guide*, no. 3A, pp. 27–31.

——(1981), 'Bristol', in G. Milne and B. Hobley (eds), 'Waterfront archaeology in Britain and northern Europe', *CBA Research Report*, no. 41, London, CBA, pp. 103–4.

——(1985), 'Bristol's medieval waterfront "the Redcliffe project"', in A.E. Herteig, *Conference on Waterfront Archaeology in North European Towns*, no. 2, Bergen, Historisk Museum, pp. 112–21.

——(1986), 'Bristol' in M. Aston and R. Iles (eds), *The Archaeology of Avon*, Bristol, Avon County Council, pp. 144–59.

Price, R. (1979), 'Excavations at the town wall, Bristol 1974', in N. Thomas (ed.), 'Rescue archaeology in the Bristol area', vol. 1, *Bristol Museum and Art Gallery, Monograph*, no. 2, pp. 15–28.

Proudfoot, B. (ed.) (1983), 'Site, environment and economy', *British Archaeological Reports, International Series*, no. 173, Oxford.

Quirk, R.N. (1957), 'Winchester cathedral in the tenth century', *Archaeological Journal*, vol. 114, pp. 28–68.

——(1961), 'Winchester New Minster and its tenth-century tower', *Journal of the British Archaeological Association*, third series, vol. 24, pp. 16–54.

Radley, J. (1971), 'Economic aspects of Anglo-Danish York', *Medieval Archaeology*, vol. 15, pp. 37–57.

——(1972), 'Excavations in the defences of the city of York: an early medieval stone tower and the successive earth ramparts', *Yorkshire Archaeological Journal*, vol. 44, pp. 38–64.

Rahtz, P. (1977), 'The archaeology of west Mercian towns', in A. Dornier (ed.), *Mercian Studies*, Leicester, Leicester University Press, pp. 107–27.

Rahtz, P. (ed.) (1975), *Rescue Archaeology*, London, Penguin.

Ramm, H. (1976), 'The church of St Mary Bishophill Senior, York, excavations 1964', *Yorkshire Archaeological Journal*, vol. 48, pp. 35–68.

RCHM (1962), *An Inventory of the Historical Monuments in the City of York, vol. 1, Eburacum, Roman York*, London, HMSO.

——(1972), *An Inventory of the Historical Monuments in the City of York, vol. 3, South-West of the Ouse*, London, HMSO.

Reece, R. (1980), 'Town and country: the end of Roman Britain', *World Archaeology*, vol. 12, no. 1, pp. 77–92.

Reynolds, S. (1977), *An Introduction to the History of English Medieval Towns*, Oxford, Oxford University Press.

Rivière, S. and Thomas, A.B. (1987), 'Excavations at 94–97 Fenchurch Street and 9 Northumberland Alley', *Archaeology Today*, vol. 8, no. 9 (October), pp. 13–17.

Roach Smith, C. (1859), *Illustrations of Roman London*, printed by subscription.

Robinson, M. (1980), 'Waterlogged plant material and invertebrate evidence', in N. Palmer, 'A beaker burial and medieval tenements in The Hamel, Oxford', *Oxoniensia*, vol. 45, pp. 199–206.

Rogerson, A. and Dallas, C. (1984), 'Excavations in Thetford, 1948–59 and 1973–80', *East Anglian Archaeology*, vol. 22, Gressenhall, Norfolk Archaeological Unit.

Ross, A. (1967), *Pagan Celtic Britain*, London, Routledge & Kegan Paul.

Rowsome, P. (1987), 'Roman street life', *Archaeology Today*, vol. 8, no. 9 (October), pp. 22–5.

Rowsome, P. and Wooldridge, K. (1989), 'Swept under the carpet: excavation and preservation at Huggin Hill', *Rescue News*, no. 48, p. 3.

Rumble, A.R. (1980), 'HAMTUN alias HAMWIC (Saxon Southampton): the place-name traditions and their significance', in P. Holdsworth, 'Excavations at Melbourne Street Southampton, 1971–6', *CBA Research Report*, no. 33, London, CBA, pp. 7–20.

Ryder, M.L. (1983), 'Hair and wool from Perth High Street', in B. Proudfoot (ed.), 'Site, environment and economy', *British Archaeological Reports, International Series*, no. 173, Oxford, pp. 33–42.

Schofield, J. (1981), 'Medieval waterfront buildings in the City of London', in G. Milne and B. Hobley (eds), 'Waterfront archaeology in Britain and northern Europe', *CBA Research Report*, no. 41, London, CBA, pp. 24–31.

——(1984), *The Building of London from the Conquest to the Great Fire*, London, Colonnade.

Schofield, J. and Leech, R. (eds) (1987), 'Urban archaeology in Britain', *CBA Research Report*, no. 61, London, CBA.

Scottish Urban Archaeological Trust (1984), *Perth, The Archaeology of the Medieval Town*, Perth.

Sheldon, H. (1989), 'The curious case of the Queen's Hotel', *Rescue News*, no. 47, p. 1.

Sheldon, H. and Tyers, I. (1983), 'Recent dendrochronological work in Southwark and its implications', *London Archaeologist*, vol. 4, no. 13, pp. 355–61.

Shoesmith, R. (1982), 'Hereford City Excavations 2, excavations on and close to the defences', *CBA Research Report*, no. 46, London, CBA.

Spearman, M. (1988), 'The medieval townscape of Perth', in M. Lynch, M. Spearman and G. Stell (1988), *The Scottish Medieval Town*, Edinburgh, John Donald, pp. 42–69.

Spence, C. (ed.) (1990), *Recording Manual*, London, Museum of London.

Stell, G. (1988), 'Urban buildings', in M. Lynch, M. Spearman and G. Stell (eds), *The Scottish Medieval Town*, Edinburgh, John Donald, pp. 60–80.

Stenton, Sir F.M. (1934), *Norman London*, London, The Historical Association.

——(1971), *Anglo-Saxon England*, Oxford, Oxford University Press (third edn).

Stirland, A. (1985), 'The human bones', in B. Ayers (1985), 'Excavations within the north-east bailey of Norwich Castle, 1979', *East Anglian Archaeology*, vol. 28, Gressenhall, Norfolk Archaeological Unit, pp. 49–58.

Tatton-Brown, T.W.T. (1974), 'Excavations at the Custom House site, City of London', *Transactions of the London and Middlesex Archaeological Society*, vol. 25, pp. 117–219.

——(1975), 'Excavations at the Custom House site, part 2', *Transactions of the London and Middlesex Archaeological Society*, vol. 26, pp. 103–70.

——(1977), 'Canterbury, is there a future for its archaeology?', *Rescue News*, no. 13, p. 2.

——(1990), 'The history of St Gregory's Priory', in *Canterbury's Archaeology 1988–9*, Canterbury, Canterbury Archaeological Trust, pp. 20–4.

Taylor, H. and Taylor, J. (1980), *Anglo-Saxon Architecture*, Cambridge, Cambridge University Press.

Thacker, A.T. (1988), 'Early medieval Chester: the historical background', in R. Hodges and B. Hobley (eds), 'The rebirth of towns in the west', *CBA Research Report*, no. 68, London, CBA, pp. 119–24.

Thomas, C. (1981), *Christianity in Roman Britain to AD 500*, London, Batsford.

Thompson, E.A. (1983), 'Fifth-century facts?', *Britannia*, vol. 14, pp. 272–4.

Thompson, F.H. and Whitwell, J.B. (1973), 'The gates of Roman Lincoln', *Archaeologia*, vol. 104, pp. 129–207.

Timby, J.R. (1988), 'The middle Saxon pottery', in P. Andrews (ed.), 'The coins and pottery from Hamwic', *Southampton Finds*, vol. 1, Southampton, Southampton City Museums, pp. 73–124.

Todd, M. (1989), 'The early cities', in M. Todd (ed.) (1989), 'Research on Roman Britain 1960–89', *Britannia Monograph*, no. 11, London, pp. 75–90.

Todd, M. (ed.) (1989), 'Research on Roman Britain 1960–89', *Britannia Monograph*, no. 11, London.

Tomlin, R. (1986), [untitled] in D. Brinklow, R.A. Hall, J. Magilton and S. Donaghey, 'Coney Street, Aldwark and Clementhorpe, minor sites and Roman roads', *The Archaeology of York*, vol. 6, no. 1, London, CBA, pp. 63–7.

Tweddle, D. (1984), *The Coppergate Helmet*, York, York Archaeological Trust.

——(1987), 'Later Anglian and Anglo-Scandinavian sculptured fragments' in L.P. Wenham, R.A. Hall, C.M. Briden and D.A. Stocker, 'St Mary Bishophill Junior and St Mary Castlegate', *The Archaeology of York*, vol. 8, no. 2, London, CBA, pp. 118–22.

——(1990), 'Craft and industry in Anglo-Scandinavian York', in P.J. Corfield and D.J. Keene (eds), *Work in Towns 850–1850*, Leicester, Leicester University Press, pp. 17–41.

——(forthcoming), 'Anglian York – a survey of the archaeological evidence', *The Archaeology of York*, vol. 7, no. 1, London, CBA.

Tylecote, R.F. (1986), *The Prehistory of Metallurgy*, London, Institute of Metals.

Urry, W. (1967), *Canterbury under the Angevin Kings*, London, Athlone Press.

Vince, A. (1984), 'The Aldwych: middle Saxon London discovered', *Current Archaeology*, no. 93, pp. 310–12.

——(1988), 'The economic basis of Anglo-Saxon London', in R. Hodges and B. Hobley (eds), 'The rebirth of towns in the west', *CBA Research Report*, no. 68, London, CBA, pp. 83–92.

——(1990), *Saxon London: An Archaeological Investigation*, London, Seaby.

Vince, A. and Jones, M.J. (1990), *Lincoln's Buried Archaeological Heritage*, Lincoln, City of Lincoln Archaeological Unit.

Wacher, J. (1974), *The Towns of Roman Britain*, London, Batsford.

——(1979), 'Silver Street', in C. Colyer and M.J. Jones (eds), 'Excavations at Lincoln, second interim report: excavations in the lower walled town 1972–8', *Antiquaries Journal*, vol. 59, pp. 50–91.

——(1989), 'Cities from the second to the fourth centuries', in M. Todd (ed.), 'Research on Roman Britain 1960–89', *Britannia Monograph*, no. 11, London, pp. 91–114.

Wacher, J. and McWhirr, A. (1982), 'Early Roman occupation at Cirencester', *Cirencester Excavations*, vol. 1, Cirencester, Cirencester Excavation Committee.

Wade, K. (1988), 'Ipswich', in R. Hodges and B. Hobley (eds), 'The rebirth of towns in the west', *CBA Research Report*, no. 68, London, CBA, pp. 93–100.

Wade-Martins, P. (ed.) (1983), 'Waterfront excavation and Thetford ware production, Norwich', *East Anglian Archaeology*, no. 17, Gressenhall, Norfolk Archaeological Unit.

Walker, J.S.F. (1977), 'Excavations in medieval tenements on the Quilter's Vault site in Southampton', *Proceedings of the Hampshire Field Club Archaeological Society*, vol. 35, pp. 183–216.

Walthew, C.V. (1983), 'Houses, defences and status: the towns of Roman Britain in the second half of the second century AD', *Oxford Journal of Archaeology*, vol. 2, no. 2, pp. 213–24.

Walton, P. (1989), 'Textiles, cordage and raw fibre from 16–22 Coppergate', *The Archaeology of York*, vol. 17, no. 5, London, CBA.

Ward, S. (1988), 'Excavations at Chester: 12 Watergate Street, 1985', *Grosvenor Museum Archaeological Excavation and Survey Reports*, no. 5, Chester, Grosvenor Museum.

——(forthcoming), 'Excavations at Chester, Saxon occupation within the Roman fortress', *Chester Archaeological Service, Excavation and Survey Report*, no. 7, Chester, City Council Department of Leisure Services.

Warwick, R. (1968), 'The skeletal remains', in L.P. Wenham, 'The Romano-British Cemetery at Trentholme Drive, York', *Ministry of Public Buildings and Works Archaeological Report*, no. 5, London, HMSO, pp. 113–76.

Waterman, D.M. (1959), 'Late Saxon, Viking and early medieval finds from York', *Archaeologia*, vol. 97, pp. 59–106.

Watkinson, D. (ed.) (1987), *First Aid for Finds*, Hertford, Rescue.

Watts, L. and Rahtz, P. (1985), 'Mary-le-Port, Bristol – Excavations 1962/3', *City of Bristol Museum and Art Gallery Monograph*, no. 7.

Webster, G. (1975), *The Cornovii*, London, Duckworth.

——(1988), 'Wroxeter', in G. Webster (ed.), *Fortress into City*, London, Batsford, pp. 120–44.

Webster, G. (ed.) (1988), *Fortress into City*, London, Batsford.

Wellbeloved, C. (1842), *Eburacum*, London, Longman.

Wells, C. (1982), 'The human burials', in A. McWhirr, L. Viner and C. Wells, 'Romano-British cemeteries at Cirencester', *Cirencester Excavations*, vol. 2, Cirencester, Cirencester Excavations Committee, pp. 135–202.

Wenham, L.P., Hall, R.A., Briden, C.M., and Stocker, D.A. (1987), 'St Mary Bishophill Junior and St Mary Castlegate', *The Archaeology of York*, vol. 8, no. 2, London, CBA.

Wheeler, R.E.M. (1920), 'The vaults under Colchester Castle: a further note', *Journal of Roman Studies*, vol. 10, pp. 87–9.

——(1921), 'An *insula* of Roman Colchester', *Transactions of the Essex Archaeological Society*, second series, vol. 16, pp. 7–41.

——(1930), 'London in Roman times', *London Museum Catalogue*, no. 3.

——(1954), *Archaeology from the Earth*, Oxford, Oxford University Press.

——(1956), *Still Digging*, London, Michael Joseph.

Wheeler, R.E.M. and Laver, P.G. (1919), 'Roman Colchester', *Journal of Roman Studies*, vol. 9, pp. 136–69.

Wheeler, R.E.M. and Wheeler, T.V. (1936), 'A Belgic and two Roman Cities', *Report of the Research Committee of the Society of Antiquaries of London*, no. 11.

Whimster, R. (1981), 'Burial practices in Iron Age Britain', *British Archaeological Reports, British Series*, no. 90, Oxford.

White, R. (1990), 'Excavations on the site of the baths basilica', in P. Barker (ed.), *From Roman Viroconium to Medieval Wroxeter*, Worcester, West Mercian Archaeological Consultants.

White, W. (1988), 'The cemetery of St Nicholas Shambles', *London and Middlesex Archaeological Society Special Paper*, no. 9.

Whitelock, D. (1955), *English Historic Documents*, no. 1, c.500–1042.

Whittingham, A. (1980), 'The foundation of Norwich cathedral', *Archaeological Journal*, vol. 137, pp. 313–14.

Williams, B. (1981), *Excavations in the Medieval Suburb of Redcliffe, Bristol*, Bristol, City of Bristol Museum and Art Gallery.

Williams, J.H. (1984), 'From "palace" to "town": Northampton and urban origins', *Anglo-Saxon England*, vol. 13, Cambridge, Cambridge University Press, pp. 113–36.

Williams, J.H., Shaw, M. and Denham, V. (1985), 'Middle Saxon palaces at Northampton', *Northampton Development Corporation Archaeological Monograph*, no. 4, Northampton.

Williams, T. (1989), 'The palace of Allectus – archaeology and late Roman history in action', *Young Archaeology*, April, p. 7.

——(1990), 'The foundation and early development of Roman London: a social context', *Antiquity*, vol. 64, pp. 599–607.

——(forthcoming), 'Public buildings in the south-west quarter of Roman London', 'The Archaeology of London', vol. 3, *CBA Research Report*, London, CBA.

Willshaw, E. (forthcoming), *Chester Rows Trail*, Chester, Chester City Council.

Wright, T. (1872), *Uriconium*, London.

Yorke, B.A.E. (1982), 'The foundation of the Old Minster and the status of Winchester in the seventh and eighth centuries', *Proceedings of the Hampshire Field Club Archaeological Society*, vol. 38, pp. 75–84.

Yule, B. (1990), 'The dark earth and late Roman London', *Antiquity*, vol. 64, pp. 620–8.

INDEX